# MENACING ENVIRONMENTS

NEW DIRECTIONS IN SCANDINAVIAN STUDIES

Andy Nestingen / *Series Editor*

BENJAMIN BIGELOW

# Menacing Environments

## Ecohorror in Contemporary Nordic Cinema

University of Washington Press | *Seattle*

*Menacing Environments* is freely available in an open access edition thanks to TOME (Toward an Open Monograph Ecosystem)—a collaboration of the Association of American Universities, the Association of University Presses, and the Association of Research Libraries—and the generous support of the University of Minnesota.

Additional support for the book's publication was provided by the Department of Scandinavian Studies at the University of Washington.

Design by Mindy Basinger Hill | Composed in Adobe Caslon Pro

UNIVERSITY OF WASHINGTON PRESS | *uwapress.uw.edu*

LIBRARY OF CONGRESS CATALOGING-IN-PUBLICATION DATA

*Names*: Bigelow, Benjamin (College teacher), author.
*Title*: Menacing environments : ecohorror in contemporary
Nordic cinema / Benjamin Bigelow.
*Description*: Seattle : University of Washington Press, 2023. | Series: New directions in Scandinavian studies | Includes bibliographical references and index.
*Identifiers*: LCCN 2023009368 | ISBN 9780295751634 (hardcover) |
ISBN 9780295751641 (paperback) | ISBN 9780295751658 (ebook)
*Subjects*: LCSH: Motion pictures—Scandinavia—History and criticism. |
Horror films—Scandinavia—History and criticism. | Environmental protection and motion pictures. | Nature in motion pictures.
*Classification*: LCC PN1993.5.S2 B54 2023 | DDC 791.430948—dc23
LC record available at https://lccn.loc.gov/2023009368

♾ This paper meets the requirements
of ANSI/NISO Z39.48-1992 (Permanence of Paper).

# CONTENTS

═══

CONCLUSION
Nordic Ecohorror as Social Critique | *164*

# ACKNOWLEDGMENTS

─────

I am grateful for the unwavering support and sage advice of Andy Nestingen, series editor for New Directions in Scandinavian Studies, as this book took shape over the last few years. Andy showed admirable flexibility as my idea for the book changed in both topic and scope, and has been a generous sounding board and adviser as I worked to complete the manuscript. Larin McLaughlin, editorial director at University of Washington Press, also deserves recognition for supporting my work and shepherding this book through the rounds of peer review, revision, and publication. Larin always made herself available and patiently talked this first-time author through the many questions I had at every step of the process. I am thankful for the wisdom and insight she brought to the project. Special thanks go out to Caroline Hall and the entire UW Press editorial staff for their work on the layout, design, and many other practical matters that helped make this book a reality. I am also deeply grateful for the detailed and productive feedback I received from two anonymous peer reviewers. Their input helped me hone my argument and smooth out the manuscript's many rough edges. I am indebted to them for their careful and generous reading of my work.

The entirety of this book was written amid the restrictions and upheavals of public and private life brought about by a global pandemic. I am grateful that, despite this strange new reality of isolation, my work benefited from robust and inspiring conversation with colleagues in Nordic film studies in both Europe and North America. In the final stages of revision—when I most needed support—I was invited to take part in a virtual Nordic film writing group that provided a valuable accountability mechanism to help me keep my deadlines. I am grateful to the participants in that group—Amanda Doxtater, Kimmo Laine, Arne Lunde, Anders Marklund, and Anna Estera Mrozewicz—for their support. I'm especially grateful to Arne Lunde—and his cat, Ingrid—for continuing the meetings with me and cheerleading my work this summer even when other members of the group couldn't make it. Arne has always been beyond generous with his time and encouragement, and it has been a privilege to keep the virtual connection alive over the past couple of years. For her generous encouragement, support, and time over the last several years, I am grateful to Claire Thomson.

It is no exaggeration to say that this book probably would not have been completed without the support of my other virtual Nordic studies writing group, SSAWA—an acronym whose origins remain murky to those of us in the group. Meeting with my dear SSAWA colleagues, Amanda Doxtater, Benjamin Mier-Cruz, and Liina-Ly Roos, roughly every other week for the past two years has provided a steady rhythm of incisive feedback and shared conversations about our professional and personal lives. An invaluable intellectual alchemy has emerged from this group that had to do with reading and responding to so much of each other's work in progress—a process that has been as pleasurable as it has been productive. *Heia SSAWA!*

In the final stages of writing this book, I was supported by a generous faculty fellowship from the Institute for Advanced Study here at the University of Minnesota, which allowed me to take a leave from my teaching duties during the fall of 2021. I am grateful to former IAS director Jennifer Gunn and to the amazing group of scholars she and the staff of IAS brought together. The interdisciplinary exchange of ideas during that semester inspired me to think critically about my assumptions and exposed me to new methodologies and ways of thinking that have had an immense impact on the direction of my work. I am grateful to Susannah Smith and the rest of the staff at IAS, who helped keep our cohort connected and supported amid the many practical challenges of remote work and an ongoing pandemic.

Throughout this process, I have enjoyed the support of an exceptional group of colleagues in the Department of German, Nordic, Slavic, and Dutch (GNSD) at the University of Minnesota. I am forever grateful to Charlotte Melin, chair of the department when I was hired in 2017, who welcomed me to Minnesota and subsequently drew me into a community of environmental humanities scholars here in Minneapolis. In that connection, I am thankful to Charlotte and her co-organizers of the Environmental Humanities Initiative, Christine Marran and Dan Phillipon, for involving me in the initiative and for organizing many inspiring workshops, talks, and colloquia. In GNSD, I have been fortunate to have received the tireless mentorship and generous counsel of Leslie Morris, who has gone above and beyond as chair to advocate for my work, shepherd the department through the disruptions and stress of the pandemic, and share her insights and advice. Jim Parente has been an exceptional mentor whose deep knowledge of the institution and commitment to the future of Nordic studies at the University of Minnesota have been an inspiration. I am grateful to my current and former Nordic language colleagues here at Minnesota—Aija Elg, Dan Haataja, Kristiina Jomppanen, Kyle Korynta, Lena Norrman, Liina-Ly Roos, and Hanna Zmijewska-Emerson—who have generously shared their wisdom and insights, and have inspired me with their hard work and commitment to keeping Finnish, Norwegian, and Swedish studies alive and well here at the U of M. Former colleagues Rüdiger Singer and Ross Etherton deserve special acknowledgment for collaborating with me and sharing many great conversations about professional and personal life during their time in Minnesota. I am inspired by the work of fellow GNSD faculty members Matthias Rothe and Jamele Watkins, and have benefited greatly from their ideas and support. I am grateful to the graduate students I have worked with during my time in GNSD, who have shared their work and scholarly interests with me and contributed to an increasingly productive dialogue in the department. I am especially grateful to Kathleen Ibe for participating in a reading group on material ecocriticism and to Olivia Branstetter for participating in a research mentorship on folk horror with me last summer—both experiences that led to fruitful dialogues at different stages in the process of writing this book.

The research I undertook for this book came directly out of my experience designing and teaching a course at the University of Minnesota called Scandinavian Gothic: Horror and the Uncanny in Nordic Literature and Media. I am grateful to the graduate and undergraduate students who took part in that course during the spring semesters of 2020 and 2022. Their enthusiasm for the horror genre and their commitment to probing the many complex ideologies and cultural implications reflected in texts that are easy to dismiss as low-brow entertainment have been a source of intellectual inspiration and joy. Thank you to all my students for contributing to an ongoing conversation that has helped me grow as a scholar and a person.

Although this book is in some ways a departure from the work I did in graduate school, I am deeply grateful for the mentorship I received as a PhD student in the Department of Scandinavian at University of California, Berkeley. Linda Rugg and Karin Sanders were supportive and incisive readers of my work, from whom I learned to think more precisely and creatively. Mark Sandberg has remained a generous adviser and friend to whom I will always be indebted. Mark's unwavering attention to detail and his uncanny ability to ask *precisely* the right question have helped me challenge my assumptions and test the strength of my arguments as they are being shaped.

I am grateful to my family for supporting me, encouraging me, and bringing happiness and joy into my life. My parents, Wil and Vicki Bigelow, deserve special thanks for always being there for me and supporting me and my family. I am thankful for my sister, Alyson Horrocks, who inspired an early love of scary stories and horror films. Such interventions on the part of an older sibling may have led to some nightmares in my early childhood, but they also inspired an enduring fascination with the thrill of being scared and an interest in the traditions and histories that horror narratives tapped into. I am grateful to my children—Lucy, Clio, and Felix—for being inexhaustible sources of laughter, joy, and energy. In very different ways, each has given me much happiness, and they have never ceased to surprise and delight me with their creativity and intelligence. Finally, I am forever grateful to Sophie—the best partner I could ever have asked for. It has been an adventure navigating the joys and challenges of parenthood, full-time careers, and the adjustment to life in four very different locations and cultures, but Sophie has brought real joy, spontaneity, love, and laughter during our now seventeen years together. Writing this book would not have been possible without your patience and support, Sophie. Thank you.

# MENACING ENVIRONMENTS

# Uncanny Ecologies

Picture a nation where the air is clean, the food is plentiful, and the state looks after the material needs of all its citizens. This society emerged from the destruction and misery of World War II and rallied around a collective vision of a society where people were safe, labor unions were robust, and the comforts of middle-class life were accessible to all. Decades of public consensus around labor-friendly, social-democratic principles ensued. Child rearing, previously a physical burden borne entirely by the mother and financed by the wages of the father, was now aided by state programs ensuring months of paid parental leave along with generously subsidized public day care programs to look after the child once their parents returned to the workforce. Egalitarian housing programs were instituted, public transportation networks were expanded, and a renewable energy infrastructure was built up to power the nation's collective aspirations. The land's most treasured wilderness areas were protected from industrial development, and its people enjoyed free access to roam its pristine landscapes and bask in the sunlight of its long summer days. As this nation's prosperity grew, its government earmarked a significant portion of its GDP to generous humanitarian giving and international aid programs to share some of this wealth with the developing world. The nation's material prosperity, democratic freedoms, natural beauty, rationally ordered communities, and habits of international benevolence produced citizens who have been measurably among the world's happiest people for many years running.

Do you recognize any particular nation-state in this description? Chances are, one or more of the Nordic countries—with their expansive welfare states and sterling international reputations for generosity, environmentalism, and gender equality—spring to mind. Indeed, parts or all of the description could fit any one of the countries belonging to the Nordic Council: Denmark, Finland, Iceland, Norway, or Sweden. One reason the description might sound so familiar, even for those who live outside the region, is that some version of this utopian narrative has been exported for decades to the outside world, establishing a global reputation for Nordic exceptionalism in multiple areas—environmentalism, diplomacy, and gender equity, to name just a few.[1] This narrative is reinforced by the annual publication of the World Happiness Report (WHR), a yearly study completed under the auspices of the UN Sustainable Development Solutions Network.[2] Over the last five years, the top rankings on the WHR Happiness Index have been claimed by Finland (three times), Norway, and Denmark. Depending on the year, Iceland and Sweden have closely trailed their Nordic neighbors, while the Netherlands and Switzerland are the only non-Nordic countries to have ranked in the top five in recent years. As outsiders look to the Nordics to learn the secrets of achieving happiness, a cottage industry has sprung up to preach the wisdom of supposedly untranslatable cultural concepts that are key to well-being within these cultures. Thus, terms like *hygge* (Danish for "coziness"), *lagom* (Swedish for "good enough"), or *sisu* (Finnish for "tenacity") have been commodified by Nordic happiness gurus in the form of how-to manuals that seem to have found particularly fertile ground in the self-help markets of the United Kingdom and the United States in recent years.[3] The Nordic exceptionalism narrative has also been perpetuated by the ascendent political discourse of Democratic Socialism in the United States, with the likes of Bernie Sanders urging voters to "look to countries like Denmark, like Sweden, and Norway and learn from what they have accomplished for their working people": subsidized early childhood education programs, rational and sustainable public infrastructure, and a universal, single-payer healthcare system.[4]

Does this utopian narrative seem suspect? Look closer at Nordic societies, and you'll find that indeed less rosy accounts of the region are being told as well. And in the twenty-first century, Scandinavian crime fiction—which has come to be branded as Nordic noir—has provided precisely that kind of counternarrative for millions of readers and viewers across the globe. In the transmedial accounts of murder and detection that have reached a massive global audience, readers and viewers are urged—along with the investigative team—to examine the supposedly utopian Nordic society more closely and regard its dark underbelly. In the fictional worlds conjured by Nordic noir, readers and viewers are confronted with the limits and blind spots of the Nordic welfare state, an institution that not only harbors diabolical killers in these narratives but also enables more everyday forms of violence against women, queer communities, indigenous people, and minority ethnic and religious communities. Daniel Brodén describes this tendency toward social and political critique in Scandinavian crime fiction as a fixation on the dark sides, or "shadow images" (*skuggbilder*) of the Swedish welfare state, an intervention that casts the virtues of the so-called people's home (*folkhemmet*) of Swedish society in a sinister and uncanny light.[5] Similarly, Jakob Stougaard-Nielsen echoes the broad critical consensus that Scandinavian crime fiction "has insisted on painting rather grim pictures of societies in which the welfare state is overburdened and unable to care and where, even after half a century of social engineering, crime appears as present and widespread as ever."[6] Nordic noir insists that behind the reassuring façade of happiness and prosperity, human misery persists in many forms.

Look closer still, though. Examine not only the harmful prejudices and reactionary politics that Nordic noir draws our attention to, but also the very bodies that inhabit these societies. Look closer, at the material practices they undertake to survive and become prosperous. Look at the ways they interface with the environments they find themselves in. Look at the symbiotic, multispecies collectives they are enmeshed with. Look at the substances they take in and the waste they leave behind. Look at their patterns of industrial and postindustrial development—how supposedly environmentally friendly Nordic societies have reshaped landscapes, how their transportation networks have lubricated the channels through which global capital flows while expanding the carbon-heavy sprawl of human habitation. Look at the ways their settlements are always predicated on brutal displacements—of other people *and* of other species—and the ways their material prosperity is built on the planetary violence of mineral and chemical extraction. Look closer and also look *lower*: direct your gaze to the very earth on which Nordic societies are built, and the flows of substances between this particular ground and the human inhabitants who have settled upon it. This magnified gaze, which looks *behind* and *beneath* the individual person to reckon with the unsettling kinds of material interconnection between people and their environments, is precisely what contemporary environmental horror narratives confront their audiences with. While Nordic noir draws our attention to the shortcomings of ostensibly exceptional societies—to the *human violence* that persists in the Nordic welfare state—Nordic ecohorror frightens us with the *material and environmental violence* that lurks behind and beneath these societies.

Consider the following scene as an exemplar of Nordic ecohorror: a sickly yellow light seeps through a dense mist in an ancient marshland. Our view sweeps across the watery landscape, taking in the skeletal, leafless branches of ancient trees and the weary forms of washerwomen soaking and scrubbing their soiled laundry, only faintly visible through the steamy vapors. We hear the drips and splashes of washing over a bleak undertone of whistling wind passing over the sodden wasteland. A deep and ponderous voice begins to narrate the scene for us: after centuries as a communal laundry marsh, a national hospital has been built over the bog, and instead of washerwomen, doctors and scientists—the "best brains in the nation"—have come to occupy the site, bringing with them the advanced scientific apparatuses of modern medicine. As the technocratic arm of the nation-state supplanted the modest, grimy labors of the ancient peasantry, ignorance and superstition were swept aside to make room for a fortress of scientific positivism. Organic life was to be studied and defined according to rigorous, impartial regimes of observation and experimentation, says the voice. Our gaze turns downward, passing through the depths of the marsh and into the murky underworld beneath it: a space permeated by a dense mesh of roots that reach farther and farther into the soil, seeking out nutrients and forming an expansive web far below the surface of the marsh. The voice tells us that signs of age and fatigue have started to show on the otherwise solid medical edifice that has been built on top of the marshes—a visible reminder of the oozing, unstable foundation on which it was established. As we go farther down, suddenly something emerges from the depths: a human hand rises up out of the earth, and then another appears next to it, reaching toward the light like the germ of a plant piercing the surface of the soil to gather rays from the sun. Although nobody knows it yet, the voice tells us, the portal to this primordial underworld has begun to open up again. The image cuts to a shot of an apparently solid wall that suddenly springs cracks in its surface through which blood begins to seep, then trickle, and then burst into a deluge as the wall finally crumbles. Over the course of ninety seconds, a bastion of modern medicine has been undermined by the uncanny bodies and subterranean fluids emerging from the depths of the earth beneath it.

What I have just described is the precredit opening sequence that played at the beginning of each episode of Lars von Trier's television series *Riget* (*The Kingdom*, 1994–97, 2022), a groundbreaking, tongue-in-cheek blend of supernatural horror, pulpy medical procedural, and off-beat melodrama in the mold of David Lynch's *Twin Peaks* (1990–91).[7] This brief precredit sequence conveys several of the thematic and formal features of contemporary Nordic ecohorror that I will draw out and examine in this book.[8] To begin with, Nordic ecohorror depicts material environments as *transcorporeal meshworks*.[9] Formally and materially, the meshwork constructed by the opening sequence of *The Kingdom* is transcorporeal—to use the term coined by Stacy Alaimo— because it is made up of interpenetrating bodies and material forms that have grown together and respond to each other in ecological webs. These webs can encompass both positive feedback loops—as in symbiotic mutualism between codependent species—as well as negative feedback loops, as in the frequently toxic interchanges between the human and more-than-human worlds.[10] In *The Kingdom*, we see this transcorporeal enmeshment between human and the environment in the way the humble figures of the washerwomen do not transcend their watery environments but instead plunge into it to carry out the tasks of daily life. Nor is their immersion in the boggy landscape in the service of a quintessentially Romantic bodily communion with "nature"; it is instead a plunge into a deidealized ecological mesh that exerts an unsettling pull on their bodies. The horror of *The Kingdom*, then, is framed by the precredit sequence as a horror of (trans)corporeal immersion in a viscous material landscape to which the precarious figures of the washerwomen must submit their constitutionally porous and vulnerable bodies. In the series, their immersive submission to the landscape prefigures the unknowingly vulnerable, ecologically entangled modern society that has been constructed atop this watery ground.

It is crucial to note, however, that the uncanny emergence from the chthonic spaces beneath the hospital is *not* depicted as an alien environmental force: it is instead a pair of human hands pushing up through the more-than-human earth where they have been submerged. Though it is predicated on the tangible enmeshment of human bodies and more-than-human environments, *The Kingdom* is no "revenge of nature" narrative that pits human civilization and nonhuman nature against one another in an antagonistic existential struggle. As the hand emerges from the depths of the earth, it is a "naturecultural" force that returns to threaten the society above it—one that emerges from the discursive and material inseparability of human societies from the natural environments with which they are entangled.[11] To describe the environment as *transcorporeal*, moreover, is to acknowledge along with Alaimo that the human body is not closed in on itself, shut off from the world of material flows and ecological interchange, but rather is "always intermeshed with the more-than-human world."[12] In this meshwork, there can be no clean spatial or ontological separation between a bounded human domain of *culture* and a wild, untamed realm of *nature*. The sequence presents us, in the useful formulation of ecocritic Timothy Morton, with an image of "ecology without nature": the world as a boundless mesh of symbiotic entanglements rather than one that is divided into stable and sequestered domains of human "culture" and nonhuman "nature."[13] There is, indeed, no possibility of a human culture free from the material conditions of "nature," just as the "natural" landscape of the earth has become indelibly marked by the carbon-heavy industries of human culture in the Anthropocene.

Secondly, because these environmental meshworks are framed within the generic conventions of horror, they *depict material interconnectedness as a threat*, revealing an undercurrent of ecophobia in Nordic culture that belies the region's reputation for environmental friendliness. In ecohorror, the loss of clear distinctions between human and nature hastens the disquieting realization that human agents are not transcendent, autonomous individuals who can live in comfortable material separation from the rapidly changing natural environment. The disquieting transcorporeal embeddedness of human beings within material environments refigures them as precariously embodied *ecological subjects*. In the opening to *The Kingdom*, we see this dangerous interconnectedness in the way an ecophobic human institution that has suppressed and paved over the natural environment is undermined by the encroaching fluidity of the earth itself, which confounds all human efforts to relegate it securely to a nonhuman domain. As blood erupts through the man-made wall bearing the legend RIGET (THE KINGDOM), we get a hint of the haunting environmental forces that threaten to topple a key piece of Denmark's healthcare infrastructure. As the serial narrative develops, we see that the hospital is haunted not only by spectral, apparently immaterial figures, but more troublingly by environmental forces such as groundwater, which emerge from the depths to destabilize the physical structure of the hospital. The impending eruption of uncanny forces emerging from the earth is the result of the shortsightedness of modern scientific development, which has supposed it can establish its edifices wherever it pleases and keep the leaky environment at bay. The affective responses of dread, tension, and fear that are generated by ecohorror, then, can be framed both as fear *of* the natural environment and as fear *for* the natural environment, as Christy Tidwell and Carter Soles point out in their recent book.[14]

Finally, these dangerously interconnected ecological meshworks provide a vehicle for a searing *social critique* that takes on the revered institutions, unquestioned ideological orthodoxies, and claims of cultural exceptionalism in contemporary Nordic societies. In the opening sequence of *The Kingdom*, the leakage begins to undermine the material foundations of not just a single medical facility but Denmark's *national* hospital—a cornerstone of the entire kingdom that has stood for decades as a proud monument to scientific and technical progress, and to the benevolent medical care provided by the Nordic welfare state. Its threatened downfall, then, is a moral indictment of the entire social enterprise it stands in the service of—an enterprise that is pointedly depicted as resting on a leaky and unstable foundation.

## NORDIC ENVIRONMENTAL EXCEPTIONALISM

In the Nordic region, the environmental anxieties expressed in sequences like the opening of *The Kingdom* meet a context-specific set of cultural assumptions, societal structures, and material conditions that make ecohorror a particularly potent and unsettling narrative mode. An immediate sign of this is the way ecohorror undermines one of the major foundations of regional identity in the Nordic countries, namely the widely held perception of Nordic "environmental exceptionalism" in the global context.[15] Sustainable development and other pro-environmental initiatives have been a major priority of the Nordic countries since the early 1980s.[16] Along with Germany and the Netherlands, the Nordic EU member countries of Denmark, Finland, and Sweden have taken on leading roles in European climate initiatives, bringing a Nordic model of regional cooperation to bear on environmental issues.

Although typically framed in terms of contemporary concerns about climate change and sustainability, this Nordic "environmental exceptionalism" is part of a more deeply seated ecological tradition in the Nordic cultures that has its origins in nineteenth-century nature mythologies and the cultural fixation on wilderness landscapes in the local variations of national Romanticism that took hold in the region. If the Nordic countries are praised as being exceptionally "environmentally benign" in the twenty-first century,[17] it is merely one manifestation of the Nordic "regime of goodness" that cultural historian Nina Witoszek has tied to the ecohumanist impulses of the nature discourses that developed in Scandinavian cultures in the nineteenth century. Witoszek indicates that this environmental tradition is concerned first and foremost with the priorities of the human subject in the natural landscape by labeling this Nordic environmental tradition "eco-humanism," which she describes as "a cosmology based on humanist ideals, but one in which the symbolic referents of identity derive from nature imagery and from a particular allegiance to place."[18] In ecohumanism, the main premise of humanism—namely, "the recognition of the inherent dignity and of the equal and unalienable rights of all members of the human family"—is "modified by values springing from man's experience of nature."[19] Though ecocritic Ursula Heise has pointed out the problematic aspects of the "sense of place" this kind of ecohumanist approach to nature has inspired—with Norwegian eco-philosopher and theorist of "deep ecology" Arne Næss as one of its major proponents—Nordic ecohumanist ideals have been a central part of the region's reputation for environmental sustainability, due in no small part to the regional self-branding strategies propagated by the Nordic Council of Ministers.[20] Perhaps the most visible token of this ecohumanist tradition today is Everyman's Rights—known in Finnish, Norwegian, and Swedish respectively as *jokamiehen oikeudet, allemannsretten*, and *allemannsrätten*—a Nordic approach to wilderness recreation that is prominently highlighted on the official tourism websites of most of the Nordic countries.[21] The tradition of Everyman's Rights, which guarantees the right to freely roam on uncultivated land—whether privately or publicly owned—has codified into law the easy and relatively democratic access to the wilderness that everyone enjoys in the Nordic region. This legal fact thus reinforces the region's reputation for egalitarian environmentalism, as well as a Nordic ecohumanist mythology centered on the ideal that modern city dwellers periodically escape their urban settlements and wander unmolested into the wilderness to enjoy the salubrious effects of fresh air and sunlight. Moreover, featuring this right to roam prominently on the Nordic countries' official tourism websites signals that egalitarian environmentalism is a central element of the region's cultural self-image and regional branding strategies.

Against this backdrop of Nordic ecohumanism, Lars von Trier's depiction of nature in *The Kingdom* presents the viewer with a disquieting image of the natural environment as an intractable and possibly malevolent meshwork that evades all human efforts at rationalization and containment. Far from portraying Danes as responsible stewards of the natural world—as the ideology of Nordic environmental exceptionalism would suggest—*The Kingdom* suggests that modern Danish society has sought to subdue "nature" in the pursuit of material progress.[22] What makes the opening sequence to *The Kingdom* an example of ecohorror at work as a media and narrative mode—rather than simply wilderness horror that frames nature as an enemy to be subdued—is that it goes beyond the "revenge of nature" narrative, fixating not on the unknowable alterity of "nature" as an alien force bent on the destruction of humankind but rather on the human-nature interface as caught up in a dense, transcorporeal mesh that blurs the boundaries between the two categories.

This fixation on blurring boundaries between the human and the more-than-human world is a central feature of ecohorror, particularly when it is considered as a media mode rather than only a genre. Stephen A. Rust and Carter Soles discuss the potential of this focus on ecohorror as a mode, writing that such an expansive definition can include "texts in which humans do horrific things to the natural world, or in which horrific texts and tropes are used to promote ecological awareness, represent ecological crises, or *blur human/ non-human distinctions more broadly*."[23] Christy Tidwell has further reinforced this expansive emphasis on ecohorror as a mode or "an effect that may surface" not just in overtly ecocritical texts but "within other horror narratives as well."[24] This definition rests on the "blurring of lines" and "the lack of solid demarcations" between human and nature, making ecohorror a mode that draws our attention to the "dangers of interconnectedness."[25] In their recent book on ecohorror, Tidwell and Soles compare ecohorror to Linda Williams's theorization of melodrama as both a genre and a mode, meaning that ecohorror both "has identifiable characteristics of its own while also appearing within other genres," and allowing for the possibility of "moments of ecohorror" in otherwise non-ecocritical works.[26]

The grounding of the precredit sequence of *The Kingdom* in an oozing landscape harboring both anthropogenic and ecological horrors is a far cry from the Nordic region's reputation for benign and progressive environmental policy. The comforting rhetoric of sustainable development—which presupposes that industrial modernity can be reconciled with low-impact or even carbon-neutral environmental practices through innovative technologies and international climate cooperation—is challenged by von Trier's uncanny images of more-than-human material forces literally reaching out from the earth to undermine the technocratic and cultural edifices of the human societies that have paved over the land. Nordic ecohorror, then, takes the form of a blistering critique of the region's supposed environmental exceptionalism. As with the unrelenting bleakness of the crime fiction produced in the region, ecohorror is a dissident voice that articulates a counterdiscourse to this reputation for benign, ecohumanist environmentalism. Nordic ecohorror, however, goes farther than Nordic noir, which is widely acknowledged for its social-realistic revelations of the hidden misogyny, inequality, and racism of Nordic societies. Ecohorror extends this social critique to a more fundamental level, taking on the very material basis of the region's discursive and environmental practices as well, using tension, dread, and fear as potent affective tools in its discursive arsenal. As Alexa Weik von Mossner argues in her book *Affective Ecologies*, the role of the reader/viewer's embodied cognition and emotional response is particularly relevant to the critical examination of environmental narratives, since these narratives develop fictional environments for which viewers' bodies "act as sounding boards."[27] While socially critical narratives of all kinds might appeal to higher-order intellectual ideals of morality and justice, the affective appeals of ecohorror aim straight for our gut.

## ECO-FEAR, ECOPHOBIA, ECOHORROR

Climate anxiety has become a potent rhetorical device in the impassioned pleas of environmental activists, whose calls for radical urgency often appeal to existential fear and dread for the prospects of life on our rapidly warming planet. This is especially the case with Swedish climate activist Greta Thunberg's public discourse, which, as Tidwell and Soles point out, is characterized not by optimism or clever, market-friendly proposals for sustainable development, but rather by dire pronouncements of almost unavoidable environmental catastrophe. Thunberg reserves her most pointed rhetoric for the older generations of world leaders, whom she accuses of not being *terrified enough* about the calamitous environmental consequences already manifesting themselves. As Thunberg said in a widely seen speech at the World Economic Forum in January 2019, "Adults keep saying, 'We owe it to the young people to give them hope.' But I don't want your hope. I don't want you to be hopeful. *I want you to panic. I want you to feel the fear I feel every day.* And then I want you to act. I want you to act as you would in a crisis. I want you to act as if the house was on fire. Because it is."[28] Building on Thunberg's call for a demonstrative response of environmental fear, a group of Norwegian climate activists organized an event in August 2019 called the "climate roar" (*klimabrøl*), which gathered a group of thirty thousand people outside the Norwegian Parliament in Oslo in a collective, simultaneous scream to register anger, concern, and panic at the possibility that global warming could continue unabated. The event has been described as the largest climate-related public action in Norway's history and has since been reenacted every summer in Oslo and launched as a digital forum for individuals and businesses to join the *klimabrøl*.[29] As participants clutched their faces and opened mouths wide in a primal scream for the environment, they echoed a native iconography of climate angst, effectively reenacting the tortured expression captured in Edvard Munch's *The Scream* (1893), a painting originally exhibited under the German title *Der Schrei der Natur* (The Scream of Nature). Munch's painting is one of the most widely reproduced images in modern art, even circulating in modern horror cinema through the similarly iconic mask worn by the killers in the hugely popular meta-slasher *Scream* (1996) and its sequels. More importantly for a cultural history of environmental awareness in the region, Munch described his painting as a moment of expressionistic identification between human and nature, in which the pain of the natural environment finds expression in a profound moment of human anxiety and dread. In a short poem that documents his inspiration for the painting, Munch describes a moment of personal crisis he experienced as he stood on a promontory overlooking the Oslo Fjord at sunset one evening:

I stopped, leaned
against the fence tired
as death—over the
blue-black fjord and city
there lay blood in tongues of fire. My friends moved
on and I remained
behind shivering
in angst—
and I felt that there went
a great infinite
scream through
nature.[30]

In the image, then, the distinctions between human and "nature" melt away in the unsettling experience of environmental trauma, and the screaming figure becomes a fully ecological, transcorporeal subject. Building on a Nordic tradition of environmental anxiety dating back to Munch's famous painting, Thunberg and the *Klimabrøl* movement have harnessed the rhetorical power of eco-fear in their climate activism to draw international attention to the horrors of climate inaction, in the process publicly giving voice to the rage younger generations feel at the apathy of older generations.[31] The prominence of these recent collective performances of climate anxiety is one indicator of the productive potential of negative affect in environmental discourse.[32] The potency of the fear-based appeals made by Nordic ecohorror media is another.

Though Thunberg and the *Klimabrøl* movement embody a style of environmentally aware panic and dread, there is also a more reactive and phobic response to the natural environment driven by entirely more anthropocentric concerns—a reaction ecocritic Simon C. Estok has called *ecophobia*. As Estok explains, understanding the potentially dangerous ensnarement of human bodies in a complex of material agents and discursive systems is a challenging and unnerving task: "Imagining a menacing alterity of the natural environment (an otherness often represented as ecophobic life-and-death confrontations for humans) means imagining materials and their *intractable grip* on our lives and deaths."[33] In this book, I follow Estok in referring to this reactionary aversion to environmental enmeshment as ecophobia, a response that can manifest itself at individual and systemic levels. Unlike the environmental anxiety, dread, and rage performed by climate activists in the service of promoting environmental awareness, ecophobia typically supports an anthropocentric status quo and justifies unfettered industrial development. The apparent bravado of ecophobic claims of human invulnerability to the environment should not obscure the anxiety and fear at the heart of this disavowal. In this way, ecophobia is a potent feature of ecohorror, expressing a reflexive resistance to the agents of ecological connection. The films I examine in this book make use of ecophobia in complex ways, however, sometimes appearing to reinforce ecophobia's stance of reactionary anthropocentrism and at other times appearing to challenge it in graphic and unnerving ways. It is important, though, to draw a firm distinction between the environmentally aware anxiety expressed by figures like Thunberg and the *Klimabrøl* movement and the reactionary impulse of *ecophobia*. While climate anxiety can be used in the service of en-

One of several versions of *Der Schrei der Natur*
(the scream of nature), popularly known as *The Scream*
in English (*Skrik* in Norwegian), produced by
Norwegian artist Edvard Munch between 1893 and 1910.

Climate activists participating in the Klimabrølet (the climate roar), screaming
in unison to express the urgency of the climate crisis outside the Norwegian Parliament
in 2019. Frame grab from "Klimabrølet 2019," Thought Leader Global Media,
https://www.youtube.com/watch?v=6dILmQgzv_c.

vironmental activism to showcase the precarious enmeshment of humans and nature, thereby encouraging action to mitigate climate change, the impulse of ecophobia imagines the incursion of the environment into the human domain as an unwanted contamination that must be avoided at all costs. Ecophobia, then, is caught up in a rhetoric of purity and contagion, and seeks to shore up the physical and symbolic boundaries between "nature" and "culture," while eco-fear or climate anxiety acknowledges enmeshment in order to encourage a more ecological understanding of the human's place in the material world.

One technique harnessed by Nordic ecohorror is to activate the viewer's ecophobic impulses and thereby elicit feelings of fear and dread centered on the threats posed to human subjects by the lively environments they are enmeshed with. Material environments harbor vibrant presences that become terrifying because they are unanticipated. Since ecophobia adopts the anthropocentric view that the natural environment is an inert backdrop to human affairs, when these seemingly static environments become animate and begin to confront the human subject, they are not only startling and surprising; they threaten to destabilize the foundational epistemological and existential assumptions of modern humanism. As Jeffrey Jerome Cohen writes, the unexpected liveliness of the environment unsettles the stable ontological categories that humans have lived with for centuries and also challenges anthropocentric time scales: "A rock jumps. Every hiker has had the experience. The quiet woods or sweep of desert is empty and still when a snake that seemed a twig writhes, a skink that was bark scurries, leaves wriggle with insectile activity. This world coming to animal life reveals the elemental vibrancy already within green pine, arid sand, vagrant mist, and plodding hiker alike. When a toad that seemed a stone leaps into unexpected vivacity, its lively arc hints that rocks and toads share animacy, even if their movements unfold across vastly different temporalities."[34] The unexpected liveliness of nature can inspire gentle reflection on the strange temporal mismatches between rocks and humans, inviting us to ponder geological time and adopt a more ethical approach to the environment. However, it is just as easy to see how unanticipated animacy can inspire more primal and reactive responses of fear and aversion. The writhing twig, the scurrying bark, and the wriggling leaves that Cohen describes here similarly recall the hallucinatory vivacity of the apple trees that assail Dorothy and the Scarecrow along the yellow brick road in *The Wizard of Oz* (dir. Victor Fleming, 1939), a moment of ecohorror on the path to the Emerald City that takes the form of a "revenge of nature" motif. Just as the trees suddenly spring to life, slap Dorothy's hand, and start hurling apples at her and the Scarecrow, there is no reason to automatically presume that strange environmental presences are benign. Indeed, ecohorror appeals to the more primal impulse, inciting an instinctual fight-or-flight response rather than the calm contemplation of temporal and perceptual discrepancies that Cohen describes.

Unlike the climate-based panic that Thunberg and other young climate activists have called for, ecophobia's reactionary aversion to environmental animacy and entanglement means that when it is deployed in ecohorror, it can run the risk of reinforcing the anthropocentric, antienvironmental impulses it uses to elicit fear and horror, as Christy Tidwell and Carter Soles have pointed out.[35] That this possibility exists for anthropocentric ecophobia to be reinforced by ecohorror, however, simply indicates that the discourse of cinematic ecohorror is, like all art, an open-ended, polyvocal discourse that can encompass contradictory positions and impact its viewers in divergent ways. Unlike the activism of an environmentalist like Thunberg, which appeals to the audience with urges to adopt *particular* ideas and act in *particular* ways, the rhetorical appeals of ecohorror are more diffuse and difficult to pin down. Because ecohorror uses the instinctual fear of unexpectedly lively environments to promote an unsettling style of environmental awareness, insufficiently nuanced approaches to ecohorror run the risk of assuming that viewer responses to this environmental animacy will be uniformly negative and averse to the ecological awareness it engenders. This book draws out the internal complexities in contemporary Nordic ecohorror and shows how its use of ecophobia has the effect of promoting a more attuned and ecologically grounded sense of environmental awareness. Deployed in this way, ecohorror can strategically provoke an ecophobic reaction in order to encourage socially critical, ecologically grounded ideas about human bodies, social communities, and the material worlds they are enmeshed with. One crucial effect of Nordic ecohorror's complex engagement with ecophobia is that it works to destabilize an alliance that has been central to notions of social life and society in the region, namely the figure of the autonomous, individual human subject and that of the sovereign, holistic national community that can protect the dignity and autonomy of that individual.

## UNSETTLING THE INDIVIDUAL

As a media mode, ecohorror is fixated above all on the experience of being unsettled. But this experience of environmental unsettling is not universal: instead, it is marked locally by the particular social and cultural assumptions that prevail in any given region, especially as they relate to the relationships among individuals, communities, and their environmental surroundings. In the Nordic countries, one of the most idiosyncratic of these prevailing social attitudes is the philosophy that historians Henrik Berggren and Lars Trägårdh call "statist individualism," a concept that describes the "seeming paradox" of a social ethos in Nordic societies that is "based on a strong alliance between the state and the individual aiming at making each citizen as independent of his or her fellow citizens as possible."[36] The provocative claim Berggren and Trägårdh make is that although Swedes (along with other inhabitants of the Nordic region) are renowned for their amenability to social collectives—with the Swedish concept of the *folkhem* (the people's home) standing as an ideal figuration of this benign, cooperative social-democratic collectivism—they are at their core self-interested individualists. It is, in fact, the profound individualism of Nordic societies that has (paradoxically) contributed to the exceptional alliance between individuals and public institutions in the region. According to this theory, Nordic societies—with their long-held traditions of egalitarianism, agrarian self-sufficiency, and social democracy—are deeply suspicious of intimate relationships based on mutual dependency. Such relationships hobble individual autonomy, binding individuals in most societies to romantic partnerships and families that constitute "unequal and hierarchical social relations." The Nordic approach, which Berggren and Trägårdh also call the "Swedish theory of love," is to reject the idea that romantic alliances require giving up individual sovereignty, instead adopting an ethos of love based on a radical egalitarianism and positing that "all forms of dependency corrupt true love."[37] Because of the necessity of a stable social order, however, the radically sovereign individuals of Nordic society have aligned themselves with state authorities, which benefit from the relative economic equality and high productivity of individuals and in turn offer the protections of a robust social-democratic welfare state.

The delicate balance between the countervailing forces of individual autonomy and state authority enshrined in Nordic "statist individualism" has culturally specific consequences for the modes of storytelling that prevail in the region. If Nordic societies are deeply suspicious of intimate relationships based on mutual dependency, this suspicion can also be seen in narratives about the material environment. Ecological enmeshment, after all, is just another form of mutual dependency that requires permeable boundaries between individuals and takes the form of intimate (and invasive) relationships of material interconnection. And the sovereign, independent individual imagined in the "Swedish theory of love" is a profoundly antiecological subject, relying as it does on a sense of robust boundaries between the self and the world. One of the arguments of this book is that anxieties about human entanglements with one another and their symbiotic dependency on other organisms and material environments have a particular cultural inflection in the Nordic region, where robust state authority has for centuries gone hand-in-hand with an abiding respect for democratic values and individual autonomy. Locked in a mutually beneficial but paradoxical entanglement, the delicate alliance between the sovereign state and the autonomous individual is vulnerable to becoming destabilized if their shared understanding of the material conditions of life is threatened. And that is precisely what happens as environmental awareness brings the fact of (a potentially menacing) material intimacy and ecological interdependence to the fore. Nordic ecohorror, then, is a particularly destabilizing and socially critical narrative mode, since it has the potential to topple the twin pillars of social order and democratic values in the region: the autonomous individual and the sovereign state. Indeed, a basic implication of ecohorror is that autonomy and sovereignty are flawed, even indefensible concepts in material or ecological terms, since organisms are always dependent on other organisms and particular environmental conditions, tangled as they are in transcorporeal webs of life. In the Nordic social context, then, it is hard to imagine a mode of storytelling that is more fundamentally unsettling to the cohesion of Nordic societies than ecohorror.

The structure of this book traces the ever-increasing radius of destabilization brought about by ecohorror. Starting with the individual human body, the first two chapters fix their gaze on the most intimately personal structures of epistemological and ontological stability, categories that have ossified in Western intellectual traditions into a rigid binary opposition between the self and the physical world. Under the philosophical sway of Cartesian dualism, the individual has been imagined as an interiorized, self-aware subject defined by its intellectual and empirical—rather than corporeal—capacities. In chapters 1 and 2, I examine two films that build ecohorror narratives on the deconstruction of that disembodied subject position and the emergence of a precariously embodied, ecologically enmeshed subject in its place. This is an appropriate starting point, since *ecology* is a neologism that directs our attention to intimate spaces and relationships. In coining the term, the German zoologist Ernst Haeckel brought together *logos* (word, reason) and *oikos* (home), signaling etymologically that ecology would be concerned with the domestic, private, intimate spaces of the material world.[38] If our body is a kind of incarnate home that is vitally, materially interconnected with other ecological phenomena, environmental awareness must start with a material-ecological sense of our own corporeality. In ecohorror, this awareness of our own ecological, symbiotic coexistence with material agents presents us with a different kind of threat than the alien, monstrous foes that conventional horror narratives frequently revolve around—a threat that is at once startlingly material and threateningly intimate. By causing us to shift our gaze away from the anthropocentric view of nature as a distant space fundamentally separate from the human domain, ecology posits a material world in which nature is everywhere around us and within us—indeed, the human body is inseparable from the natural environment.

The discursive shift from remote natures to intimate ecologies in ecohorror thus makes us aware of material transgressions into the formerly protective boundaries between the individual self and the surrounding world. In ecohorror, so-called surroundings are no longer only *around* the human body; they are also *within* it. Living organisms, dependent on material interchange as they are, have evolved to encompass symbiotic relationships of ecological interconnection. Human existence, then, is always *coexistence*, not only with other humans but also with other species and agencies, including animal, vegetable, mineral, bacterial, chemical, and viral agents. This is made clear in the influential work of evolutionary biologist Lynn Margulis, who refers to living organisms not as unified and autonomous beings, but rather as "holobionts" that are more accurately described as a collective comprised of a host organism and the colonies of different life forms in symbiotic relationships of interdependence, both externally (exosymbiosis) and internally (endosymbiosis).[39] In the words of anthropologist Tim Ingold, human bodies should, then, be regarded not as "blobs of solid matter with an added whiff of mentality or agency to liven them up," but rather as "*hives of activity*, pulsing with the flows of materials that keep them alive."[40] Human beings depend on humble (and invisible) symbiotic entanglements with bacteria and viruses, which more often than not *sustain* human life rather than threaten it. Against the backdrop of Berggren and Trägårdh's argument about "statist individualism," such an ecological re-orientation of the self as a multispecies collective—a "hive of activity" rather than an autonomous individual—underscores the degree to which ecohorror gets right to the heart of foundational concepts of the Nordic social model.

In an ecological sense, then, ecohorror reminds us that our bodies are not our own—or at least not ours exclusively. Thus, we do not *shape* these ostensibly external domains through human interventions; instead we *are shaped by* the very dynamic ecological meshworks we are entangled with. The bacterial cultures that flourish in the digestive tracts of living bodies, for instance, make proprietary claims on food ingested by the host organism from the environment, meaning that our digestive health is *shaped by* the organisms symbiotically enmeshed within our guts. After the death of the organism, forms of bacterial, fungal, animal, and vegetable life make more lasting and violently territorial claims on the material left behind by dead bodies, reshaping these organic forms by breaking them down and returning them to the material economies of the surrounding environment. Relationships of interdependence also radiate out into spheres surrounding an organism during its lifespan, becoming, in the words of Richard Dawkins, an "extended phenotype." In this sense, the beaver's dam is a phenotypical expression of the beaver genome just like the creature's prominent front teeth. DNA, then, is just like the mind in the influential "extended mind thesis" of cognitive philosophers David Chalmers and Andy Clark: it is a "leaky organ, forever escaping its 'natural' confines and mingling shamelessly with body and with world."[41] Cartesian divides between the internal and the external, the self and the other, the cultural and the natural, become less fundamental and more tenuous, even hopelessly blurred. To underscore the porousness of bodily boundaries in ecological enmeshment, ecohorror confronts the viewer with images of bodily dissolution, abjection, and interpenetration, presenting the human body as a fundamentally transcorporeal form. In that sense, this book adds an ecological upgrade to Carol J. Clover's influential thesis that horror is, along with pornography, a "body genre," in that it depends entirely on direct appeals to sensational and affective response within the body of the viewer.[42] Horror and pornography, writes Clover, "exist solely to horrify and to stimulate, not always respectively, and their ability to do so is the sole measure of their success."[43] Rather than thinking of horror as entirely bent on stimulating the body—that is, a mode of *corporeal* media—thinking of ecohorror as a mode of *transcorporeal* media means acknowledging that it works not only by directly appealing to the body as such, but also by making us aware of the commingling of body and environment as a necessary—though sometimes horrifying—condition of material life.

The first two chapters focus directly on these bodily appeals of ecohorror, drawing our attention to the mechanics and politics of ecological embodiment in a contemporary Nordic context. In chapter 1, I examine Lars von Trier's experimental metahorror *Epidemic* (1987), a film about the making of a film that traces the narrative of an idealistic young doctor who ventures across a plague-infested landscape to treat the victims of a novel virus, disregarding the public health directives of his higher-ups in the process. Reading *Epidemic* as an ecologically conscious iteration of what Priscilla Wald has termed the "outbreak narrative," chapter 1 traces how the film uses transcorporeal body horror to unsettle the idealistic and dematerialized subject posited by scientific objectivism, paving the way for a fully ecological subject to emerge. Moreover, this critique of objectivist embodiment may also be seen as a dismantling of the humanist logic Nordic ecohumanism retains—with its blithe assumptions that human subjects can go out into nature for physical and spiritual rejuvenation without being caught up in the toxic material interchanges demanded by ecological enmeshment. Fixating on abject images of bodily (and media) disintegration, *Epidemic* portrays the process of contagion and infection in an especially overt way and, as such, serves as a useful case study for understanding the way ecohorror can be generated by a fixation on the transcorporeal mechanics of ecological embodiment. Chapter 2 continues this examination of ecohorror's elaboration of the transcorporeal body, analyzing Norwegian auteur Joachim Trier's supernatural thriller *Thelma* (2017). Appearing three decades after *Epidemic*, Trier's film works within a tradition of telekinetic horror about the psychosexual awakening of psychically gifted young women, in this case packaged within a queer horror narrative centering on a repressed young woman's growing same-sex attraction to a classmate. Although *Thelma* activates some of the same thematic concerns with the transcorporeal enmeshment of the physical body as *Epidemic*, it brings questions of gender and sexuality into the mix. *Thelma* posits that despite its reputation to the contrary, Norwegian society continues to be haunted by regimes of misogynistic paternalism—regimes that are all the more unsettling because of the ways they are intimately bound up with Nordic environmental imaginaries.

## UNSETTLING THE COLLECTIVE

Going beyond this now-troubled notion of the autonomous individual body, the final three chapters trace the consequences of Nordic ecohorror for how social collectives are reimagined and resituated by our changing awareness of environmental enmeshment. How human communities and more-than-human collectives are conceived is a crucial question for the future of human societies in a rapidly changing climate, a future that is less and less taken for granted in recent examples of ecohorror. As these chapters make clear, competing notions of social cohesion and collectivism have characterized Western social orders and sociological theory. On the one hand, there are dominant models of social life that figure the individual as fully autonomous and self-sufficient, an idea rooted in liberal individualism and neoliberal economic policies, and legitimized in classical sociology through the seminal work of Herbert Spencer. On the other hand, as Tim Ingold has pointed out, there are notions of social coherence that imagine the community as a kind of externally bounded, collective superorganism.[44] In classical social theory, this notion of society as a seamless collective is best exemplified by the work of Émile Durkheim, who in the preface to his influential manifesto *The Rules of Sociological Method* compares society to an alloy formed when separate metals are melted down and melded together: "The hardness of bronze lies neither in the copper, nor in the tin, nor in the lead which may have been used to form it, which are all soft or malleable bodies. The hardness arises from the mixing of them."[45] To follow the material logic of Durkheim's metallurgical metaphor, society is formed when individual identities are melted down so that discrete individuals may be melded into a seamless whole that is greater than the sum of its parts. These kinds of communities are based on a principle of social solidarity that can tend toward a troubling style of exclusionary and inhumane holism, as Timothy Morton has pointed out. This kind of holism, writes Morton, is "one of the most profound inhibitors of world sharing."[46] As Ursula Heise writes, ideologies of transcendent holism have been central to modern environmentalism, with a "sense of planet" emerging as photography started to capture distant images of the planet Earth from space. Although such a "sense of planet" can lead to a feeling of collective environmental responsibility that cuts across the arbitrary boundaries of nation-states to encompass the entire globe, such a planetary scale also tends to eradicate difference and disregard the needs of marginal communities in favor of a holistic view of the entire biosphere.[47]

As we have seen, Nordic societies, according to Berggren and Trägårdh, have sought to overcome the potential for abuse and inequity in social collectives by embracing a paradoxical philosophy of "statist individualism," insisting on both the autonomy of the individual and the sovereignty of the state. The films discussed in the final three chapters challenge this Nordic model of social life, showing how in practice Nordic societies have the potential to operate as meld-like, holistic social collectives, which exclude unwanted or supposedly "unnecessary" individuals through frequently horrifying practices of social engineering, including the exclusion or eradication of marginalized and unwanted individuals and groups. Techniques of exclusion highlighted in this section run the gamut from relatively subtle forms of inequity such as environmental privilege and racism to more violently exclusionary, far-right ideologies such as ethno-separatism and ecofascism. In Nordic ecohorror, then, environmental critique works alongside social critique to reveal the ways that Nordic societies base themselves on principles of both bounded, interiorized individual subjects and transcendent social collectives. These twin pillars of social cohesion in the Nordic region are unsettled by ecohorror's fixation with transcorporeality, material flow, and the dynamic correspondences between organisms and environments. Nordic ecohorror shows us how supposedly objective measures of collective happiness that are frequently touted as indicators of the success of the Nordic model are belied by the hidden violence committed in the service of social solidarity.

The final three chapters are preoccupied with issues of collectivity, national identity, and belonging in contemporary Nordic ecohorror, with a particular focus on the way social and environmental collectives are imagined and critiqued in such films. Chapter 3 examines the Icelandic horror film *Reykjavik Whale Watching Massacre* (2009) as an example of what Pietari Kääpä has termed the ecoslasher. Focusing on the potency of the cultural trope of Iceland as an isolated island nation, I argue that the film oscillates between the microcosmic scale of the nation and the macrocosmic scale of the planet to undermine the material logic of eco-nationalism and isolationism. As one example among many in the growing subgenre of Nordic slasher and splatter films—a group that includes wilderness horror films like *Fritt vilt* (*Cold Prey*, 2006) and *Bodom* (*Lake Bodom*, 2016), as well as the Nazi zombie franchise *Død snø* (*Dead Snow*, 2009; *Dead Snow 2: Red vs. Dead*, 2014)—I approach *Reykjavik* as a case study in the kinds of national and transnational environmental discourses Nordic horror films have explicitly engaged with in recent years. Chapter 4 analyzes Iranian-Danish director Ali Abbasi's debut film, *Shelley* (2016), a film about the horrors of pregnancy and surrogacy that draws direct connections between modern eco-sustainability in the region and the predatory and parasitic dimensions of Nordic environmental privilege. I connect the film's environmental imaginaries with discourses of health and rural living that have their roots in Nordic vitalism and protofascism of the early twentieth century, arguing that the film's horror derives from the uncanny persistence of such ethno-nationalist, neo-Romantic formulations of the national landscape in contemporary Nordic societies. Chapter 5 analyzes the connections between cultural belonging and ecofascism in American horror auteur Ari Aster's Swedish folk horror film *Midsommar* (2019). Like Abbasi's film, *Midsommar* focuses on the horror of isolation in the Nordic countryside from the perspective of the cultural outsider. *Midsommar* draws spectacularly horrifying connections between the ostensibly benign modern yearning for territorial belonging—a longing for a sense of environmental connectedness with the land—and the brutal ideologies of ethno-nationalism and white supremacy.

## CONTEMPORARY NORDIC HORROR

The reader may notice a historical imbalance in the films discussed in this book, which skews markedly toward twenty-first-century examples. There are structural and systemic reasons why any representative account of environmental horror in Nordic cinema will tend to overrepresent contemporary examples. As Gunnar Iversen writes in his chapter on contemporary Nordic horror cinema, few horror films were produced in the Nordic region until the 1990s, despite some well-known exceptions, such as Victor Sjöström's *Körkarlen* (*The Phantom Carriage*, 1921), Benjamin Christensen's *Häxan* (*Witchcraft through the Ages*, 1922), and Carl Th. Dreyer's *Vampyr* (1932). A "long and coherent horror tradition" in the Nordic countries has been elusive, writes Iversen, because government financing polices and strict film censorship have discouraged a film genre that was long viewed as outré and morally deficient. According to

Iversen, a few horror films were made in the postwar era as coproductions with US producers, such as *Rymdinvasion i Lappland* (*Terror in the Midnight Sun*, dir. Virgil W. Vogel, 1959) and *Reptilicus* (dir. Sidney W. Pink, 1961). Several other low-budget horror exploitation films were produced in the 1960s and 70s as well, such as *Dværgen* (*The Sinful Dwarf*, dir. Vidal Raski, 1973) and *Thriller: En grym film* (*Thriller: A Cruel Picture*, dir. Bo Arne Vibenius, 1973). Tommy Gustafsson and Pietari Kääpä similarly note the exceptional status of horror films in the mid-century Nordic film cultures, with examples like the Finnish *Valkoinen peura* (*The White Reindeer*, dir. Erik Blomberg, 1954) and the Norwegian *De dødes tjern* (*Lake of the Dead*, dir. Kåre Bergstrøm, 1958) finding commercial success and critical acclaim precisely because they used the conventions of horror lightly, mixing horror and fantasy sequences with elements of the ethnographic film (in the case of *The White Reindeer*) and crime fiction (in the case of *Lake of the Dead*).[48] Such films were palatable in a state-sponsored Nordic film production context because they struck a balance between art and genre film, bearing out Andrew Nestingen's theorization of the "medium concept" film—a style of filmmaking that has been prevalent in the Nordic region because it "involves the adaptation of genre models and art-film aesthetics." Publicly funded production schemes can thus regard the medium concept film as having "cultural significance" while also courting the broad appeal of genre film.[49] While certain forms of "pure" genre cinema flourished in state-sponsored Nordic film industries in the twentieth century—especially comedies and crime thrillers—horror remained a denigrated and infrequently produced genre until recently. This dearth of horror, as scholars have argued, is the result not of a cultural prejudice against horror but of government funding policies that explicitly favored the cultural prestige of art-house and social problem films.[50] This tendency shifted in the 1990s, when new government film financing schemes were introduced and more liberal censorship policies enacted, which combined to make horror much easier to finance and produce. The so-called 50/50 production scheme, which was introduced in Denmark in 1989 (and subsequently imitated in other Nordic countries) allowed for high-quality popular genre films to be coproduced by the national film institutes if private producers could come up with half the budget, a change that had the effect of making cinema more of a profit-driven industry in the Nordic region and less centered on fully state-sponsored prestige films. As

Gustafsson and Kääpä note, by the turn of the millennium, the tide of film production had completely shifted in the Nordic region: whereas "art house, social problem films or historical films were the norm before, nowadays it would not be overstating the case to suggest that domestic productions more often than not follow competitive genre strategies."[51]

A side effect of the structural disadvantages faced by horror cinema in Scandinavia was that many examples of Nordic horror were genre hybrids, with very few "pure" horror films being produced until the 50/50 production schemes were introduced in the late 1980s and 1990s. Ingmar Bergman made films that have been seen as existential and psychological art-horror hybrids, such as *Persona* (1966), *Vargtimmen* (*The Hour of the Wolf*, 1968), and the historical rape-revenge film, *Jungfrukällan* (*The Virgin Spring*, 1960), whose violence, brutality, and fixation on vengeance suggest a connection to horror. Because these films were made by a vaunted and world-renowned auteur, however, they have seldom been described as horror films, although they have clear connections to the genre.[52] There is also a strong sense of existential pessimism and even nihilism in many of Bergman's films that has been taken up by contemporary Nordic auteurs like Lars von Trier and Nicolas Winding Refn, who have provocatively combined graphic violence and body horror with noirish philosophical pessimism in more overt homages to genre filmmaking.

Gunnar Iversen has described the growth of horror in the Nordic region under the rubric of New Nordic Horror, emphasizing the hybrid space horror occupies "between art and genre" filmmaking in the Nordic region. In an expansive and efficient survey of Nordic horror over the last few decades, Iversen identifies several tendencies. Among them is the use of the vampire figure to critique the Swedish welfare state, most memorably in *Låt den rätte komma in* (*Let the Right One In*, dir. Tomas Alfredson, 2008);[53] the exploration of the personal and national traumas of the historical past in Finnish horror (*Sauna*, dir. Annila Antti-Jussi, 2008); and Lars von Trier's singular importance as the influential director of the art-horror hybrids *The Kingdom* and *Antichrist* (2009). More relevant for a study of ecohorror is Iversen's discussion of the reevaluations of gender and national landscapes in Norwegian slasher films such as *Villmark* (*Dark Woods*, dir. Pål Øie, 2003), *Fritt vilt* (*Cold Prey*, dir. Roar Uthaug, 2006), and *Død snø* (*Dead Snow*, dir. Tommy Wirkola, 2009). Iversen suggestively describes how these backwoods slasher films critique the instrumental ways modern city dwellers exploit natural resources for their personal enjoyment, "using nature as a way of escaping urban boredom," as well as critiquing "traditional ways of looking at nature and landscape in Norway." In its critique of Norwegian Romantic environmentalism, the wilderness slasher "transforms nature and landscape from an idyllic place for recreation to a place of violence and terror," challenging the "religious or even erotic" relationship with rural nature that modern Norwegian culture has cultivated.[54]

Approaching contemporary Nordic cinema through a more overtly ecocritical lens, Pietari Kääpä includes a chapter on ecohorror in his book *Ecology and Contemporary Nordic Cinemas*. In his survey of contemporary ecohorror, Kääpä describes how recent Nordic horror cinema has given rise to "reinterpreted versions of national narratives, where nature appropriation combines with the conventions of anthropocentric logic," and has centered on the "historical particularities of the different Nordic countries, from the history of eugenics to welfare ideology."[55] Like Iversen, Kääpä emphasizes the prolific output of wilderness slasher films in Norway, analyzing the oscillation between anthropocentric civilization and bestial wildness in these films through the Deleuzian concept of "becoming-animal." Kääpä also describes how Iceland's first horror film, *The Reykjavik Whale Watching Massacre* (dir. Júlíus Kemp, 2009)—a film that I examine more closely in chapter 3—similarly adopts an eco-slasher format, situating horror within a particularly fraught national and international debate about the sustainability of the whaling industry in Iceland. Additionally, Kääpä's chapter emphasizes the role of Nordic mythical creatures, such as trolls in the Norwegian fantasy found-footage film *Trolljegeren* (*The Troll Hunter*, dir. André Øvredal, 2010) and elves in the Finnish film *Rare Exports* (2010). This tendency has only become more pronounced in the years since Kääpä's book was published, with fantasy-thriller films and television series such as *Jordskott* (2015–17) and *Gräns* (*Border*, dir. Ali Abbasi, 2018) leading some to speak of an emerging hybrid genre centered on the mythical and the supernatural under the rubric of "New Nordic Magic."[56]

As a more expansive examination of ecohorror in contemporary Nordic cinema, *Menacing Environments* adds to this existing scholarship with a more granular analytical focus on individual films, adopting a pointed use of material ecocriticism as a theoretical framework for this analysis. Running the cultural gamut from high to low—from auteur-driven, art house horror to campy, self-aware slasher—the films examined in this book serve as case studies that are intended to stand in for the broad range of ecologically oriented horror films being produced in the Nordic region today. Undermining both the foundations of the autonomous individual and the social collective of the sovereign state—two crucial pillars of society in the contemporary Nordic region, according to the theory of statist individualism—ecohorror proves to be an exceptionally unsettling media mode.

# CHAPTER ONE

# The Plague Is Here

Transcorporeal Body Horror in *Epidemic*

Stripped to its material essence, ecohorror is a media mode about the frightful dissolution of the apparent boundaries between human bodies and more-than-human environments. In place of an anthropocentric separation of culture from nature, ecohorror makes us aware of the ways human bodies are always frighteningly enmeshed with their environments. One of the primary techniques horror films have used to draw attention to the ecological entanglement of bodies and environments is to center on narratives of biological and supernatural contagion. To take one illustrative example, Bram Stoker's *Dracula* (1897)—along with its numerous cinematic adaptations—is built on a migration narrative that generates a xenophobic fear of the vampiric and cultural other, in this case an undead, hypnotically attractive and monstrously repulsive Eastern European aristocrat. The cultural terror at the heart of the narrative is that as Count Dracula feeds parasitically on the bodies of modern Londoners, he threatens to spread his disease—and his cultural otherness—throughout the cosmopolitan center of modern commerce, which in turn is positioned to infect the entire globe. The efforts of Van Helsing and his collaborators to subdue the vampiric contagion thus become a project of biological containment: keeping the horrifically infectious bodies of vampires contained within themselves and preventing the exchange of diseased fluids beyond their bodily bounds. The model of embodiment required for such containment is fundamentally anti-ecological, since it requires the insulation of organic bodies from one another and generates fear of xenobiotic contact. This same fear of contagion also forms the basis of werewolf and zombie films, which similarly center on an infectious monstrosity whose potentially irrepressible spread reveals the disconcertingly fluid boundaries between bodies and environments. In a

Nordic context, contagion horror can be seen in contemporary vampire films such as *Låt den rätte komma in* (*Let the Right One In*, dir. Tomas Alfredson, 2008), zombie films like *Sorgenfri* (*What We Become*, dir. Bo Mikkelsen, 2015) or *Død snø* (*Dead Snow*, dir. Tommy Wirkola, 2009), and werewolf films like *Når dyrene drømmer* (*When Animals Dream*, dir. Jonas Alexander Arnby, 2014). Although films like these can be categorized separately according to the figures of monstrosity they center on—vampires, zombies, and werewolves—the underlying cultural fear at their core is that the infectious spread of contagion will prove uncontainable. In that sense, these films can also be grouped together under the rubric of outbreak ecohorror, fixating as they do on the mechanisms of viral infection through bodies that are precariously enmeshed with their social and environmental surroundings.

In modern Nordic cinema, it is hard to find a film that more clearly illustrates the material mechanics of this contagious ecological enmeshment than *Epidemic* (1987), the second feature film of the then up-and-coming Danish auteur Lars von Trier. Offering an unusual blend of art-house metacinema and epidemiological horror, *Epidemic* activates age-old anxieties about the penetrating, intractable grip the natural environment has on human bodies. Specifically, *Epidemic* provokes horror through the specter of emerging disease and rampant viral infection that spreads through the very tangible ways human bodies are enmeshed with environments through eating, drinking, and breathing. At its material core, then, the film is about the fear of biotic contact with potentially diseased bodies and environments. With von Trier's tendency to playfully mix filmmaking modes, styles, and tones, *Epidemic* veers chaotically between the horrific and the ridiculous. But underlying the moments of self-reflexivity and irony in *Epidemic* is a consistent fixation on the ecophobic and xenophobic fear of infection across biological and national borders. Occupying an important historical moment in the prehistory of modern Nordic horror just before new production schemes encouraging genre filmmaking in the region took hold in the early 1990s,[1] *Epidemic* establishes an ecologically grounded representation of embodiment that Nordic ecohorror has returned to again and again in the three-plus decades since its premiere. Examining the way *Epidemic* situates human figures as precariously caught up in infectious environments thus provides an important perspective on how modern Nordic horror developed a fixation on the emergence of the precariously·exposed ecological body.

The metafictional structure of *Epidemic* opens with a frame narrative about two young filmmakers named Lars and Niels (played respectively by von Trier and his real-life writing partner, Niels Vørsel) who must write a film script from scratch under a rapidly nearing deadline. Having suffered the loss of a previously completed manuscript when a floppy disk becomes damaged just days before they were set to present it to their producer, Lars and Niels decide they do not actually like their previous idea after all and instead choose to write a script from scratch. The scenario they land on is a film set in a plague-ravaged Europe, with a narrative about an idealistic young physician named Mesmer who thinks he can make a difference. As the alarmingly contagious new disease spreads fear across the continent, a syndicate of doctors based in an unnamed metropolitan capital take charge of the government response to the outbreak. They claim the plague has spread across the country—infecting the very soil, air, and water of the rural landscape, making the land itself diseased—and impose a quarantine to keep the city safe from the advancing virus within its protective city walls. The naive Mesmer, however, goes against their orders and heads out to the countryside to provide medical care to the sick who live outside the protective boundaries of the city. In his idealistic quest, Mesmer fancies himself a heroic figure of medical enlightenment who will generously minister to the sick and dying whom other doctors have left to their own devices for fear of contracting the infection themselves. The irony of his mission, as the scriptwriters explain, is that the medical experts are wrong—the plague is, in fact, confined to the urban center. When he leaves lockdown to minister to the supposedly infected, then, Mesmer himself becomes the agent of viral transmission, spreading disease wherever he goes. As Lars and Niels research, outline, and write their new script, we see the scenes they imagine play out before our eyes as an intercut film within a film, a narrative structure that sets up a series of metafictional parallels between the filmmakers and the film they are scripting. As this plot summary makes plain, the fictional scenario Lars and Niels come up with is all about the ways in which viruses—as nonhuman agents that can spread disease and panic—unsettle the very notion of stable, dependable boundaries between the human body and the material world.

Analyzing the film through a material-ecocritical lens, this chapter reads *Epidemic* as an ecohorror film about the fundamental *transcorporeality* of the human body, to borrow a term from Stacy Alaimo. To view the body through the lens of transcorporeality is to see it as a permeable, porous form that is constitutionally inseparable from the surrounding world. The shift in perspective that comes with seeing the human body as fundamentally *open* to the surrounding world rather than enclosed and insulated from it has profound consequences for how we understand the traditional conceptual divides and implicit hierarchies that have been imposed in Western humanist traditions: "Imagining human corporeality as trans-corporeality, in which the human is always intermeshed with the more-than-human world, underlines the extent to which the substance of the human is ultimately inseparable from 'the environment.' It makes it difficult to pose nature as mere background. . . . Indeed, thinking across bodies may catalyze the recognition that the environment, which is too often imagined as inert, empty space or as a resource for human use, is, in fact, a world of fleshy beings with their own needs, claims, and actions."[2] As Alaimo makes clear here, thinking transcorporeally draws our attention to the more-than-human materials and agencies that surround us and flow through us. This reorientation demands a new kind of environmental ethics—one that is nonanthropocentric and that recognizes the agency of the "fleshy beings" with which we are joined in relationships of ecological enmeshment. But as Alaimo also acknowledges, this corporeal openness to the environment also constitutes a very material kind of vulnerability, which is a source of legitimate ecological unease. The so-called natural world is transcorporeally entangled with the carbon-heavy industries of capitalist modernity, seeding toxins in the environment that are in turn taken up by bodies enmeshed in these environments. Because the concept of transcorporeality acknowledges the agency of the nonhuman material world, it "not only traces how various substances travel across and within the human body but how they *do* things—often unwelcome or unexpected things."[3]

*Epidemic* takes advantage of this potential for transcorporeal horror by fixating on the ways in which viruses exert a kind of agential force that dissolves the material boundaries of the human body and unsettles the cohesion of human societies. In this sense, the emergence of the ecological subject in *Epidemic*—figured as a constitutionally porous, entangled body that is viewed as a multispecies collective or a "hive of activity"[4]—shows the degree to which ecohorror has the potential to unsettle the foundational principles of the Nordic social model that Berggren and Trägårdh have labeled "statist individualism" (a concept described at greater length in the introduction). If the autonomous individual is no longer viewed as *autonomous* nor *individual,* then a Nordic social model that relies on the paradoxical alignment of the individual and the state cannot stand.

Viruses are an ideal site for this destabilizing kind of transcorporeal horror, since they are environmental agents that engage in just the kind of transit *across* bodies that Alaimo describes above, and the effect of that transit is often pain, sickness, and death. In crossing the divide between the interior of the human body and the external realm of nature, the virus dismantles the humanist conceit that the environment is "inert, empty space" or merely a repository of natural resources that may be extracted by human societies. Viruses are, then, agents of humiliation, removing the human body from its anthropocentric pedestal and bringing it into more intimate proximity with the earth. Seen through the lens of material ecocriticism, however, this kind of abasement is not in the service of an ontological reduction of the human to nonhuman—as if the transcorporeal human, in its entanglement with the natural environment, has slid precipitously down the "animacy hierarchy" theorized by Mel Y. Chen.[5] Instead, depicting the human body as transcorporeally enmeshed with the environment encourages what Karen Barad calls "agential realism": that is, shifting away from an oppositional ontology that situates the human *against* nature—where humans may interact with the natural world as an ontological other—and instead positing an ontology in which the human and the more-than-human world are caught up in a relational, mutually constitutive relationship of *intra-activity*.

This is the fundamental distinction, as I see it, between "revenge of nature" or "nature strikes back" horror and ecohorror: while the former builds on an oppositional ontology of interaction and threat between the binary figures of the human and the natural world, the latter generates unease and horror by depicting the dissolution of boundaries between the two.[6] In that sense, *Epidemic* functions as ecohorror because it undoes the conventional binaries of the outbreak narrative. Rather than fixating on the otherness of viruses as alien invaders penetrating the barriers of the human body, the film instead shows how humans themselves are the agents of viral contagion. Entangled in material webs of intra-activity that bring them into transcorporeal relations with all kinds of viruses, human bodies are inseparable from their environments. It makes little sense, then—as the spokesmen of medical expertise in *Epidemic* do—to frame epidemics as eco-genic emergencies that result from the "contamination" of the human body by the natural environment. Neither is viral infection entirely anthropogenic; to frame the human as the sole cause of epidemics is to reify the ontological binary of human/nonhuman. Instead, epidemics are a prime example of a naturecultural phenomenon—to draw on the terminology of Donna Haraway—since they reveal the inseparability of the two categories and the ways human and nonhuman mutually constitute each other in relationships of agential intra-action.

Shifting away from the anthropocentric fantasy of nature as "mere background" and drawing our attention to the way material environments teem with invisible, nonhuman agencies that threaten to infect and kill their human hosts, *Epidemic* provokes fear based on the menacing strangeness of a resurgent nature. Ecocritical theorist Simon C. Estok has coined the term *ecophobia* to describe the kind of reactive "contempt and fear we feel for the agency of the natural environment."[7] Since it posits nature as an alien and potentially threatening external force against humanity, ecophobia presupposes that human culture and nonhuman nature are sequestered from one another, occupying separate domains divided by relatively robust and stable spatial and ontological boundaries. Ecophobia centers on the realization that some of the nonhuman agencies in the natural environment "threaten to dissolve us," in Estok's words; it is part of a long-standing "history of hostility to agentic forces outside of ourselves" that informs "how we respond emotionally and cognitively to what we perceive as environmental threats and as a menacing alienness."[8] Central to its affective appeal to the viewer as a work of ecohorror is the way *Epidemic* activates these deeply rooted feelings of fear and hostility to the perceived "menacing alienness" of the natural environment.

It would be an oversimplification, however, to assume that because *Epidemic* activates an ecophobic response in its audience, the film ultimately reinforces the anthropocentric logic of ecophobia. Just as there are embedded metafictional levels within *Epidemic*, there are also complex and contradictory discursive positions in the film, some tending to reinforce ecophobia and others supporting more ecologically sound models of environmental enmeshment. Indeed, the most unsettling scenes in the film center precisely on the transcorporeal economies of contagion the human body is caught up in, showing how necessarily vulnerable the human body is to unwanted intrusions from the environment. Although the images of bodily intrusion, abjection, and fluidity in *Epidemic* are undoubtedly unsettling and transgressive, such a fixation on transcorporeal flows between the body and the environment paints a more ecologically realistic form of material enmeshment. The film's transcorporeal realism ultimately gives the lie to the anthropocentric sequestration of culture and nature through its images of bodily dissolution, abjection, and unsettling fluidity. Although *Epidemic* has no overt, univocal environmentalist rhetoric to impart, the horrors with which it confronts the viewer effectively challenge the arrogance of humanist positivism that Dr. Mesmer stands for. *Epidemic* does what Estok claims the best material-ecocritical discourse can do: it "challenge[s] human exceptionalism and unseat[s] humanity from its self-appointed onto-epistemological throne, its imagined singular embodiment of agency, subjectivity, and ethical entitlements."[9] Like most of the other ecohorror films I discuss in this book, then, *Epidemic* activates ecophobia only to critique it and dismantle its very premises. Though it uses ecophobia for its most unsettling affective appeals, ecohorror works through the anthropocentric logic of ecophobia in order to arrive at a materially realistic, ecocritical worldview.

In this chapter, I analyze the particular style of transcorporeal body horror Lars von Trier develops in *Epidemic*. Body horror has been described as "the explicit display of the decay, dissolution, and destruction of the body, foregrounding bodily processes and functions under threat, allied to new physiological configurations and redefinitions of anatomical forms."[10] Conventionally, body horror is equated with the depiction of horrifically exceptional or extreme forms of embodiment; it is a mode that "generates fear from abnormal states of corporeality, or from an attack upon the body."[11] Christy Tidwell notes that with its fixation on the shifting boundaries of the biological body, body horror lends itself to ecocritical readings: "It is often difficult to separate a focus on nature and environment from issues related to the body; as a result, the lines between ecohorror and body horror are not always clear."[12] Adopting an ecocritical understanding of body horror, this chapter goes beyond the notion that the corporeal processes and intrusions into the body are *abnormal* states. On the contrary, the transcorporeal exchanges between the interiority of the living body and the exteriority of the material environment that body horror makes such spectacular use of are not, in themselves, abnormal or exceptional. They are instead merely an exaggeration of the everyday kinds of material interactions between body and environment that living organisms depend on. Stylistically, von Trier's transcorporeal body horror uses imagery of bounded bodies giving way to horrifyingly abject and fluid bodies. In transcorporeal body horror, abject bodily fluids like pus and blood take on greater material significance than mere vehicles for sensational gore. Instead, these fluids are the very substance of transcorporeal interchange—a material flow of vital traffic between the insides of living bodies and the environments that surround them. In *Epidemic*, this phenomenon of material interchange and traffic extends the notion of the transcorporeal body outward, encompassing not only the living bodies of individual organisms but also the structures of the buildings and the boundaries of the nation-states they inhabit. This metonymic extension beyond the individual body into the proximate "bodies" of architecture and nation is symptomatic of the logic of contagion at the heart of the outbreak narrative, a form that by definition is concerned not only with individual cases of infection but also with the global spread of infectious diseases. As part of its macroscopic focus, *Epidemic* combines the visceral abjection of diseased bodies with images of the global traffic of people and goods through cities and across borders as a way of figuring the modern nation-state as another kind of transcorporeal body—an organism whose vitality depends on material pathways of circulation that, like all ecological interfaces, can also carry the seeds of illness and death.

## TRANSCORPOREALITY AND THE OUTBREAK NARRATIVE

In terms of genre, *Epidemic* could be considered a metacinematic take on what Priscilla Wald calls "the outbreak narrative"—a narrative form that spans fictional and nonfictional accounts of disease emergence in an increasingly globalized world. According to Wald, "the outbreak narrative" is "an evolving story of disease emergence" that has appeared in an increasing number of guises in recent decades, proliferating since the AIDS epidemic of the 1980s. Narratives of outbreak "put the vocabulary of disease outbreaks into circulation"; they are driven by "a fascination not just with the novelty and danger of the microbes but also with the changing social formations of a shrinking world."[13] Because of its fixation on traffic and circulation, the outbreak narrative offers a look at viral disease in materially realistic terms. There are moments in any outbreak narrative, then, when we catch a glimpse of the material mechanisms of viral exposure. These are the pivotal seconds when uninfected people are unknowingly exposed to the invisible virus, when the infection is allowed to enter their bodies and take residence there. At these moments, a crucial turn takes place. Now smitten with the virus, passive observers become active agents of viral transmission who silently spread the infection to others whose paths they cross. These crucial turns in an outbreak narrative are only possible through the transcorporeal mingling of an invading virus with its human host, a chance alliance that effectively situates the human body as an open receptacle for environmental incursion.

One such moment in *Epidemic* comes when Lars—deeply engrossed in research for the new film script—is invited by Niels's pathologist friend to observe an autopsy. The body in question numbers among an unlucky vanguard who have been infected with a novel virus that has just begun to spread in Copenhagen. Lars stands over the body alongside two pathologists, all three dressed in surgical gowns, gloves, and masks to protect their uninfected bodies against the emerging disease. Pelle, one of the pathologists, has just made an incision to reveal the telltale pea-size nodules that have grown on one of the victim's lymph nodes. He urges Lars to "take a look at this" and announces that the two nodules they have just found are the largest discovered so far among the victims—a sign, perhaps, that the outbreak is becoming more severe. Obeying the pathologist's suggestion, Lars leans toward the body to take a closer look.

The scene sets up clearly visible distinctions between the living—who are upright, clothed in protective garments, and intact—and the dead, laid out on the table, naked, and cut open. Such a dichotomy between the enclosed corporeal presentation of the living human agents and the exposed, open, inert materiality of the dead body serves to reinforce the binaries of anthropocentric humanism. The dead body, it seems, is an inert material *object*—a former person whose body has now been reclaimed by nature—while the living are culturally situated human *subjects*, insulated from the brutal grasp of nature through their belonging within a human society. But as the dissected corpse is cut open and the observers lean in to see the physical tokens of disease more clearly, there is a *double exposure*—not of the photographic but of the *biotic* kind. While the dead body is quite literally opened up by surgical instruments so that the disease may be exposed and posthumously diagnosed by the pathologist, the uninfected observers are rendered more exposed to the infection as they lean in. After cutting into the corpse, one of the pathologists uses a rake retractor to hold back layers of skin and flesh to reveal the nodule to their gaze. A side effect of this revelation, of course, is that the infection is brought into closer proximity to their uninfected bodies. Betraying his lack of medical knowledge, Lars has left his surgical mask untied, an omission that effectively offers up his nostrils and mouth to the air above the exposed nodules. In his eagerness to see the signs of contagion firsthand, Lars seems unaware or unconcerned that he might be lowering his defenses and presenting his body as a new host for the virus.

Stacy Alaimo has used the term *exposure* to analyze different styles of embodied interactions with nature, contrasting the enclosed, armored stance of "carbon-heavy masculinity" with the receptive stance of "insurgent vulnerability" carried out—frequently in the nude—by environmental activists and artists.[14] The distinctions Alaimo draws between ecophobic hypermasculinity and ecocritical feminism are arrayed along a continuum that runs from corporeal *enclosure* to *exposure*. Unlike Alaimo's notion of insurgent exposure, *Epidemic* presents such corporeal openness as a terrifying kind of vulnerability—one that, particularly in an environmental or epidemiological emergency, must be counteracted and resisted through practices of isolation and enclosure.

A more down-to-earth way of describing the exposed, transcorporeal bodies of living organisms is to say that they are "leaky," the term favored by cultural anthropologist Tim Ingold in his ecological approach to material culture studies. Citing an anthropological study of the uses of ceramic pottery in premodern Argentina, Ingold notes that rather than being seen as "obdurate matter," pots were treated with the same concern as living bodies "to compensate for chronic instability and shore up vessels for life against the ever-present susceptibility to discharge that threatens their dissolution or metamorphosis." The living body is similarly susceptible to leakage, and indeed depends on the "continual taking in of materials from its surroundings and, in turn, the discharge into them, in the process of respiration and metabolism" in order to survive. Just like ceramic pots, then, living bodies "can exist and persist only because they *leak:* that is because of the interchange of materials across the ever-emergent surfaces by which they differentiate themselves from the surrounding medium. The bodies of organisms and other things leak continually: indeed their lives depend on it."[15] In Ingold's description, we find a helpful model for understanding the fundamental quality of leakiness that gives the body its emergent, vital character. Part of the dynamic quality of bodies is that they must negotiate a precarious equilibrium between stability and leakiness. If the body becomes too obdurately stable and solid—in other words, enclosed and shut off from the fluid interchange of materials across its surfaces—it succumbs to suffocation, thirst, or starvation. However, if the body becomes too leaky and fluidly open to the environment, it becomes vulnerable to constant infection or, more horrifically, dissolution. In pointing to the vital importance of the "leakiness" of living bodies, Ingold thus situates the body as precariously balanced between fluid and solid. This perilous equilibrium makes the body a dynamic center of transcorporeal interchange that can never stand in material isolation from the surrounding world and the flows of biotic traffic that take place in such an environment.

As this autopsy scene makes clear, the spread of viral disease takes advantage of the exposed, leaky qualities of both the infected and the uninfected bodies. Stacy Alaimo's concept of transcorporeality draws our attention to the fundamentally open, unbounded quality of organic bodies, which must be constructed with porous surfaces that allow for constant material circulation between their insides and their surroundings. The leakiness of living bodies, then, is a crucial *feature* rather than a bug. The setting of *Epidemic* in a context of viral outbreak, however, pathologizes this corporeal virtue, turning transcorporeality into an apparent defect. In the midst of an epidemic, the otherwise health-promoting material traffic between the insides of bodies and their external environments becomes an existential threat to a living organism, and possibly even to an entire species. By focusing on the transcorporeal mechanics of infection—including the microscopic transit of viruses across bodily surfaces and the macroscopic flow of people and goods across borders—*Epidemic* develops a style of ecohorror that is preoccupied with the threatening interchanges between human bodies and their environments. These threatening flows between body and environment, which allow for a kind of biological invasion of the natural world into the most intimate recesses of the human organism, counter the tradition of Nordic environmental exceptionalism and instead present the environment as a threatening, alien force that will ultimately secure our destruction.

Although this autopsy scene is not a pivotal moment in the plot development of *Epidemic*, it clarifies the competing models of embodiment at play in the film. These models of embodiment also play crucial roles in discourses of all kinds, including the competing frameworks of environmental activism and unfettered industrial development. As Alaimo suggests, these models of embodiment might be described as closed and open bodies. The ideological framing of those positions, however, becomes attenuated when the threat of environmental incursion into the body is so directly existential, as it is in the midst of viral outbreak. In an epidemiological emergency, *all* bodies should aspire to a certain amount of protective closure from the environment. The uninfected must isolate themselves from others, wear masks when they come in close contact with possibly infected bodies, and otherwise impose practical impediments to incursions of the environment by restricting transcorporeal flows of traffic between the body and its surroundings. As ultimately untenable as the model of corporeal enclosure is, *Epidemic* dwells on the way this corporeally shut-off body is situated as the ideal in epidemiological discourse. The closed body, indeed, becomes a source of visceral terror in the film.

## CLOSED BODIES, SEALED BUILDINGS

The slippage between individual bodies and the larger structures they inhabit—homes, nations—is apparent from the very beginning of the writing process Lars and Niels undertake. They begin research for their new film script at the Danish National Archive, a site that houses "Danmarks hukommelse" (Denmark's memory), in the words of a helpful archivist who assists them. They have come to the archive to learn about the history of communicable diseases in Europe as they start to write their script. Lars and Niels immediately become fixated on the atmosphere of misdirected paranoia, suspicion, and brutality that characterized plague-infested landscapes of the historical past. As the archivist holds forth on the epidemics that gripped medieval Europe—reading directly from primary sources housed at the archives—the filmmakers learn about the techniques of physical isolation that proliferated in response to such plagues: "Fathers left their children, wives left their husbands, brother left brother, for the disease attacked both through breathing and sight. And thus they died, and no one could be induced to bury them at any price. Family members dragged their dead to open graves without the benefit of clergy, eulogy, or tolling of bells. Throughout Sienna, mass graves were filled with victims. . . . Some were covered with such a thin layer of dirt that dogs dug them up and devoured their bodies." Though medieval Europe lacked the microbiological models of disease used by modern medicine, the archival source quoted here suggests that there was a recognition that face-to-face human contact and the breathing of shared air spread the disease. In their desperation to remain healthy, the uninfected forsook their infected family members and did all they could to isolate themselves from the horrible disease. In his narration from primary sources, the archivist also uncovers a quality of irony to their efforts, showing how an aversion to the disease led to ineffectual burials in open or shallow graves. This lack of isolation from the dead bodies of victims allowed the plagues to worsen as the virus infected the dogs who ate the diseased corpses. The desperate survivors made evasive efforts that in fact worsened the spread of disease, undertaking incomplete burials and imposing ineffectual quarantines that would inevitably lead to further death.

As this visceral archival anecdote makes clear, the basic physical problem that must somehow be overcome to slow the spread of the disease in an epidemic is the transcorporeal leakiness of the living body. Once figured as a virtue that helps the body negotiate a fragile equilibrium between corporeal openness and enclosure, viral infection tips the scales and turns this leakiness into an acute existential threat that must be neutralized. The body must somehow become enclosed, cut off from the potentially contagious, infectious exchanges that would bring illness, suffering, and death. What can be done to overcome the body's transcorporeal leakiness and avoid such virulent disease transmission? As *Epidemic* makes clear, the traditional response to viral threat is to impose isolation, to cut off flows of human traffic, and to put protective physical barriers in place between households. The public sphere withers, and the types of social interactions that take place in the agora cease. Populations become atomized, and life is increasingly rendered private and cloistered.

In conditions of viral outbreak, however, the cure is often worse than the disease. The kind of claustrophobic isolation imposed in an epidemic can, in fact, be fatal, an irony that makes the perverse public health measures imposed during plagues a potent vehicle for environmental horror. As the archivist continues telling historical anecdotes about plagues in medieval Europe, the filmmakers' fascination is piqued by the atmosphere of epidemiological panic, isolation, and public health brutality that prevailed in such epidemics. "The Great Plague of 1348 saw harsher methods employed," says the archivist. He describes the clerical response when the first plague victims were detected outside Milan: "Archbishop Bernabo Visconti ordered all plague-infested houses to be sealed up with bricks with the family inside. Thus Milano escaped the plague. Three families were sealed in to die of plague and hunger." This frightening image of infected bodies walled up in their own homes to die of starvation presents us with the uncanny mirror image of the leaky bodies Alaimo and Ingold theorize. To protect the community from the infectious fluidity of diseased bodies during the plague, Milanese health officials used the walls of homes as an obdurate material prosthesis to shore up the body and protect others from dangerous transcorporeality.

It is not surprising, then, that there is an easy metonymic slippage in the archivist's words between infected bodies and the architectural structures those bodies inhabited—it is the *houses* that are described as "plague-infested" here, rather than the bodies themselves. This substitution of architecture for body is telling because it justifies the public health response of sealing the houses those bodies inhabited. To protect the community, transmitters of virus must be isolated, literally walled off from the outside world. In an epidemic, then, environments—including built environments—become their uncanny mirror images: homes, in this case, become tombs. The irony of such brutal public health measures, according to the archivist, was that they only delayed the inevitable. Far from providing a durable enclosure against the escape of the virus, these sealed houses actually made the community more susceptible to mutated viral strains that would give rise to later epidemics. When Niels asks the archivist if Milan "had no plague because it isolated itself from other plague-ridden cities," he responds that the strategy of sealing off infected houses worked initially, but the city "was hit that much harder when the next plague came." Aspiring to firmly enclose dangerously leaky bodies, then, is hardly effective public health policy in the long run. The horror of this anecdote, however, centers not so much on the ravages of the disease itself but instead on the radical diminution of public space and the claustrophobic terror of the fatal, enforced isolation that went along with it. It is, in other words, a horror of shrinking environments. In this style of epidemiological ecohorror, the troublingly porous bodies of the infected are increasingly equated with their rapidly diminishing and insulated surroundings.

As we find out later in the film, the way houses effectively became tombs for the infected in medieval Milan inspires Lars and Niels to literalize the house-as-tomb metaphor by imagining a terrifying scene of live burial. Lars and Niels are doing double duty, driving through the industrial heart of northwestern Germany to visit their friend, the actor Udo Kier, while they talk out the plot of their film and produce the script on a portable typewriter. As the 16-mm film captures grainy images of passing freight trucks, smokestacks, and the smog-congested factory landscape they pass in their car, Lars imagines what will befall "our friend Mesmer" as he embarks on his journey to "disease-ravaged Europe." They bandy a few ideas back and forth before Niels says, "During the plague, people died in a matter of hours and were buried quickly. In the rush, some people were buried alive." Niels speculates that it "might be a good idea if Mesmer's girlfriend, the nurse, met this fate. That would fit in with Mesmer's mission." As they consider this idea, their Mercedes descends into a tunnel beneath a passing city, and the frame is plunged into the darkness of the tunnel, which is broken only by a line of incandescent light along the roof of the tunnel that traces the curve of the road. An eerie electronic drone begins on the soundtrack, and the film cuts to the live burial scene Niels has imagined. We see the scene in cross-section: a cutaway of a simple wood casket surrounded by earth with the unfortunate nurse lying within on top of a thin layer of wood shavings, her hands crossed at the waist. As the still-alive nurse comes to, she begins gasping for air and feebly groping the casket lid in front of her. The camera zooms in to capture the hopelessness of her situation registering on her gasping face. The horrifying scenario of live burial not only connects the imagined film to historical incidents that supposedly took place during medieval epidemics, but is also the most visceral depiction of the kind of horrifically confined, insulated, enclosed body of the infected that premodern epidemiology posited as the ideal. In its eagerness to isolate the virus and staunch the spread of infection, such live burials were in fact the logical extension of medieval epidemiology's ecophobic aversion to the transcorporeal expressions of the diseased body.

Indeed, the way *Epidemic* frames epidemiological experts as agents of suffocation—figures who prescribed the asphyxiation or starvation of the infected by confining them to radically enclosed and sealed-off spaces in the name of public health—aligns medical expertise with an ideology of ecophobia. This is particularly apparent in the first scene the imagined film *Epidemic* stages for the viewer. In it, the young Dr. Mesmer is confronted by a syndicate of medical experts who, in the epidemiological emergency that has gripped the land, have taken over control of the government. The head of the syndicate tells Mesmer, "I understand that you wish to undertake a medical practice in the infected areas outside the city, knowing full well that the academy of doctors has decided that no treatment can be given for this disease. Dammit, Mesmer—I could never give you permission to leave for these areas." According to the doctors on the council, Mesmer wouldn't have a chance of surviving a single day, because infection has seeped into the very material environment outside the city. "The air is infected," one of them intones. "And the soil," adds another, before a third doctor chimes in, "And the water." The schematic landscape portrayed by this public health discourse, then, is one in which rural nature itself is teeming with microbial contagion, and public safety demands that medical experts remain safely contained within the protective walls of the city—here figured as a kind of fortress of human civilization that must be cut off from the material flows of the external world if it is to survive. Though the doctors eventually give the idealistic young Mesmer leave to venture out on what they consider a suicide mission, the abject fear they express at the corporeal interchange between human bodies and a supposedly contagious environment outside the city walls gives voice to the kinds of ecophobic responses that are awakened by epidemiological emergencies. Although *Epidemic* gives voice to and activates a sense of ecophobia in the viewer by highlighting the potential dangers of transcorporeal interchange with the environment, it ultimately *works through* this phobic response and reveals that the horrors of epidemics emerge from human hostility toward corporeal interchange. It is, then, the suffocating human responses to outbreak that become the source of horror in *Epidemic*.

## OOZING BUILDINGS, ABJECT BODIES

If the horror of live burial implicit in the archivist's unsettling anecdotes of the public health response in medieval Milan represents the apotheosis of transcorporeal denial—that is, the sealing off of bodies and the structures they inhabit—the scene at the archive also provides us with some startling imagery showcasing the irrepressible leakiness of bodies and structures. As Lars and Niels accompany the archivist into the depths of the national archive, he shares with the filmmakers an especially telling story about the archive itself, one that seems to form the basis for the material logic of infection in *Epidemic*. Describing the time-worn architectural structure that houses the understories of the national archives, the archivist remarks that "the walls are probably not what you'd expect to find" in such a crucial site of cultural memory. He explains that the building has a problem with saltpeter gradually oozing out of the walls and speculates that it probably owes to the dampness of the ground underneath the building. "In the old days," he explains, "some of the staff were afraid to come down here, especially in the dark, because of the strange sounds, pops, when the saltpeter cracked off more plaster." As the archivist tells his story, the camera fixes on the silhouetted, backlit figure of Lars as he inspects the archive. The lighting is noirish and moody. The archivist's voice echoes resonantly in the brick-lined depths of the structure. The camera zooms in to look more closely at the cracks in the ancient walls, cutting to a shot of Lars gazing at the walls and apparently contemplating the words of the archivist, who concludes by saying that the saltpeter oozing out of the building is a sort of "wall disease." As he does so, the soundtrack starts to capture subtle cracking noises, as if to provide empirical proof of the archivist's claims.

In this lingering shot of the apparently oozing, audibly popping walls, we experience the first note of environmental horror in the film. It is as if the supposedly inert walls of the building have taken up a voice and started to speak, audibly reminding human visitors to the building that architectural structures have agency too: they change, they move, they leak. Indeed, in their gradual shifts the walls take on an uncannily fluid quality. As they move, flow, and explosively pop, then, the oozing walls draw our attention to the surrounding environment—a space conventionally thought of, in the anthropocentric logic of humanism, as an inert background for human activity. No longer background, this supposedly inanimate environment lurches into unsettling motion, emerging uncannily into the foreground.

Timothy Morton has recognized the potential for horror in this emergence of the environment into the foreground of human consciousness, an effect Morton attributes to environmental awareness. "Since everything is interconnected," writes Morton, "there is no definite background and therefore no definite foreground."[16] Morton's interest in the darker implications of environmental awareness leads him to describe the model of material interconnection posited by ecology as the "mesh"—an image that implies both connectivity between organisms and environments as well as the potential for feeling precariously caught up and trapped in such a viscous, weblike material domain. This sensibility lends itself to the study of ecohorror because of the way it highlights the unnerving moments when inert backgrounds seem to come to horrifying life and assert themselves in the foreground: "The mesh isn't static. We can't rigidly specify anything as irrelevant. If there is no background and therefore no foreground, then where are we? We orient ourselves according to backgrounds against which we stand out. There is a word for a state without a foreground-background distinction: madness."[17] In their uncanny emergence from the background into the foreground, then, the walls of the Danish National Archives house not a site of rational order and collective memory but instead the potential dissolution of those rationalizing structures as the environment looms menacingly into the foreground of human consciousness. It is not the *contents* of the archives that are important in such an ecological consciousness, then; it is, in a literal sense, the structures and environments that matter.

The protracted close-up of the pockmarked surface of the wall as Lars stares at it, contemplating the idea of a "wall disease" that turns the supposedly stalwart structure of the national archive into a slowly oozing, fluid form, gives us an unsettling view of the transcorporeal environments human bodies are enmeshed with. Human-made structures meant to hold the natural environment at bay and stake a territorial claim for human culture are revealed to be porous, susceptible to the flowing intrusions of the outside world. The natural world suddenly shifts from being an externality—an inert backdrop for the playing out of human endeavors—to being at the very center of the action, asserting its agential role in the environmental dramas unfolding at center stage. The anecdote about the oozing walls is an important clue to understanding the metacinematic focus of the film as well, since it points not only to the physical media on which cultural memory is preserved but also to the material structures that house those sources. This focus betrays a media-critical impetus behind *Epidemic*, as it is not so much the actual ideas, memories, and diseases transmitted person-to-person that matter, but rather the physical mediations that allow such transmissions to take place at all. The ecohorror of *Epidemic*, then, points not only to the porous transcorporeality of living bodies but also to material mediations of all kinds.

In addition to introducing an ominous note of environmental horror in the film, the image of slowly leaking, diseased walls is a crucial distillation of the material logic of infection in *Epidemic*. The protective enclosure provided by a building depends not only on the stability of the ground the structure is built on but also on the solidity of the walls that hold the building upright. Walls must be solid and strong if they are to support the roof, and they must be effectively insulated if they are to provide protection from potential infringement of the environment outside the structure. Any intrusion from the outside world—be it the encroachment of wind, rain, or an infestation of rodents—represents a failure of the structure to live up to its idealized protective form.

Furthermore, by invoking the biological notion of disease in his description of the structure, the archivist's words blur the distinction between architectural horror and body horror. The idea of the archive as a kind of site of spectral terror—as a memory- and trauma-saturated "haunted house" of sorts—gives way to a startlingly visceral mode of body horror as we become aware of the unsettling hybridity of the architectural-biological structure the filmmakers are exploring. In this sense, the physical structure of the archive is imagined not as a *metaphorical* body but as a *literal* one. In its oozing, porous, dynamically changing character, the building is figured as an actual body, and thus assumes the animacy, agency, and transcorporeal character of the biological body. That we as viewers enter the film within a film at this point suggests that the imagined film is based on this notion of oozing, leaking, liquifying walls that uncannily allow the outside world to infect the interior space of the building. In this kind of oozing structure, interior and exterior cease to be meaningfully distinct as the environment promiscuously mingles with the insides of buildings. Lars, the viewer, and the film he is concocting thus become aware that buildings are never impermeable fortresses that keep the world absolutely at bay, but rather are always transcorporeal structures that allow transit between the building's interior and the outside world.

This environmental "infection" of the human domain works not only at the biological and architectural levels but at the level of media as well. As the outside world slowly leaks into the archive through the porous walls of the structure, the imagined film within a film also leaks into the film we are watching. As Lars's gaze slowly pans across the jagged surface of "diseased" wall, the shot dissolves to a gauzy close-up of the contents of a medical case—we see bandages, vials of medicine, and surgical tools—rummaged through by a man in a lab coat (played by Lars) whom we will soon come to know as Dr. Mesmer, the naive idealist who thinks he can stop the plague singlehandedly with his epidemiological interventions. In the scene that follows, we learn about Mesmer's plan. He is meeting with a panel of older, more distinguished doctors and scientists who decry his intentions to leave the safe confines of the medieval city and travel out to the supposedly plague-infested regions of the countryside. The doctors speak of the "protective walls of our city" and warn that out in the open world "the elements" will turn against him: "It may start as a light cough, but quickly and without mercy, the respiratory organs are disabled by the infected air. The bacteria in the soil penetrates the skin and the flesh by the mere contact. And the water you drink will destroy you from inside." The epidemiological picture the eminent physicians paint for Mesmer is a grim one. The only hope, it seems, is to remain in the city, isolated from the disease outside.

The model of infection deployed by the representatives of the medical establishment in this scene is characteristic of the siege-like practices of isolation and interiority that prevail in an epidemiological emergency. To protect oneself in such a situation, boundaries must be reinforced, and distance from the disease must be maintained. In other words, the walls of human habitation must be kept robust and impermeable, just as one must ensure that the disease does not enter through the surfaces of one's own body. The intellectual categories "in here" and "out there" correspond neatly to the view of the natural environment that has prevailed in the Western humanist tradition. In this anthropocentric worldview, "in here" represents the safety of human communities, which have developed physical structures that can keep the natural world isolated from the cultural centers of civilization. Safety, in other words, means keeping nature "out there," beyond the walls of the city.

While this worldview may seem to provide some measure of prudent protection in the midst of a viral epidemic—quarantine, after all, is a tried and true epidemiological safeguard—it is also based on assumptions about the distinction between culture and nature that are characteristic of what Simon Estok terms ecophobia. This phobic human response to the natural world asserts that impermeable boundaries can be maintained between culture and nature—*here* lies order, civilization, safety; *there* lies madness, chaos, and death. As *Epidemic* demonstrates, ecohorror invokes ecophobia in order to undermine its material logic. While the eminent doctors claim that Mesmer can stay safe if he remains in the city, the imagined film within a film is based on a fundamental irony: it is the city, the *polis*, the center of human civilization, that is actually infected, while the supposedly infected areas in the countryside are in fact free of the disease before Mesmer travels out to them. Though the film seems to set up a dichotomy between Mesmer's doe-eyed idealism and the world-weary pragmatism of the more aged physicians, the materially meaningful distinction in the film is between the unhealthy ecophobia of the city and the free-flowing ecological relationships that can flourish in domains less marked by human habitation.

The oozing, unexpectedly leaky quality of the walls at the archive is also evident in the presentation of infected bodies in *Epidemic*. As Lars and Niels continue to draft the script for their film, they consider the tangible qualities of the boils associated with the bubonic plague in gruesome material detail. In one scene, Lars reads aloud from an unnamed archival source describing the plague, choosing a passage that parallels the image of the leaky walls from earlier in the film. "And no matter how hard and firm the boils might seem," Lars reads, "it could rupture unexpectedly, to the victim's surprise, and spill forth into a two-colored pus. It was startling that the colors didn't mix, but came out together, by God's will, without compounding into a third color." The grotesquely specific image of the two-colored pus suddenly rupturing from the infected body reminds Niels of a toothpaste called Signal that he recalls from advertisements as a white paste with a red stripe down the side, speculating that the boil might work along the same principle as the Signal toothpaste tube. Later in the film, Lars and Niels buy a tube of Signal toothpaste and see that when the tube is squeezed, the paste does indeed come out in two distinct colors, with a red stripe along the side. But when they cut open the tube to discover if the red and the white parts of the paste are arranged in stripes within the tube, they find that this is not the case, and they are left with an oozing mess of red and white paste on their hands as a reward for their inquisitiveness. As an image of environmental fluidity, the dissected toothpaste tube reinforces the messiness and inseparability of the transcorporeal enmeshment of organisms and environments.

Just like the unexpectedly oozing walls of the archive, the bodies of infected plague victims are unpredictable, permeable vessels prone to sudden rupture and leakage. The fluids that pour forth from these leaky bodies are themselves unpredictable and strange substances that display some qualities of solid matter, maintaining their distinct colors rather than mixing into a compound. The distinctions between solid and liquid matter are, then, contingent and fleeting, just as the boundaries between the inside and outside of transcorporeal bodies are subject to sudden dissolution.

The ultimate agent of contagion in the film, however, is not the supposedly "infected" environment feared by the medical experts. Instead it is Mesmer himself—with his naive objectivism and his assumption that he can investigate and treat disease without his own body being implicated in the process—who spreads the illness across the land. As the film shows Mesmer triumphantly riding a Red Cross helicopter across the supposedly diseased landscape, his idealistic medical ministry would seem to be a brave one, since he is subjecting himself to the possibility of infection in order to come to rescue of the country-dwelling people he assumes to be infected. Such a retreat to the countryside under the sway of humanist idealism—an idealism that is ignorant of the transcorporeal exchanges of ecological enmeshment—is an effective representation of the assumptions of a Nordic approach to the environment that cultural historian Nina Witoszek has labeled *ecohumanism*, which she describes as "a cosmology based on humanist ideals, but one in which the symbolic referents of identity derive from nature imagery and from a particular allegiance to place."[18] In ecohumanism, the main premise of humanism—namely "the recognition of the inherent dignity and of the equal and unalienable rights of all members of the human family"—is "modified by values springing from man's experience of nature."[19] Although Witoszek does acknowledge this point, it is important to note that this "ecohumanist" stance remains fundamentally grounded in humanism and therefore assumes that human subjects can go out into nature for physical and spiritual rejuvenation without being caught up in the toxic material interchanges ecological enmeshment demands. *Epidemic*'s critique of the naive objectivism of medical epistemology is therefore also a critique of Nordic approaches to nature, which reinforce the optimistic, neo-Romantic instrumentalization of the wilderness as a site for the rejuvenation of the human subject. The emergence of the transcorporeal ecological subject in *Epidemic* thus comes at the expense of the Nordic ecohumanist subject.

## INFECTIOUS MEDIA AND THE METACINEMA OF OUTBREAK

The oozing fluidity of bodies presaged in the beginning of the film explodes into full corporeal abjection in the final scene. In it, Lars and Niels host a dinner for Claes, a production consultant from the Danish Film Institute (played by Claes Kastholm Hansen, the actual DFI consultant for *Epidemic*). The purpose of the dinner is to showcase their completed script for the project and convince Claes that the Film Institute has made a wise investment in their film. But since Lars and Niels have lost their previous finished script, they have to fill out the scant twelve-page manuscript they have actually completed with some performative narration of their own. Lars begins the narration, saying that he will "explain the ending" of the film, since the scene has apparently

Lars and Niels imagine a possible scene in their film depicting the accidental live burials that could take place during a plague, specifically suggesting that Mesmer's wife could be depicted as a victim of this terrifying fate. Frame grab from *Epidemic* (dir. Lars von Trier, 1987).

In contrast to the techniques of bodily enclosure and isolation advocated by the public health officials attempting to limit viral infection in *Epidemic*, Dr. Mesmer naively exposes his own body to the supposedly infectious landscape outside the city and in the process becomes a vehicle for contagion and spreads the plague across the countryside. Frame grab from *Epidemic* (dir. Lars von Trier, 1987).

not been included in the partially completed script: "Our hero, Mesmer . . . after having traveled around this infected environment, he's entrenched in this underground cave. . . . But as everyone else around him has died, he hides in this cave so he won't fall ill, but discovers that he's the disease carrier. And then he breaks out of this cave by crawling along this long, steep passage and comes up, kneels and thanks God for the life which once had been." The Danish verb *bryde ud* (break out), which Lars uses to describe Mesmer's emergence from his cave, has exactly the same resonance as its English translation: it is related to the noun *udbrud* (outbreak), a term that has a similar implication of viral contagion in Danish. In that sense, Mesmer's emergence at the end of the film as the agent of infection, from a cave where he has attempted to hide from the (nonexistent) contagion of the environment around him, serves as a metaphor for the transcorporeal fixations of the entire film. Claes is not impressed with Mesmer's idealistic and reverential turn to the divine in the final scene, however. "He crawls in a cave, comes out and thanks God?" he asks incredulously. "It's pathetic at best. I had expected there to be a little more action in it. You know, the classic tragedy where all the main characters finally fall down dead. 'Oh, I'm dying,' you know?" Lars protests that he had hoped to contain the death to the offscreen space, asking Claes frustratedly if he'd "like a bloodbath" in the final scene. Claes—whom the film has depicted as a crass, America-loving cultural tourist—answers in the affirmative: "Well, in films—particularly Danish films—and that's what fate has forced me to work with, there are lots of stories where people don't die when they should, or fewer people die than ought to. And there's fewer screams and less blood than there ought to be. Where things ebb away, right? As if an evening fog rolled in and everything disappeared." The image Claes settles on serves as a damning commentary on what he views as the frustrating timidity of Danish film: as everything ebbs away and a fog rolls in, Claes suggests, Danish films become steeped in a kind of idealistic, dematerialized haze. What Danish films lack, he suggests, is the gory materiality of the American horror film.[20] In the final scene of *Epidemic*, the metacinematic conflation of the frame narrative and the embedded narrative becomes more salient. As (fictional) Claes requests an action-packed final bloodbath, actual Claes (the producing consultant for *Epidemic*) gets one.

The bloodbath comes in the form of a hypnotist show Lars and Niels have arranged for the evening. True to the self-reflexive quality of the film, the hypnotist Svend (Svend Hamann) is played by an actual hypnotist, whom von Trier would later cast again for the first season of his TV series *The Kingdom*.[21] Svend has been hired to fill out the script and Lars's narration with a demonstration for Claes of the acute spectator response Lars and Niels hope their film will inspire. To that end, Svend hypnotizes a young woman named Gitte (Gitte Lind) into the fictional world of the film. As Svend induces Gitte to "relax," "think about sleeping," and "sink into your chair," with all the trancelike repetitiveness one would expect from such a show, her head sinks to her chest, and she appears to enter a deep sleep. At this sight, Lars and Claes smile, savoring the voyeuristic pleasure of watching the unconscious, hypnotized spectator. Reminding Gitte that she has read the script before their arrival, Svend commands her to "enter the film. Enter *Epidemic!*"

In her suggestible and uninhibited state, Gitte embodies a certain version of the action-packed ending Claes has requested better than any words on a page. Her performance begins in a verbal register but slowly moves into a more immediate, bodily demonstration of corporeal abjection. "I'm walking down the street," Gitte narrates. "There are . . . people. They . . . they look terrible. They . . . they're screaming. They're screaming so terribly loudly." Gitte's breathing becomes labored as she evidently takes in the horror she sees before her hypnotized consciousness. "They cry out," she continues. "They shout for God, I think. They want help. And there are rats. Rats with tails . . . such long tails. Longer than their bodies. Everyone walks alone. Nobody wants to talk. They're scared of each other. Scared of infection and death." When she tells Svend that she thinks there is a dead body in one of the houses, the hypnotist commands her to enter. Horrified, Gitte narrates, "She's covered with boils. She's lying there . . . staring. The children begin to whine softly. They're so terribly frightened." She goes on to describe the blackened, boil-covered bodies of the children. The contagion, it appears, has spread throughout the village. Gitte grows more and more frantic in her terror, hyperventilating and grabbing at her face and neck. As Svend becomes concerned at her pronounced reaction, he attempts to count her down to get her out of the film, but Gitte seems unable to escape. "There are lots of holes everywhere with children . . . human bodies. They're dying in the streets. They lie everywhere and . . . and die." Tears begin streaming down Gitte's face. Her crying becomes wailing. She is inconsolable, screaming, writhing. The camera cuts to a close-up of a boil on Niels's wrist peaking out from under the cuff of his tuxedo jacket. Gitte's screams become piercing, shrill, terrified wails. It is an expressive, anxious, Munchian scream—a scream that seems to go through nature and through the body of the beholder. As Gitte's screams become more frantic, we see boils have sprouted all over her neck. She leaps onto the table and grabs for a fork. As the camera cuts to shots of the now clearly infected dinner guests, writhing and vomiting, we see a close-up of the tines of a fork piercing the boil on Gitte's neck, blood and pus streaming forth and running down her body. In the final shots of the film, the camera pans across the aftermath of the scene—plates and food are everywhere; infected bodies are collapsed in heaps; vomit, blood, and wine are splattered across the wall. As the camera settles on Lars, he looks up to the sky—the last image we see before the credits roll.

In this final sequence, we are not only given the kind of action-packed bloodbath Claes wished for; we are also treated to the kind of abject transcorporeal body horror the film has been hinting at all along. Such an explosive ending seems to be the natural response to the rigid, suffocating practices of corporeal containment during historical plagues and epidemics, as the film makes clear. In place of this ecophobic, rigidly contained individual and collective body, *Epidemic* poses a model of environmental and medial fluidity. Just as the body is a transcorporeal organism that must be allowed to freely mingle with the environment to maintain its life, and the vitality of a nation-state depends on free movement of people across borders, *Epidemic* models a fluid sort of metacinematic narrative. The material world, the film posits, has become infected by a disease originating in the fictional world they have come up with. Fully material and ecologically fluid, *Epidemic* draws film into a relationship of transcorporeal interchange with the real world.

In his sojourn into the supposedly infected countryside outside the city walls, Dr. Mesmer brings his dualistic model of embodiment with him. Assuming he can transcend the environment in his idealistic efforts to bring medical care to the rural folk, Mesmer exemplifies the Nordic approach to nature that has been described by cultural historian Nina Witoszek as ecohumanism. *Epidemic* forwards an eco-materialist critique of such an approach to nature—with its naive disregard for the transcorporeal interchanges between the body and the material world. The film's fixation on the oozing, leaky, abject qualities of the transcorporeal body draws attention to the entanglement of living bodies and the environment. One of the techniques the film uses to do this is by bringing the background unsettlingly into the foreground—showing how both the natural and built environments do not serve as an inert backdrop for human endeavors but rather are intimately connected to the bodies that interact with them. Such a shift in focus from the centrality of the human subject to that of the physical surroundings effectively undermines the enclosed model of embodiment posited by the ecophobic approaches of public health authorities in the film. By showing how such closed-off notions of embodiment are suffocating and ecologically unsustainable—and that it is the human figures disregarding the realities of transcorporeal interchange who spread disease, rather than a supposedly "infected landscape"—*Epidemic* activates an ecophobic response in its viewer, only to dismantle its material logic. Though the film ends on a note of abject body horror and unsettling corporeal leakiness, the infection that comes spectacularly to the surface in the film's final scene similarly results from the naive investigations of the filmmakers Lars and Niels, who have disinterestedly studied historical and contemporaneous diseases as they have hurriedly scripted their film, without supposing that their bodies are implicated in the transcorporeal interchanges that result from such a project.

# CHAPTER TWO

# Abject Ecologies

## Patriarchal Containment and
## Feminist Embodiment in *Thelma*

Norwegian auteur Joachim Trier's fourth feature film, *Thelma* (2017), opens
with a flashback. A young girl and her father walk across a frozen lake. The
camera captures them in an extreme long shot as they make their way across
the wintry landscape, emphasizing the deep space of the scene as the ice recedes
into the background. A forest in the distance forms an undulating horizon,
hiding the late-afternoon winter sun that has just gone down. The surface of
the lake is as smooth as a mirror, giving us a reflection of the two figures as
they slowly trudge across it. A cut to a close-up of the girl's face as she walks
shows her looking down at the lake. Her point of view reveals fish swimming
just beneath her feet, clearly visible through the transparent layer of ice. The
scene cuts to an underwater shot looking up at the girl from underneath the
ice, and we see that the fish-eye view of the world above is similarly unhindered
by the transparent ice. Cutting back to the surface, the camera follows the girl
and her father as they continue their hike toward a snow-decked forest just
on the other side of the lake, the father carrying a hunting rifle on his back.
As they get to the forest, the pair stops and rests, the girl enjoying a cup of
hot cocoa from her thermos while the father readies his gun for the hunt.
Continuing their hike through the snowy forest, the two come across a deer,
and the father signals to the girl that she should stop and watch. Transfixed by
the confrontation with the young doe—who seems blissfully unaware of any
human presence in the scene—the girl's gaze is unwavering. Her father raises
the gun and gets the deer in his sights, holding the barrel level and steadying
his aim. In the silence of the scene—with her eyes still locked on the doe—the

father slowly shifts his aim to the back of his daughter's head. After a tense few moments without taking his shot, the father lowers the gun, and the doe runs off through the forest. The girl looks up at her father, still apparently unaware of the peril she had been in moments before. The scene cuts to black, and the title card flickers to life in bold letters on the screen: THELMA.

*Thelma* is a supernatural thriller about a young woman's queer awakening and the unsettling telekinetic powers that accompany her gradual emancipation from her repressive upbringing as she moves away from her parents to begin university studies in Oslo. Because of its indebtedness to the tradition of horror movies about psychic powers—with films like *Carrie* (1976) and *The Fury* (1978), both directed by Brian De Palma, as clear reference points—*Thelma*'s fixation on the usual tropes of the genre comes as no surprise. The overbearing, fundamentalist Christian faith of parents who have kept their daughter sheltered from the world; the coming-of-age narrative, focusing on Thelma's belated sexual awakening; Thelma's gradual mastery of her psychic abilities, which accompanies a painful process of gaining autonomy from an authoritarian parental regime—all of these elements come straight from the playbook of the telekinesis horror film.

But the setting of *Thelma*'s opening flashback scene in the wintry landscape of the forested Norwegian countryside signals from the very beginning that the film is concerned with the role of the natural environment in the expression of Thelma's psychic abilities. Seen in a Norwegian cultural context, the opening scene begins the film with a paradigmatic representation of *friluftsliv*—a term literally meaning "open-air life" (but often translated as "outdoor recreation") that has deep roots in Nordic cultures. Though the English translation of *friluftsliv* suggests something banal—as if it were merely an umbrella term for recreational activities like camping, fishing, or hiking—scholars have studied the concept's connections to Nordic environmental attitudes and imaginaries, suggesting that it may present a kind of conceptual underpinning to the region's environmental exceptionalism. Some have attempted more expansive definitions of the term in an effort to capture the wide semantic range *friluftsliv* encompasses. Thomas H. Beery notes that the concept "fuses ideas of outdoor recreation, nature experience, philosophy and lifestyle."[1] Picking up on the first part of the compound term (*fri*, meaning "free" or "open"), Gelter adds that *friluftsliv* is "based on experiences of freedom in nature and spiritual connectedness with the landscape."[2] Combining, as the term does, concepts of freedom, the outdoors, and lifestyle, the overwhelmingly emancipatory and harmonious connotations of *friluftsliv* have been used to explain the exceptionally positive valence of nature and the wilderness in the Nordic cultural imagination. So although the Nordics are regarded as technologically advanced and progressive societies in which most inhabitants live in urban or suburban settings, their famously leading role in promoting ideals of environmentalism and sustainable development has led the Nordic countries to be seen as exceptionally nature-loving.

Seen in the light of the concept of *friluftsliv*, the opening scene of *Thelma* registers as all the more unsettling. As the cinematography captures the deep space of the landscape Thelma and her father walk through, the scene is set up to emphasize the open, boundless, and emancipatory spaciousness of the wilderness setting. As we see Thelma enjoying hot cocoa and being guided in how to track an animal and engage with nature in a quiet, unobtrusive way, the scene could hardly seem more wholesome. In the moment that her father, Trond, turns the gun from the deer to the back of Thelma's head, though, the overwhelming sense of harmony in nature is shattered. The scene oscillates suddenly from the freedom and wholesomeness of *friluftsliv* to the terrifying specter of paternal violence. This violence, we come to learn, does not come in the form of random or arbitrary attacks, but rather is part of a systematic effort to contain Thelma's body—to keep her psychosomatic powers bottled up within her. This paternal regime of rigid boundary maintenance is suggested by the icy imagery of the opening scene, which young Thelma seems to ponder as she glances down at the fish swimming just beneath her feet. The hard surface of the ice forms temporarily firm boundaries that will soon give way to fluid interchange between the lake and its surroundings. Set against the celebrated Norwegian love of *friluftsliv*, the film suggests, Trond's efforts to keep Thelma's body rigidly contained strike a strident note, underscoring the hypocrisy of a culture that embraces the supposed freedom to roam unencumbered in nature on the one hand, but also works to systematically repress and contain female bodily expression on the other. Such efforts at corporeal containment cannot be reconciled with the material realities of ecological enmeshment, evident in the transcorporeal porousness of organic bodies.

Rather than reading the film through the lens of genre—through which we might examine how it adheres to or departs from a set of conventions characteristic of telekinesis horror films—I examine the ways *Thelma* contributes to the emerging mode of ecohorror, especially in terms of its ecocritical presentation of paternalistic and feminist models of embodiment. Such an ecocritical reading of *Thelma* reveals the ways contemporary Nordic cultures are reimagining women's bodies in terms of their fundamental ecological and material characteristics. As a film about the unsettling power unleashed by a young woman's psychosexual awakening, *Thelma* fixates on the emancipatory energy expressed by the unruliness of the female body. In eco-materialist terms, *Thelma* is a horror film about the social conflicts that play out along the contested boundaries between a woman's body and the external world. The film suggests that ostensibly progressive and egalitarian societies like Norway continue to be haunted by deeply rooted traditions of misogynistic paternalism, a social regime that insists—among other demands—on the rigid containment of the female body. Following the opening scene, lingering shots of the wilderness landscape throughout the film repeatedly suggest there is more than a passing connection between this uncannily persistent misogyny and human attitudes toward the environment in the region. As we have already seen in the case of Lars von Trier's outbreak horror film *Epidemic*, total corporeal containment is an ecologically untenable form of embodiment that derives from an ecophobic fear of the mingling of human bodies and their environments. In *Thelma*, these paternalistic and ecophobic containment strategies, far from permanently suppressing Thelma's psychosomatic powers, in fact have the effect of amplifying them. Refused the possibility of giving vent to her internal life—her impulses, desires, states of mind, and her own kinetic energy—Thelma's body builds up an explosive pressure that is unleashed throughout the film as a series of uncontrolled, involuntary, and highly material episodes of psychokinetic and transcorporeal abjection.

To set the stage for Thelma's rebellion, the film posits that—far from its reputation as one of the most gender-equal countries in the world—contemporary Norwegian society has remained mired in a misogynistic tradition of policing and attempting to contain the expressive force of women's bodies. Against the backdrop of Norwegian nature discourses like *friluftsliv* and *allemannsretten* (Everyman's Rights), *Thelma* shows how cultural misogyny has been "naturalized" in contemporary Norway, as Nordic nature imaginaries have centered the masculine subject and provided nature-based explanations for the supposedly hysterical expressions of female bodies. In service of this gender critique, *Thelma* situates the subtle kinds of biopolitical power contemporary societies exert on women's bodies within a historical continuum of misogyny that can be traced back to medieval witch burning. Seen through the lens of Nordic film history, then, *Thelma* situates itself in relation to a problematic "tradition of torturing women" in Nordic cinema, in the words of Linda Haverty Rugg—a tradition that encompasses some of the most canonical films of auteurs like Carl Th. Dreyer, Ingmar Bergman, and Lars von Trier. That Joachim Trier overtly places his film in a homegrown Scandinavian cinematic tradition that includes canonical films about witchcraft and female victimhood suggests that we ought to reconsider what the "tradition of torturing women" might include in a contemporary context. Without using Rugg's terms, Joachim Trier has remarked that *Thelma* was his response to the regressive gender politics of horror films invested in spectacularizing the suffering of women's bodies: "Unfortunately some of the films that we look back on, in the '70s for example, were old-fashioned in their approach to the female body. You fall into the trap of them being more exploitative. I'm riffing off some of the best themes. . . . I'm trying to do a modern empowerment tale of a young person while riffing off some of those classical traditional tropes from horror movies."[3] For the purposes of this chapter, triangulating *Thelma's* place in relation to the Nordic tradition of torturing women and a broader trend of female exploitation in horror is not a question of assigning a genre to the film. Instead, as Trier's comments suggest, these troubling traditions present a certain view of the female body that he wants to both respond to and work against. To do so, Trier presents on screen a version of Norwegian society that is not far removed from the medieval patriarchal societies that burned witches. Moreover, the continuity of misogyny even in ostensibly enlightened Norway—with its internationally regarded achievements in gender equality—is expressed in terms that lend themselves to an eco-materialist understanding of embodiment. Though the tortures that *Thelma* depicts are indirect and ostensibly more humane forms of paternalistic social control, the film suggests that any regimes that constrain female physicality—even in indirect and more "humane" ways—will be met with direct and emphatically material resistance from oppressed women who acknowledge and perform their own ecological embodiment. Rather than holding out hope for female spiritual transcendence through martyrdom—as the films in the tradition of torturing women do—*Thelma* advocates instead for confrontational acts of abjection and transcorporeal resistance.

## ABJECT TRANSCORPOREALITY

The central plot conflict of Trier's film arises when Thelma (Eili Harboe) moves away from her apparently loving—but decidedly overbearing—parents (Henrik Rafaelsen and Ellen Dorrit Petersen) and her rural childhood home to the capital city of Oslo to begin studying at the university. In addition to her fundamentalist Christian faith being challenged by her new, culturally secular friend group, as well as experiencing an intense and (for her) unsettling same-sex attraction to her classmate Anja (Kaya Wilkins), she has had seizure-like episodes that she assumes must be symptoms of epilepsy. As Thelma's attraction to Anja grows, they become friends and share a passionate kiss in the lobby of the Oslo Opera House. Unsettled by the total upheaval of her conservative social values, Thelma starts to suspect that her strong feelings for Anja are associated not only with her seizures but also with an inexplicable—and possibly malign—psychic force that begins manifesting itself within her. Her uncontrollable telekinetic powers seem to have a direct connection to her most transgressive and deeply felt desires, as if an internal "sinfulness"—to use the moralizing language of Thelma's upbringing—is escaping the bounds of her mind and body and having potentially dangerous consequences in the real world. After being admitted to a specialty clinic where she is subjected to a draining regime of induced seizures—all of which are recorded by a host of electronic sensors and video monitors—the specialist finally reaches a diagnosis: not epilepsy but a condition called psychogenic non-epileptic seizures (PNES). The doctor explains that the seizures are just a symptom of some other disorder, a physical reaction to something that is being repressed—possibly just stress, but maybe, he says, traumatic memories. Unbeknownst to Thelma, the draining regime of induced seizures has also had a terrifying side effect. As the doctor prods her with questions about her romantic life, Thelma fixates on Anja while she is gripped by a convulsive fit. At that moment, Anja, alone in her apartment, is alarmed by a sudden flickering of lights and the blaring of a stereo she had turned off moments earlier. As she struggles to understand the sudden electrical disruptions, a plate glass window in her living room spontaneously explodes, only to immediately reassemble itself, after which Anja is nowhere to be seen. Thelma's psychic energy has somehow projected Anja—her secret object of desire—into some vacuous space beyond the physical realm. A strand of Anja's hair left ominously dangling from the now intact window suggests that Thelma, in her distress, has somehow contained her within its transparent surface. The rest of the film centers on Thelma's quest to retrieve Anja from her unwitting psychic banishment, a quest that precipitates the revelation of a secret family history and a parental regime of manipulation, gaslighting, and medical abuse to keep Thelma's frightening powers in check. In a fiery final set piece, Thelma dramatically confronts and overturns the abusive paternalism of her father, and in the process frees Anja from the abyss—setting the stage for the two to begin a romantic relationship without the constraints of her parents' prejudice.

To get a sense of the film's eco-materialist approach to the body, it helps to start with the scene of Thelma's first seizure. There we see Thelma hard at work not long after her arrival at the university. She sits at a desk in a full campus reading room, a textbook open in front of her as she takes notes. Aesthetically the room is characterized by order and rationalism. The study cubicle she sits at is echoed by mimetic copies receding into the background, the quasi-mechanical repetition of the space hinting at the orderliness of the academic system within which Thelma has assumed her place. The rows of books lining the walls, the ample natural light streaming into the room, and the minimalist simplicity of the modern academic architecture suggest enlightenment and learning, as well as the rigid uniformity imposed on individuals within Norway's egalitarian social tradition. The spare sound design includes the subdued noises of students quietly attending to their work in a library: stifled coughs, the sliding of chair legs along the floor as students settle in or get up to leave, the flipping of textbook pages, and the scratch of pens on notebook pages. Thelma bears a distinct mark of difference in this setting otherwise characterized by social conformity: a crucifix necklace. An unusual accessory in culturally secular Oslo, the necklace serves as a visual reminder of the conservative social values of her upbringing. The one obvious mark of individuality in the scene is thus also a mark of social adherence and obedience to authority in another sense.

Into this space of order and learning walks Anja, a young woman who settles into the empty seat next to Thelma and begins silently studying alongside her. We don't know it yet, but Thelma is going to fall in love with Anja. Her immediate attraction is only subtly hinted at by stolen glances and polite smiles within this rigidly quiet social setting. As Thelma and Anja quietly continue to study, a murder of crows flock in the air nearby, and we see through the window as one bird separates itself from the others and flies full speed into the surface of the window, dropping like a stone toward the ground upon impact. Immediately after the disturbance, Thelma's hand starts to quake, a convulsion that she tries in vain to still with her other hand. The effort quickly fails, as the rest of her body begins shaking violently. Thelma's eyes roll back, her head is thrown backward, and she tumbles violently from her chair, her body assuming a tense and rigid posture on the floor as the convulsions continue. While the students gather around her and try to help, we see that her pants are soaked with urine, her lack of control over her bodily functions and movements now fully on display.

The scene is an uncomfortable one—not only in a corporeal sense because of the tense rigidity of Thelma's body and the clear physical strains of the shaking, visually evident in tense bones and muscles in her arms and hands. It is also uncomfortable in a social sense. These two kinds of discomfort are clearly linked, as the mortifying experience of becoming an object of worry and pity painfully on display for a group of fellow students has everything to do with her spectacular and very public loss of bodily control. For a young person new to the university who is painfully shy and has no friends in town, the prospect of not only becoming a public spectacle by being thrown into involuntary bodily contortions but also wetting one's own pants for all to see is the stuff of nightmares—on par with arriving at school with no clothing on. The discomfort of the scene comes from the self being reduced to a quivering body, as well as from the unsettling leakage of bodily fluids no longer contained while shocked and nervous onlookers gather around.

As Thelma's body is repeatedly seized by terrifying convulsive fits, the trembling, unstable boundaries between the interior self and the exterior world are on full display. She becomes a leaky organism whose fluidity and instability violate the normative model of bodily containment. Horror has long been associated with this kind of negotiation and violation of bodily boundaries, along with the complex affective dynamics of attraction and repulsion that play into such a negotiation.[4] In her seminal book *Pouvoirs de l'horreur: Essai sur l'abjection* (*Powers of Horror: An Essay on Abjection*), Julia Kristeva argues for a psychoanalytic understanding of horror through the concept of abjection, an experience she describes as crucial to the process of subject formation. In abjection, the subject demonstratively separates itself from the maternal body through actions like spitting out food, vomiting, or otherwise expelling undesirable substances from the body. The experience of abjection thus demonstrates a certain style of contrarian individualism established in basely physical terms: "'I' want none of that element, sign of their desire; 'I' do not want to listen, 'I' do not assimilate it, 'I' expel it. But since the food is not an 'other' for 'me,' who am only in their desire, I expel *myself out*, I abject *myself* within the same motion through which 'I' claim to establish *myself*."[5] As the pre-Oedipal developmental stage is described in psychoanalytic theory as one in which the mother's body is narcissistically assumed to be an extension of the self, the process of individuation through abjection involves a complex negotiation of the boundaries of self. By rejecting material sustenance, the subject thus prioritizes personal autonomy over the nutritional needs of the body. Such abject demonstrations of the subject's individuality, moreover, frequently take the form of violent, spasmodic fits of the body, as in the convulsions of gagging and retching: "That trifle turns me inside out, guts sprawling; it is thus that *they* see that 'I' am in the process of becoming another at the expense of my own death. During that course in which 'I' become, I give birth to myself amid the violence of sobs, of vomit."[6]

Drawing on the term's etymological connection to the action of throwing or the state of being thrown away, Kristeva describes abjection as a crucial (though painful) experience in the formation of the self. Abjection comes about as the subject rebels from the caregiver through an act of expelling matter from the body. The abject substance—the vomit, pus, blood, piss, shit—now demonstrably cast off from the body, occupies an uncomfortable middle ground between the self and the environment. "Unflaggingly, like an inescapable boomerang," writes Kristeva, "a vortex of summons and repulsion places the one haunted by it literally beside himself."[7] In abjection, the otherness that haunts our very body—the filthy, unclean substances within it—is expelled for all to see. The abject thus takes the form of a "jettisoned object" that is "radically excluded" from the self, yet which retains some ambivalent material connection to the self. Abjection is an experience characterized by "a massive and sudden emergence of uncanniness, which, familiar as it might have been in an opaque and forgotten life, now harries me as radically separate, loathsome. Not me. Not that. But not nothing, either. A 'something' that I do not recognize as a thing."[8] Rather than Freud's well-known formulation of *das Unheimliche* (the uncanny) as the return of the repressed, Kristeva's description of abjection traces an opposite trajectory where a haunting otherness does not *return* but is instead expelled, rejected, cast off from the body in a movement of defiant (and sickening) individuation. And in that moment of casting off the abject substance—which, Kristeva writes, is often accompanied by nausea, involuntary spasms, and the writhing of a body in violent upheaval—the subject individuates herself from the caregiver through the defiant act of rejection, as when children spit out food they have been fed. Abjection is thus transgressive and gross: a dramatic public demonstration of private shame brought into the open. In this uncomfortable scene, then, Thelma establishes her subjectivity by abjecting herself, bringing herself low, reducing herself to a thrashing, leaking, unclean body. In her revolt, Thelma becomes revolting.

In a material sense, abjection constructs an image of the body as a transcorporeal organism. Abjection centers on violent explosions of substance and fluid from within the body into the environment. It is merely a more dramatic version of the type of transcorporeal action that is constantly taking place, vital processes that depend on the transit of substances across the porous boundaries between the body and the world. Transcorporeality is an approach to the body, first elaborated by feminist ecocritic Stacy Alaimo, that emphasizes the "interconnections, interchanges, and transits between human bodies and nonhuman natures." Transcorporeality sees the body as dynamically enmeshed with its environment, rather than transcendently above or securely separated by strategies of insulation. Embodiment is thus not situated in one location or in one type of substance in transcorporeality. Indeed, by emphasizing the transitory, the theory "acknowledges the often unpredictable and unwanted actions of human bodies, nonhuman creatures, ecological systems, chemical agents, and other actors."[9]

Without using the same term as Alaimo, cultural anthropologist Tim Ingold similarly emphasizes material transit and interchange in his ecological description of embodiment. Ingold's intent is "to think of the body not as a sink into which practices settle like sediment in a ditch, but rather as a dynamic center of unfolding activity."[10] Moreover, in this dynamic, ever-unfolding process of material interchange with the environment, transcorporeal bodies are *leaky* organisms. Like clay flowerpots—which must be open to the world in order to receive life-giving water for the plant to absorb and also include an opening underneath for draining excess fluids—the living body "is sustained thanks only to the continual taking in of materials from its surroundings and, in turn, the discharge into the them, in the process of respiration and metabolism." Living organisms, then, "can exist and persist only because they *leak*: that is, because of the interchange of materials across the ever-emergent surfaces by which they differentiate themselves from the surrounding medium. The bodies of organisms and other things leak continually; indeed, their very lives depend on it."[11] In the vital functioning of organic life, leakage is a feature, not a bug.

Thelma's "leakiness" in her first convulsive fit, though, is not included to emphasize the everyday vital processes that keep her alive. Instead, her urine-soaked jeans are for Thelma a sign that something has gone horrifyingly wrong. Because of the taboo status of bodily fluids and waste, a vital process that Ingold dryly describes as the "interchange of materials" across the surfaces of the body becomes a sign of psychosomatic dysfunction. The cultural norms that govern behavior in public space (particularly spaces as heavily laden with behavioral norms as university libraries) forbid the physical expression of bodily fluids, relegating such transcorporeal transits to designated private spaces such as restroom stalls. Clearly, then, open displays of transcorporeality are subject to a great deal of cultural circumscription. The deeply felt cultural association of such fluids with uncleanliness, moreover, indicates the degree to which dominant cultural values rest on a disavowal of the material and ecological enmeshment of human bodies. Thelma's seizure, then, is both transgressive and embarrassing because of the degree to which it demonstratively displays her own transcorporeality for all to see. In her abjection, Thelma thus not only differentiates herself from her parental caretakers (according to Kristeva's psychoanalytic take on abjection); she also sets herself apart from her social peer group, becoming a convulsive and leaky organism whose body defiantly resists social constraints.

As an act of material expulsion or leakage, abjection is, then, a transcorporeal act. Despite the universalizing language introduced by the psychoanalytic theory Kristeva works with, the cultural right to abject oneself is far from universal. Some identities, that is, are afforded more of a right to abject themselves than others. As recent scholars have moved away from the universal psychoanalytic subject—a subject without gender, race, or social standing—it has become clear that abjection is unevenly understood across different categories of identity. Abjection can be thought of as a privilege akin to white privilege or male privilege—indeed, a privilege typically only available to straight, white, cisgender men, who can more or less freely indulge in abjection. The profound irony of this is that debasing oneself is a privilege only available to normative and hegemonic categories of identity in many social settings.

In their recent volume *Abjection Incorporated*, Maggie Hennefeld and Nicholas Sammond are highly responsive to the ways abjection maps onto cultural privilege, bringing potent and relevant political realities to bear in their analysis. They write that, for feminist/queer and critical race theorists "the individualizing drive toward abjecting unwanted elements from the body politic intrinsically forms the basis of normative, white, patriarchal, and heterosexual iterations of the (unmarked) self, which underpin the sovereign subject."[12] The political extension of abjection, then, provides a basis for defining the social collective by excluding unwanted groups. At the same time, abjection has been co-opted by regressive political movements such as the alt-right, becoming a platform for dominant groups "claiming an abject status in order to adopt, ironize, and undermine the markers of marginalization by which damaging social and power hierarchies have traditionally been administered and enforced."[13] Abjection, perversely, has become a contested ideological zone that has fueled the rise of the trollish politics of white male resentment. "If social authenticity is a currency that derives from a wounded identity," write Hennefeld and Sammond, "abjection is its lingua franca."[14]

One potent trend of popular moving-image media in recent years has run counter to this alt-right co-optation of abjection, namely the reclaiming and dramatic embodiment of abjection by women and other marginalized communities, especially evident in the genres of comedy and horror. Women have traditionally been denied the possibility of embodying overtly visceral and frequently grossly physical performances by social and media norms that deem improper such open displays of unflattering female physicality. Women's reclaiming of abjection is a response not only to the performative abjection of straight, white men encouraged in right-wing hypermasculine settings but also to the long-standing tradition of disavowing the transcorporeal materiality of female bodies. Dominant and misogynistic cultural structures of patriarchy have situated women as objects of desire, scorn, or moral virtue in moving-image media. At the same time, women have been denied the possibility of acknowledging their base physicality, especially in corporeal displays that are incongruous with paternalistic notions of female virtue or heteronormative standards of female desirability. Denying a living, embodied subject the right to abjection, however, runs counter to the material realities that govern organic life. To impose such restrictions on abjection is to deny and shut off the transcorporeal pathways of material interchange that make life possible. Such a denial (to use Ingold's preferred metaphor) is akin to fully enclosing a flowerpot so that the plant no longer receives sunlight or water and has no possibility of releasing its excess fluidity. Trapped in such tightly insulated vessels, thriving plants wither away, becoming little more than fetid and rotten clumps of decaying organic matter.

## FRAGILE CONTAINMENT

The more we learn about Thelma and her upbringing, the more it becomes clear that she has been the object of unusually repressive and controlling parenting. At the outset of adulthood, Thelma is—to continue with Ingold's metaphor—like a potted plant that has been tightly sealed off from the world, insulated from the salubrious material flows that sustain life. Rather than a flower, however, it might be more accurate to picture an imposing and powerful botanical organism, as if a giant sequoia were somehow contained within a sealed clay vessel. Rather than simply withering away and dying, the massive tree would burst forth from its brittle confines in a potentially explosive act of arboreal vitality. The volatile pressure ready to burst within Thelma at the outset of the film thus does not derive from some dangerous and pathological force unique to Thelma but is instead the natural result of the parental strategies of corporeal and psychic containment to which her upbringing has subjected her.

In a pair of flashbacks toward the end of the film, we realize why her parents have adopted such a domineering and micromanaging style of child rearing. In one scene, we see a six-year-old Thelma jealous of her baby brother, who receives all of their mother's attention and care. That is when Thelma's potentially dangerous telekinetic powers first manifest themselves. When her brother starts crying out for their mother's care, Thelma closes her eyes in concentration, and the crying suddenly stops. Her brother is nowhere to be seen. Her mother becomes frightened and demands to know what Thelma did with him. Thelma glances over at a nearby sofa, and her brother's cries start back up again from underneath it. The baby is unscathed for the moment, but the scene shows the terrifying game of telekinetic hide-and-seek that Thelma's run-of-the-mill sibling jealousy has unleashed. The stakes are raised exponentially in the next flashback scene, where we see a sleeping Thelma telekinetically project her baby brother (who at the moment is sitting happily in a bath) to a frigid and watery death underneath the layer of surface ice on a lake adjacent to their home. In an unsettling scene, we see her father, Trond, frantically run out to the lake and discover the frozen corpse of his baby son peering up at him through the ice. These flashbacks retrospectively make sense of the perplexing backstory to the film's cold open. Taken together, the flashback scenes elucidate Thelma's upbringing, showing us that after the revelation of Thelma's terrifying and erratic psychic powers, Trond decided that they had two choices in how to deal with the girl: either kill her or subject her to an overbearing regime of surveillance and control. Between the two approaches to containment, Trond chooses the less overtly violent path.

Yet softer and more prolonged misogynistic violence is still violence. As philosopher Kate Manne writes, "Misogyny is a self-masking phenomenon" that benefits from flying under the radar, making use of softer forms of brutality that don't always leave marks.[15] According to Manne, the goal of misogynistic aggression is to police the speech and behavior of women who rebel against their roles in patriarchal societies. Such policing practices work best when they are covert, indirect, and unpredictable. Misogyny is often invisible and silent, and tries to enforce silence on its victims. "Silence is golden for the men who smother and intimidate women into not talking," writes Manne. "Silence isolates victims; and it enables misogyny."[16] Rather than overtly abusing his daughter, then, Trond instead adopts a low-key strategy that professes to help and care for Thelma. It is appropriate, then, that Trond acts both in ministerial and medical roles in parenting Thelma, prescribing aggressive pharmaceutical treatments and overseeing habitual self-discipline practices of prayer and other forms of religious confession and supplication. He repeatedly tells his daughter not to worry, that he wants to help her, that they can get her symptoms under control if she follows his directives. In Trond, *Thelma* presents the often misleadingly benevolent face of systemic misogyny, an ideology that often claims to want to help women and maintain the stability of the social order. Followed assiduously, the habitual strategies of self-control that Trond prescribes may not overtly read as violent and misogynistic practices. Yet such treatment is aimed at containing Thelma's dangerous powers within her body. To understand the real violence of these measures, it is helpful to read them in transcorporeal terms, since such a reading understands Trond's behavior toward his daughter as a form of smothering or strangulation, forms of violence that Kate Manne sees as "paradigmatic of misogyny."[17]

Yet the film offers some hope of escape from misogynistic strangleholds. One sign of this hopefulness is found in the figures of containment the film returns to, which are images that hint at the fragility and impermanence of such repressive paternal strategies. In the flashback scenes, the icy surface of the frozen lake is the substance of containment. A low-angle shot from below the ice layer during the film's cold open shows us a view of young Thelma walking on the surface above while fish swim in the frigid waters below. The relative thinness and transparency of the surface Thelma and her father walk on is an unsettling reminder that this barrier will not last. Its rigidity is a seasonal condition that will soon be superseded by a more seamless relationship between the water and the air above it. The life teeming below the icy surface may be visually obscured to the humans who walk above, but soon the ice will melt. As a representation of *friluftsliv*, the opening scene thus presents the characteristically Nordic approach to nature as one that is permeated by a rigid sense of boundaries. In the last of the film's flashback scenes—which chronologically takes place before the cold open—the icy surface of the lake serves as a barrier between Trond and the corpse of his infant son. Ice is a figure of tenuous containment in the scene since it is where Thelma has inadvertently stashed her brother in an involuntary act of telekinetic projection. It is thick enough to ensure the baby is drowned, but not so thick that he can be secreted away forever. Indeed, Trond almost immediately finds the boy's body, a discovery that angers and frightens him enough to make him consider murdering his young daughter.

A similar figure of fragile containment in the film is the surface of the glass window during the dramatic and pivotal scene in which Thelma unwittingly causes the window to spontaneously explode and reassemble itself with Anja apparently trapped inside. The rupture is a repetition of Thelma's earlier projection of her baby brother into the lake in the sense that it is an involuntary telekinetic action with disastrous real-life consequences. In this case, Thelma apparently causes the electrical disruptions in Anja's building and then psychically shatters the window, which subsumes Anja into its glassy surface while Thelma herself is unconscious in a medically induced seizure. The transparency, rigidity, and fragility of the glass are all qualities shared with the icy surface of the lake, and in that sense, both surfaces visually suggest the tenuousness and impermanence of the containment. And indeed, we see that although Anja goes missing for an extended period, she is safe and sound by the end of the film, Thelma having apparently learned how to retrieve her from the glassy abyss.

These visual signifiers of fragile and impermanent containment reflect the repressive strategies of physical and behavioral containment with which Trond inculcates Thelma throughout her upbringing. We learn about one of Trond's techniques in an early scene when Thelma and Anja are just beginning their relationship. They sit together in Anja's apartment and sip from glasses of red wine—a supremely transgressive act for Thelma, who previously abstained from alcohol—and Thelma tells Anja about her strict Christian upbringing. Using a candle burning on the coffee table in front of them to demonstrate, Thelma tells Anja that her father used to hold her hand over a candle flame, only taking it away right before it started to blister, telling the child ominously, "Remember: hell is like this all the time."

As a mark of the relative success of these techniques of parental indoctrination and coercive fear-mongering, we see the degree to which Thelma has internalized strategies of repressive self-restraint in her adult life. When she feels she has gone too far in indulging her attraction to Anja, Thelma turns to compulsive, repetitive prayers and worship services. After she and Anja share a passionate first kiss, Thelma is overcome by shame and retreats to her apartment, where we see her standing with her forehead against a wall, uttering a compulsive litany of pleas to be saved from her temptation. She prays the same line over and over with her head against the wall: "Lord, remove this from me, redeem me from these thoughts. Please, I pray, take them away." A subsequent scene shows her in a chorus of other young worshippers singing the contemporary devotional song "Graven er tom" ("The Tomb Is Empty"), written by Christian pop artist David André Østby. The chorus from the hymn takes the form of a litany repeated several times: "The tomb is empty / Jesus lives / In majesty and in power / Eternal death is subdued by him."

Such religious practices of ritualistic self-control—which involve pleas for absolution and removal of temptation, along with invoking the salvific sacrifice of Christ—have a physical analogue in the measures Thelma takes to still her own body in the midst of a seizure. The self-restraining gesture we see repeated in most of Thelma's seizure episodes is to grab her own hand in a vain effort to restrain a convulsion that threatens to overtake her whole body. The action is completely ineffectual in the first seizure scene at the university reading room;

grabbing her own wrist only prolongs and amplifies the quaking of the rest of Thelma's body in that case. In a more sexually charged scene when Thelma's body threatens to begin another convulsive fit as Anja furtively caresses her thigh during a ballet performance they are watching together, Thelma barely manages to restrain her bodily tremors by grabbing her quaking hand. The effort is shown to have dangerous external consequences, however. As she restrains herself, the building itself begins to quake as the excess kinetic energy of Thelma's body is projected to the enormous light fixture above the unsuspecting audience at the ballet, which begins swaying ominously over the crowd. Along with less directly physical practices of self-control, Thelma's clear efforts to still her irrepressible bodily paroxysms indicate the degree to which she has carried on her father's repressive efforts to contain her own psychosomatic unruliness.

These efforts at restraint are driven by ideas of mental and physical insulation from the environment that run counter to both Julia Kristeva's psychoanalytic theory of abjection and Stacy Alaimo's concept of transcorporeality, each of which situates the body as a permeable organism that can only remain viable through material interchange with the environment. Alaimo associates strategies of bodily enclosure with hypermasculine, anti-environmentalist posturing. By way of example, Alaimo mentions a type of performative masculinity found in the carbon-heavy culture of American capitalism, namely oversize-truck culture, in which it is common to adorn one's massive pickup truck with aggressive accoutrements such as armor-like grille guards or chrome trailer hitch decorations modeled after bull testicles that dangle suggestively under the phallic protuberance. More broadly, postures of corporeal enclosure can manifest themselves in many toxically masculinist practices, all of which style the body as a big, hard, impenetrable—but aggressively penetrative—corporeal fortress walled off from intrusion and insulated from transcorporeal interchange. Alaimo contrasts this posture with an opposite approach that she calls *insurgent vulnerability*: "A recognition of our material interconnection with a wider environment that impels ethical and political responses."[18] In its more activist forms, this insurgent vulnerability can become what Alaimo calls a "politics of exposure": the open recognition of one's precarious bodily exposure to the environment, which can take the form of demonstrations that use the potent symbolic value of nude bodies exposed to the ecological elements.

In *Thelma*, however, the danger that Trond's containment and control efforts seek to counteract is not his daughter's vulnerability to environmental intrusion but rather the possibility that her erratic and dangerous psychosomatic powers will instead leak out into the environment, threatening everyone around her. Trond's efforts, then, have little to do with protecting his daughter from intrusive external forces; instead, they keep internal forces safely contained within Thelma's body. As Trond sees it, the threat lurks *inside* Thelma rather than *outside* her. The question of whether to fear dangerous intrusions from without or dangerous leaks from within makes little difference in the strategy used, however; in either case, techniques of paternalistic control, containment, and solidifying psychosomatic boundaries can at best serve as temporary stopgap measures that contravene the material realities of living bodies that depend on two-way transit into and out of the body to sustain life. The similar denial of transcorporeality that underlies both Trond's parenting style and the carbon-heavy American truck culture cited by Alaimo indicates the toxically masculinist and misogynistic impulses that animate these disparate practices.

Because these efforts at total corporeal insulation are unsustainable, paternalistic containment can strategically adopt subtler, more indirect and covert forms of behavioral policing. Such is the case with another type of paternalistic containment Thelma faces, namely the many instances of parental and medical surveillance hinted at throughout the film. The first sign of Thelma's status as an object of oppressive oversight is the first shot after the film's title sequence, which brings us into the present after the precredit flashback scene. Moments after we have seen Trond aim his gun at his young daughter, we flash-forward to Thelma's student life through an aerial shot looking down at a campus square where students and campus visitors cross at random angles like so many ants far below the camera. After slowly and voyeuristically panning over the crowd for a full minute, the transcendent and godlike camera gradually zooms in to settle on Thelma, who is clearly struggling to figure out where to go in an unfamiliar setting. The film thus leaves behind Thelma's childhood with a gun aimed at the young girl's head, only to settle into her young adulthood with a different kind of repressive scope trained on her body, namely the pseudo-omniscient and voyeuristic gaze of the parental surveillance regime Thelma has grown up with. The juxtaposition of her father's gun barrel in the previous scene with the surveilling eye of the film's establishing shot in present-day Oslo in the next hints that, although the threat of immediate physical violence has gone away, soft and indirect violence through panoptic surveillance maintains a sinister grip on Thelma's life.

This move from overt violence to more covert forms of behavioral control accords with Michel Foucault's well-known discussions of panoptic surveillance in *Surveiller et punir: Naissance de la prison* (*Discipline and Punish: The Birth of the Prison*). In Jeremy Bentham's panopticon—a scheme of institutional architecture that aimed to produce a disciplined citizenry for the utilitarian benefit of modern societies—Foucault sees an image of how modern institutions impose social control through less overt, and therefore more insidious, means than in medieval and early modern societies. In the Middle Ages, states relied on grotesque public spectacles of state-sponsored corporal punishment to impose social order. Modern social institutions instead rely on panoptic technologies of rigid surveillance and minutely ordered bureaucracy. The consequence of this panoptic surveillance is that the constant possibility of authoritarian oversight becomes an internalized gaze that individuals in prisons, asylums, schools, and other institutions sense even when nobody is actually watching them. The goal of the panopticon is not absolute omniscience through total surveillance but rather reinforcement of the ever-present possibility that the eye of authority is watching you. The move from spectacles of punishment to the fostering of disciplined and docile bodies in modern nation-states constitutes what Foucault calls a "gentle way" in punishment.[19] This modern form of discipline contrasts with medieval and early modern forms of public punishment of criminals, which were intended as a display of social justice that could serve as a deterrent to the populace. In modern correctional institutions, however, "the point of application of the penalty is not the representation, but the body, time, everyday gestures and activities; the soul too, but in so far as it is the seat of habit. The body and the soul, as principles of behavior, form the element that is now proposed for punitive intervention."[20] Similarly, the object of paternalistic oversight in *Thelma* is both the body and the soul, as Trond seeks to manage Thelma's behavior and her habits. Appropriately, then, the film begins its present-day narrative with an image of panoptic surveillance— the technique par excellence of social control in modern societies, according to Foucault. After the title sequence, the film flashes forward to the present in a lingering aerial shot over the university campus whose form echoes the random sight lines of surveillance cameras ubiquitous in modern cities. Such a panoptic narrative opening hints at the broad scope of the paternalistic gaze under which Thelma has been raised. We see the degree to which this is the case as Thelma establishes herself in Oslo. Her parents keep tabs on their adult daughter's class schedule and monitor her social media accounts. Thelma calls her parents frequently on the phone, and they gently probe her about her daily schedule, making clear that they know where she's supposed to be and when. Moreover, the scene where Thelma makes Anja disappear emphasizes the voyeuristic medical surveillance Thelma is under, staging Thelma's body as the object of a medical gaze that prods and probes her for information through visual observation as well as other forms of bodily monitoring.

But no matter how insidious and pervasive these strategies of smothering containment become, the film offers some signs that their totalizing aims can never be fully realized. Trond's strategies of psychosomatic enclosure, for instance, are untenable for living organisms such as Thelma. When contained within impervious shells, transcorporeal bodies suffocate and die. But living bodies, the film shows, instinctively resist and beat back the threat of suffocation. Like *Epidemic*, *Thelma* relies in several of its most visceral scenes of dread and terror on the primal fear of suffocation or live burial and the instinctual resistance that kicks in at such moments. One of these comes late in the film, as Thelma swims laps in an empty public swimming pool. Halfway through her first lap, Thelma's attention is drawn to the ceiling as the overhead lights suddenly start flickering. Out in the middle of the pool, Thelma is unable to get back to the side before her body is overtaken by the spasms that inevitably follow flickering lights. Her arms tense up and begin to shake uncontrollably, and Thelma drops through the water like a lead weight, continuing to convulse as her body sinks deeper and deeper in the pool. Several excruciating moments later, Thelma regains consciousness and control of her body, but when she starts to swim in the direction of the surface, she is instead met with the tile floor of the pool. Thelma fights and struggles against the tiles, making every effort to break through to air. The primal terror of the scene echoes the suffocating image of Thelma's brother's corpse trapped beneath the ice in the flashback later in the film, drawing an association between her seizures, her telekinetic powers, and suffocating bodily enclosure. After struggling in vain against the tiles, Thelma finally realizes she has confused the pool floor with the surface of the water and frantically swims in the opposite direction until she surfaces.

A more potently symbolic and sexually charged image of suffocation comes earlier in the film, in a scene that may be interpreted as a fantasy or as a hallucination. Thelma—naive and inexperienced as she is—becomes the butt of a cruel joke at a party when she is tricked into thinking that a hand-rolled cigarette she takes several tenuous puffs of is in fact a joint. Under the power of the group's suggestion, she starts feeling as if she is under the influence of a powerful psychoactive drug. In a daze, the scenario quickly turns into an erotically charged fantasy of Anja passionately kissing—and then sexually stimulating—Thelma. As she closes her eyes in ecstasy and lets her head come to a rest on the sofa, a scaly black snake suddenly emerges and wraps itself around Thelma's writhing body. The snake curls around Thelma's neck, then its pointed head makes its way into the open cavity of her mouth and slithers into Thelma's throat in another unsettling image of suffocation. The scene is heavily laden with symbolic surplus, the snake fitting clearly within the Manichean moral landscape of fundamentalist Christianity. The snake becomes an obvious stand-in for the serpent in Eden who tempts Eve to transgress the interdictions of her patriarchal God. Despite the black-and-white moral binaries to which the scene alludes, however, it is a more emotionally and morally complex image of suffocation than the pool scene. Thelma's intense bodily desire for the "forbidden fruit" of same-sex intimacy equates the snake with an emancipatory—rather than evil—drive toward sexual autonomy and authenticity. The wires of pleasure and danger become crossed in the scene, then, as suffocation results from the openness to sexual penetration that Anja herself is concurrently performing on Thelma in the fantasy. As a figure of malevolence and asphyxiation, however, the snake could instead be read as a stand-in for her father's strategies of smothering behavioral control. Read in this light, the scene reverses the gender polarities of the biblical creation myth, associating evil with a suffocating and phallic figure of patriarchal control rather than with feminine moral weakness.

## PSYCHOSOMATIC ERUPTIONS

While Thelma has been subject to an exceptionally repressive parental regime of containment and oversight—given visual expression in the film's many images of suffocation—it becomes more and more evident that the psychosomatic forces within her irrepressibly rebel against such restraints. The fragile and impermanent structures of containment discussed above inevitably give way to more powerful forces that resist the tenuous and artificial boundaries thus imposed. Ice melts. Glass shatters. Thelma's tense bodily composure bursts into abject and convulsive kinesis. We have already discussed several of these instances of abjection in the film, which establish Thelma's subjecthood through the expulsion, leakage, eruption, or projection of substances and energies from the body. These moments in the film are crucial to Thelma's gradual process of assuming agency and autonomy over her own behavior, desires, and body. It is important to note, however, that they are also moments of unsettling, embarrassing, and sometimes terrifying rupture. They are unexpected and explosive moments that lead her toward individual agency and autonomy but are also painful and terrifying. As Kristeva writes of abjection, moments when the subject "gives birth" to the self are accompanied by "the violence of sobs, of vomit."[21] In that sense, abjection is a kind of explosive eruption in the fabric of the self.

The positive reading I have offered of Thelma's abjection so far, however, is tempered by the film's narrative resolution, which includes particularly violent and threatening eruptions of psychic power. During the final act of the film, Thelma takes a leave from university and returns to her childhood home, seeking parental solace and help after Anja has gone missing. Thelma's return to her parents is all the more remarkable given that she has, in the meantime, found out that a grandmother her parents told her was dead is in fact still alive and apparently suffers from the same terrifying psychic condition as Thelma. Because of revelations that have resurfaced in the medical records accessed by her doctors in Oslo, Thelma has also discovered that her father took extreme actions to repress Thelma's condition throughout her life. Not only has Trond kept Thelma's grandmother away from his daughter, hidden away in a care home, but the doctors also question the heavy doses of sedatives and other drugs her father prescribed to her as a child. Indeed, when Thelma does visit her grandmother, who at this point suffers from dementia, there is a suggestion that Trond took the same tack with his mother, subjecting her to rigid containment measures like overmedication and clinical oversight. Her grandmother suffered from the trauma of somehow telekinetically murdering or disappearing her husband while he was out fishing on a lake, so Anja is terrified that she is capable of the same dangerous psychic actions. In returning to her parents, then, Thelma takes a calculated risk that they will actually care for her rather than subjecting her to the same repressive medical interventions as her grandmother.

The danger of Thelma's return becomes frighteningly apparent almost immediately after her arrival. After Thelma tells them about her psychogenic seizures, her mother urges her not to worry about her troubles and to drink the tea they have served her. After a few sips, Thelma starts to nod off, and while she is losing consciousness, her father tells her, "Don't be afraid. We've given you something to help you calm down. We know what's happening to you, Thelma. We'll help you." An ominous drone plays underneath Trond's words of comfort, and as Thelma loses consciousness, she clearly feels terrified and betrayed by her parents. In her sedation, her parents tell her about how she had been accidentally responsible for her baby brother's death, and they explain to her that "there's something within you. If you truly desire something—with your thoughts, with your feelings—there's something within you that can make it happen." The prepositions Trond uses are telling in terms of the types of control strategies he has used in raising Thelma. If the dangerous thoughts and feelings are "within" her, then containment and restraint are the logical responses. In a subsequent scene we see that Trond has taken to locking Thelma in her bedroom, coming in periodically to check on her and give her more sedatives. He tells her that he should never have let her leave the house and says he thought her psychic powers had finally gone away. Nothing had happened since she "found God" as a young child, he explains. Trond repeatedly tells her not to worry; he's going to help her get over her condition. Besides the pharmaceutical treatment, Trond watches over Thelma as she kneels with her head against the wall and repeatedly offers prayers of contrition. She prays for mercy, saying she has "sinned in mind and deed" and has felt "a lust for evil" in her heart. As the camera cuts to Trond sitting next to her, we see that he's mouthing the words along with her, as if coaching and overseeing her compulsively repetitive prayer. When she later confesses her love for Anja to her father, Trond tells her Anja couldn't have been in love with her—that it was Thelma's psychic abilities that have attracted Anja to her. "You were probably just lonesome," he tells her. "You needed somebody." Trond then insists that it's Thelma's fault that Anja has disappeared, and it's because "deep down inside," Thelma wanted Anja gone.

Trond's professed intent to help Thelma, however, clearly takes on the smothering qualities of the soft and indirect kinds of misogynistic violence. Cloaked in reassurances of parental concern and care there lurks a violent and infanticidal impulse. In one unsettling scene, Thelma's mother becomes a Lady Macbeth figure, telling Trond that he's done all he can and it hasn't worked, and they have to "take the consequences" of this failure despite their love for Thelma. The implication is that Trond needs to take more drastic prophylactic measures against the dangerous forces within Thelma—they must either kill her or incapacitate her with stronger sedatives and long-term institutionalization. Trond prepares a syringe, filling it with an unknown medication—perhaps a lethal dose, or perhaps simply enough to render her catatonic on a more permanent basis.

The longer she stays under her father's repressive regime, the more Thelma resents it. One evening as Trond is giving Thelma her nightly pills, she tells her father that she has discovered the truth about her grandmother and, in an accusatory tone, asks if he has the same plans to overmedicate and institutionalize her. Trond refuses to answer, says goodnight to his daughter, and locks the door behind him as he leaves. Early the next morning, Trond goes out in his fishing boat and has a smoke in the middle of the lake. The scene cross-cuts between Trond on his boat and a sleeping Thelma, who thrashes anxiously in her sleep. Trond notices a murder of crows who have flocked nearby and becomes frightened when he thinks he sees Thelma on the distant shore of the lake. Seconds later, Trond gazes down at his hands as they start smoking and then burst into flames. Soon his whole body is engulfed, no matter how much he tries to smother the flames. He plunges himself into the water and stays under for several moments, but when he emerges, his body bursts into flames again. The flames drive him under the water again, and he never emerges. At the moment of her father's death, Thelma is startled awake. She walks out to the lake—the site of her grandfather's, her brother's, and now her father's deaths—and sees the empty boat floating in the middle of the lake. She plunges into the water and swims deeper and deeper, apparently losing consciousness as she dreams that she has swum back to the public swimming pool in Oslo and finds Anja there, where they share a passionate kiss. She wakes up again having washed ashore, and as she's crawling out of the water, she coughs up an apparently dead bird, who then suddenly bursts into life and flies away as Thelma's phone starts buzzing with a call from Anja. Whatever happened beneath the water, she has apparently retrieved Anja from the void and brought her back to life, coughing up and resurrecting a bird as a symbolic analogue of her revival of Anja. Following on the heels of her father's death by telekinetic immolation, Thelma's final abject act thus stands in for both a triumphant and lasting rejection of her father and the completion of Thelma's painful process of individuation. What is more, Thelma has not only "given birth" to herself through abjection but has also secured Anja's rebirth in the same action.

In terms of understanding the transcorporeal dimensions of abjection, it is important to note that the climactic eruptions bursting forth from within

Thelma are the almost predictable results of her father's most pronounced efforts to smother and contain Thelma's psychosomatic agency. If eruptions result from the buildup of extreme pressure, the repressive regime of behavioral and bodily control to which Trond subjects his daughter is to blame for the climactic burst of telekinetic energy we see in the film. By bottling up his daughter's psychic and bodily energies, Trond has only sown the seeds of his own explosive demise.

That demise comes, as we have seen, with the film's return to the Norwegian wilderness setting it opened with. Rather than the icy surface that Trond and Thelma walked across in the opening scene, however, the summertime setting of the final scene means that Trond must navigate the fluidity of the lake in search of a restorative experience of *friluftsliv*. Instead of the salubrious influence he had sought in retreating to the wilderness setting, however, he meets his demise in an unsettling scene in which Trond suffers an excruciating death by both water and fire. As a culmination of the film's imagery of bodily containment giving way to fluidity, abjection, and transcorporeality, the scene demonstrates the shortcomings of Trond's misogynistic and ecophobic approach to the natural world. Intent on containing the dangerous transcorporeality of the female body and the natural world, Trond is doomed to be consumed by the resurgent fluidity of both.

## WITCHCRAFT THROUGH THE AGES

In its climactic scene, *Thelma* returns to its conceptual origins in the "witch film" subgenre, prevalent both in European and American horror and also related to the Scandinavian tradition of torturing women that Linda Haverty Rugg writes about. This connection is signaled in part by Trond's death, which is an overdetermined witchlike execution in that he is *both* burned *and* drowned. Just like the suggestion-induced fantasy scene from earlier in the film, however, which associated the paternalistic containment of women (not feminine evil) with original sin, traditional gender polarities are reversed in this final sequence, with the father suffering a witch's death under the telekinetic power of his daughter. In framing *Thelma* as a narrative of female emancipation from smothering patriarchal control and oversight, Trier seems intent on counteracting the frequently regressive gender politics of many witch films along with films that dramatize transcendent female suffering.

In this revisionist take on misogynistic film traditions, however, Trier in fact

The rigidly contained, icy landscape of the opening scene exemplifies the strategies of containment and enclosure young Thelma's father uses to keep her telekinetic powers in check. Frame grab from *Thelma* (dir. Joachim Trier, 2017).

By the end of the film, Thelma's emancipation from the paternalistic abuse of her father is marked by a fluid, summertime landscape. Frame grab from *Thelma* (dir. Joachim Trier, 2017).

picks up where one of the earliest Scandinavian "witch films" left off: Benjamin Christensen's *Häxan* (*The Witch*; distributed as *Witchcraft through the Ages*, 1922). A remarkable and singular film, *Häxan* freely mixes documentary and dramatic storytelling to trace a history of witchcraft and the historically contingent beliefs and attitudes that guided public response to marginalized women that medieval society deemed evil but which modern society has diagnosed as suffering from pathological disorders like hysteria. The most aesthetically remarkable sequences take place in the Middle Ages, dramatizing the strange lore and superstitions that fed into the self-perpetuating mass hysteria of witch accusations and trials. Christensen himself plays Satan—complete with horns, batlike ears, pointy claws, a devious smile, and a lasciviously flicking tongue. A variety of other monsters and folkloric chimera are brought to life in the film as well, in scenes that depict the decadent and perverse Satanic orgies medieval folk beliefs assumed the accused witches were party to.

The intent of such sequences, it becomes clear as the film goes on, is not merely to dazzle the audience with Christensen's mastery of cinematic spectacle, though he succeeds marvelously in this task. Rather, the payoff comes at the end of the film, when Christensen's historical narrative brings the spectator into present-day medical and psychiatric treatments of pathological women. According to one intertitle late in the film, "There are several connections between the ancient witch and the modern hysteric." Nightly visits from the devil, according to the film, are now understood as sleep disorders like somnambulism. In one sequence, a shot of an accused witch being prodded on the back during her interrogation dissolves into a shot of a modern hysteric similarly prodded by a doctor. A condition of tactile insensitivity—which in the Middle Ages was seen as a sign that the devil had visited the witch and touched her skin, rendering the flesh insensitive—is now seen as a sign of psychosomatic disorder, since spots of numbness are now considered a symptom of hysteria. After showing how the doctor threatens to have the patient legally detained at his clinic, a subsequent intertitle empathetically comments on the plight of the woman: "Poor little hysterical witch. During the Middle Ages you came into conflict with the church. Now there are run-ins with the law."

*Häxan* ends by directly questioning the degree to which such historical shifts toward the medicalization of non-normative femininity represents progress. "The witch no longer flies away on her broom over the rooftops," remarks one intertitle, followed by a shot of a female pilot waving to the camera in front of a modern biplane. "But isn't superstition still rampant among us?" The film illustrates the persistence of superstition by showing fortune-tellers and tarot card readers plying their craft. While we no longer burn the old and impoverished, "don't they often still suffer bitterly?" The film invokes the "little woman whom we call hysterical," and asks rhetorically, "Isn't she still a riddle for us?" "Nowadays we detain the unhappy in a mental institution or—if she is wealthy—in a modern clinic. And then we will console ourselves with the notion that the mildly temperate shower of the clinic has replaced the barbaric methods of medieval times."

The final two shots of the film offer a withering critique of this self-congratulatory notion of social progress in the modern era. In the first, a modern woman—evidently a well-heeled hysteric—is ushered into a warm shower by a pair of nurses. This picture of bourgeois opulence in the gentle and humane treatments offered by modern psychiatric clinics jarringly dissolves to a shot of three bodies being burned at the stake, a shocking image of female suffering and barbaric societal cruelty that the film lingers on for the final twenty seconds of its running time. The polemical implication of this dissolve is clear: though treatments have become ostensibly gentler under the guise of modern medical practice, there is an undercurrent of misogyny that bridges the gap between the Middle Ages and the modern age, lingering in the uncanny persistence of prejudice and cruelty.

In its revisionist approach to the tradition of torturing women in Scandinavian cinema, *Thelma* takes a similar tack to *Häxan* by fixating on the persistence of misogyny in contemporary Norwegian society. Though it may have assumed the more benign guise of parental concern and medical observation, the social techniques of misogynistic control have only become more refined. Like the historical trajectory Foucault traces from the medieval public spectacles of penal punishment to the "gentler" and more covert practices of discipline and panoptic surveillance, misogynistic violence has become a softer and more insidious policing mechanism. As Kate Manne writes, misogyny is a self-effacing system that spreads more virulently when it goes undetected. By training his critique of paternalistic control of women on Scandinavian cinema, Joachim Trier is not setting up an exceptional example of misogyny in an otherwise progressive and egalitarian society. Instead, *Thelma* shows how progressivism can serve as an absolving and self-congratulatory cloak that obscures pervasive and systemic practices of gender-based violence.

# CHAPTER THREE

# Men, Women, and Harpoons

## Eco-isolationism and Transnationalism
## in *Reykjavik Whale Watching Massacre*

The final image of the Icelandic slasher film *Reykjavik Whale Watching Massacre* (dir. Júlíus Kemp; sometimes titled *Harpoon: The Whale Watching Massacre*, 2009) is an aerial shot of the open sea—a wide expanse of blue punctuated by an infinitesimal orange dot drifting on its surface in the center of the frame. We know from the preceding scenes that the dot is, in fact, the life preserver keeping Annette (Pihla Viitala) afloat and alive after she has survived a horrific attack by a band of disgruntled, bloodthirsty whalers who have turned to hunting tourists after commercial whaling is banned in Iceland. Within the ecocritical discourse of the film, which centers on issues of environmental management and national autonomy, the shot figures Annette's bobbing form as a visual metaphor for the nation of Iceland: an island isolated and adrift in a cold and inhospitable expanse of the North Atlantic.

Extracted from a global context, the drifting, desperate body of Annette clinging for life without any sign that she will be rescued by the wider world is an image of environmental precarity that accomplishes at least two important ecocritical tasks for the film. For one thing, the shot unsettles one of the central tropes of the slasher film and in the process contributes to a growing subgenre in contemporary Nordic ecohorror that Pietari Kääpä has called the *ecoslasher*.[1] True to the conventions of the slasher film, *Reykjavik* sets up clear expectations that Annette is to be the "final girl" who we anticipate will be the sole survivor to escape her murderous attackers and emerge safe and sound in the end. This trope—first named and popularized by Carol J. Clover in her influential study of gender in modern horror cinema, *Men, Women, and Chain*

*Saws*—has become one of the most ubiquitous and widely recognized critical terms in both academic horror studies and genre film fan discourse.² Rather than ending with Annette's escape from the relentless and bloody assault—as when Laurie (Jamie Lee Curtis) is rescued from the masked, teenager-mutilating madman Michael Myers (Nick Castle) in *Halloween* (dir. John Carpenter, 1978)—*Reykjavik* ends with an image of ecological uncertainty and isolation, setting the precarious body of the film's supposed final girl adrift in a hostile environment without offering much hope of her ultimate survival. Though the sadistic whalers have not succeeded in killing her, the film suggests, the environment may well finish the job—be it through thirst, hypothermia, or being devoured by a hungry orca. Contributing to a growing body of ecocritical horror films in Nordic cinema—including the Norwegian wilderness horror franchises *Cold Prey* (*Fritt vilt*, dir. Roar Uthaug, 2006; sequels released in 2008 and 2010) and *Dead Snow* (*Død snø*, dir. Tommy Wirkola, 2009; sequel released in 2014)—*Reykjavik* thus plays with the conventions of the slasher film to underscore the increasingly tenuous relationship between human societies and the natural world in the twenty-first century.

Besides contributing to *Reykjavik's* ecocritical reimagining of the slasher film, the final image of Annette drifting island-like on the surface of the ocean also raises ecocritical questions about the relationship between nature and nation, resonating with debates the film sets in motion about Iceland's uncertain position in an interconnected and globalized world. Coming at the end of a film that has pitted nationalist, pro-whaling Icelanders against international environmental activists and whaling regulation organizations and that has repeatedly questioned the apparent isolation of Iceland, the final shot clearly stands in as an image of Icelandic insularity. As Björn Nordfjörd writes, the status of Iceland as an island nation perched precariously at the meeting place of two continental plates in the North Atlantic—"too remote [from both North America and Europe] to belong culturally to either"—has been a major thematic concern of modern Icelandic cinema and remains a central pillar of Icelandic national identity.³ The cultural centrality of the island imaginary is perhaps especially prevalent in Iceland, a place many may consider the most "islandy" of all island nations, being more culturally marginal, more geographically isolated, physically smaller, less densely populated, and less geopolitically powerful than other contenders like Great Britain or Japan. As Nordfjörd notes, this intimate connection between Icelandic identity and the acutely felt sense of island-bound isolation from the outer world runs counter to the material reality of Iceland's actual enmeshment in a contemporary transnational context via tourism, immigration, and the entanglements of the global economy. In an age of globalization, Iceland is "not that different from various continental habitats," and it would therefore "seem a mistake to make claims regarding unique island identities."[4]

To ignore the importance of this island imaginary in contemporary Icelandic culture, however, would be to turn a blind eye to the crucial role played by a sense of national self-determination in Icelandic identity. Indeed, in geographical terms, the pronounced role of environmental nationalism in an island nation like Iceland makes intuitive sense, according to Nordfjörd: "If nationalism, by definition, always lays claim to the exceptional nature of the nation in question, the natural boundaries of an island's coastline would seem to make such claims all the more convincing (as compared to man-made borders on maps and arbitrarily, if strategically distributed, border controls)."[5] Being physically delimited by wide expanses of ocean, then, makes it particularly easy to naturalize the idea that Iceland is—globalism notwithstanding—an isolated and autonomous national community, and should therefore be free to determine its own destiny without the encumbrances of international intervention. As *Reykjavik* makes clear, emphasizing Iceland's status as a geographically remote island is a rhetorical move that has fueled discourses of economic and environmental nationalism in recent years.[6]

In ecological terms, imagining Iceland as a self-sufficient island society is a nationalist and anthropocentric fantasy that ignores the ways environmental currents cut across arbitrary and artificial national boundaries. The island imaginary, then, posits the collective body of the nation as an enclosed, self-sustaining system with rigid boundaries, disregarding the ecological necessity of transcorporeal interchange. This analysis of the role "islandness" plays in the Icelandic cultural imagination is a helpful starting point for examining *Reykjavik* through the lens of ecohorror—a media mode that this book argues is fixated on the frequently threatening interconnectedness of humans with more-than-human environments. Indeed, with its emphasis on material relationships of mutual dependence and symbiotic entanglement between organisms and their environments, ecology undermines the very notion of individual or national autonomy and isolation, instead directing our attention to the way the global biosphere is inextricably interconnected. As a film about exploring the limits of environmental solitude in an age of globalization, *Reykjavik* overtly situates itself within this ecocritical discourse. Seen more particularly as an ecoslasher, *Reykjavik* demonstrates the impossibility of isolation through images of horrifyingly material and sensationally transgressive interconnection.

Indeed, the viewer need only look to the film's immediately preceding shots to see that Annette's apparent isolation is misleading. Just before we get a close-up shot of Annette drifting on the surface of the sea, and then the aerial shot that ends the film, we see that the *actual* final girl of the film—counter to the expectations *Reykjavik* sets up—is Endo (Nae Yuuki), a Japanese tourist who had been aboard the same doomed whale watching excursion as Annette and has survived the vicious attack through her own cunning and her ruthless betrayal of the other passengers. Passing directly above Annette in a jumbo jet bound for her home country, Endo relaxes and enjoys a drink in her first-class seat as she disinterestedly glances at the front-page headline of the newspaper folded on her lap: "BLOODBATH ON A WHALE WATCHING SHIP."

As the final shots of the film oscillate between the national scale of Annette's drifting body as a visual metaphor for Iceland and the global scale of the Japan-bound jetliner flying above her, *Reykjavik* ends with a distillation of two opposing scales of environmental imagination that Ursula K. Heise has called a *sense of place* and a *sense of planet*. While some modern environmental movements have urged us to turn away from modern alienation and become immersed in and knowledgeable about the natural world in our immediate local surroundings—to cultivate a small-scale sense of place—others have appealed to images of global interconnectedness in order to encourage a scaled-up awareness of the ways environmental dynamics cross man-made boundaries and affect the whole planet. While a sense of place tends toward identification with hyperlocal environments and territories, a sense of planet transcends nation in a utopian global holism. As Heise has argued, both of these positions lead to problematic environmental ethics, either disregarding transnational and global dynamics in favor of fetishizing the local and reifying territorial boundaries and national identities, or disregarding individual communities and identities in favor of an abstracting, totalizing holism. For Heise, the solution is a fluid interchange between the local and global scales, maintaining an awareness of both small-scale and planetary dynamics of environmental change through a position she terms eco-cosmopolitanism. Heise's argument is useful here because it helps makes sense of the conflicting images of national isolation and global interconnection in the film. In all its cultural specificity—its fixation on debates about whaling and resource management in Iceland—*Reykjavik* seems intent on establishing a "sense of place" that is particularly Icelandic. However, as a campy, self-aware satire that critiques the isolationist, nationalist, and xenophobic impulses implicit in the pro-whaling faction of the debate, *Reykjavik* ultimately argues against such a fetishistic cultivation of a sense of place, presenting us with de-idealized images of a globalized world that societies must learn to navigate.

Examining *Reykjavik Whale Watching Massacre* as a case study in the local and global environmental discourses evoked in contemporary ecohorror, this chapter underscores how such films can make use of the formal language of cinema to put the ecological and economic concerns of the nation into dialogue with transnational and global environmental discourses. By juxtaposing and oscillating between the micro-scale view of individual bodies and the macro-scale view of national communities enmeshed in the transnational environmental and economic flows of a globalized world, the film undermines nationalist environmental discourses and highlights the transnational entanglements even apparently isolated territories are caught up in. While I have argued in earlier chapters that films such as Lars von Trier's *Epidemic* and Joachim Trier's *Thelma* are fixated on questions of ecological embodiment—depicting the alternately unsettling and emancipatory transcorporeal enmeshment of individual bodies and their environments—*Reykjavik* widens its scope to the national and global scales, fixating on the way the collective body of the nation is imagined in contemporary environmental discourse. In Nordic ecohorror, such a transnational scope helps critique and unsettle nationalist notions of collectivity. In the case of contemporary debates about environmental sustainability and economic self-sufficiency in Iceland, the film shows how environmental nationalism has contributed to a false view of the nation as naturally insulated from the outside world. To invoke an image used in chapter 2, such a position imagines the territory of the nation as an enclosed and contained body. As the film shows, Iceland is never as isolated as it seems, given its dependence on the economic influx from global commerce and tourism, yet the island imaginary is uncannily persistent, haunting ecological and economic debates in Iceland to this day.

## SCALING IN: SITUATING MASSACRE

The narrative setup of *Reykjavik Whale Watching Massacre* juxtaposes the isolationist, eco-skeptical Icelandic whaling industry with the ostensibly pro-environmental discourses of tourists who have come from far and wide to experience the natural splendor of Iceland. We follow a diverse group of international ecotourists visiting Reykjavik, who come together aboard a boat as they embark on a whale watching excursion one afternoon. Functioning as stand-ins for the international community that Icelandic isolationists would prefer to stand apart from, the tourists embody broad cultural stereotypes and reflect a particularly dim view of humanity. In the group we meet an incorrigible drunk Frenchman named Jean-François (Aymen Hamdouchi); a conservative and homophobic young American woman named Marie-Anne (Marinda Hennessy); a womanizing Japanese tourist named Nobuyoshi (Carlos Takeshi), along with his wife, Yuko (Miwa Yanagizawa), and young female assistant, Endo; a first mate named Björn (Thor Kristjansson), who we soon learn is a sexual predator; a trio of middle-aged European women who ogle a Black American tourist named Leon (Terence Anderson), discussing his physique in racist and objectifying terms; and a jolly, bearded captain named Pétur, played—in an effective bit of stunt-casting—by the Reykjavik-born American actor Gunnar Hansen, most famous for playing Leatherface in the genre-defining film *The Texas Chainsaw Massacre* (dir. Tobe Hooper, 1974). Most importantly, we meet Annette, a young tourist who seems to possess all the characteristics of the conventional "final girl" of a slasher film: she is energetic, daring, physically resourceful, and—unlike many of the other travelers—not interested in partying or casual sex.

The trouble begins not long after the boat departs. Björn corners Annette in a private cabin and attempts to rape her, while above deck, an even more spectacular violation takes place. The drunk Jean-François, who has been climbing the rigging of the boat—loudly proclaiming in a broad French accent that he wants to "look at *ze* whales!"—falls from the mast. As he plummets toward the deck, he strikes a harpoon that is secured to the rigging, projecting the blade straight down into Captain Pétur's chest and impaling him with it. As the captain lies bleeding to death on the deck, Björn is discovered in the midst of the attempted rape when the passengers seek out the first mate to step in and bring the boat safely back to harbor. Instead of filling in for his fallen captain, Björn takes the opportunity to disable the boat's ignition and escape aboard the lifeboat, leaving the captain to bleed to death and the rest of the passengers adrift on the doomed vessel.

After passengers send up emergency flares, a man aboard a small fishing boat pulls up to the whale watching vessel, whereupon the passengers begin cheering. The man reassures them in broken English that he will take the survivors to safety. Instead, he takes them to a decaying whaling ship owned by his family—a bloodthirsty group of whale hunters whose anger has been stoked by the intervention of international environmental groups calling for the end of the Icelandic whaling industry. The moratorium on whaling has, according to the disgruntled brothers and their mother—their de facto leader—left them destitute and robbed the Icelandic nation of a distinguished and traditional industry. After the rescued passengers board the troublingly dilapidated whaler, one of the murderous brothers—propelled by bloodlust when a passenger's nose starts bleeding—suddenly runs up to the passenger and plants a hammer into her forehead in full view of the horrified tourists. Several others are dispatched in quick succession. Most spectacularly, the womanizing Japanese tourist, Nobuyoshi, is hunted down with a harpoon gun as he attempts to swim away from the ship, and his body is hauled back and tethered to the ship as if it were a whale carcass, while the surviving passengers scatter and seek out hiding places aboard the ship. True to form for a conventional slasher, the passengers are sought out one by one and murdered in spectacularly gruesome fashion. Their will to live is put to the test as they find novel and increasingly claustrophobic spaces to hide, using whatever weapons they can find or fashion to fight back against their attackers. By the end of the onslaught, several possible survivors have sought avenues of escape. Leon is left as the last survivor aboard the ship, but just as it seems he is about to be rescued by the Icelandic Coast Guard, he is mistaken as the aggressor and shot by the officers—an inclusion that seems a direct reference to George A. Romero's *Night of the Living Dead* (1968), in which the surviving Black protagonist, Ben (Duane Jones), is shot and killed by police when he is mistaken for a zombie. Meanwhile, Annette and Marie-Anne have sought refuge on an inflatable lifeboat and are drifting on the sea in the midst of a rainstorm, when the boat is attacked by an orca and Marie-Anne is killed. In the end, our apparent "final girl" is left drifting on the open ocean, buoyed by her life vest, while Endo—a Japanese domestic servant who has escaped the attacks through her own cunning and subterfuge of other passengers—has assumed the identity of her wealthy employer and is on her way back to Japan. The film ends, then, by situating island-bound isolationism as the unsustainable and ecologically vulnerable position, while associating survival with a kind of cunning internationalism.

Long before the film ends with the macro-scale view of global travel, *Reykjavik* scales down to the national context, situating the viewer within the long history of whale hunting in Iceland. Opening with a credit sequence that plays over archival footage of Icelandic whale hunting from the early twentieth century, the film familiarizes us with the national tradition, which has become fetishized by Icelandic whaling interests and demonized by international environmental and animal-rights activists. To begin the sequence, we see grainy images of waves crashing against the side of a boat as it glides through the water. A crew member ascends a rope ladder to assume his perch in the crow's nest as he surveils the sea, looking for signs of whales. In a subsequent shot, the camera catches a glimpse of a whale as the creature comes up for air. In a medium close-up from behind, we see a crew member aiming a harpoon gun at the whale and firing away. The report from the gun violently shakes the camera and sends a blast of smoke into the air. As the harpoon strikes the massive creature, the gunner raises his arm in celebration. In the background, we see blasts of air emitted from the whale as it struggles against the ship it is now tethered to. A taut line of rope leading from the ship out into the water shows us the location of the struggle. Bright red clouds of mammalian blood bloom in the water. From here, the pursuit transitions to slaughter. We see a winch in close-up as it turns, hauling the massive body to the ship. Other crew members gather tools to aid in securing the whale to the craft. Rope lines are tossed out to bind the dying whale. The waters churn with blood as the whale struggles against its capture. One crew member wields a massive, handled blade reminiscent of a scythe to cut off one of the whale's fins. In the next shot, we see that the carcass has been lashed to the side of the ship. Its struggle now finished, the deep ventral pleats that run along the whale's throat have been stilled. In a subsequent shot, crew members are lined up along a dock as the carcass is hauled onto land. We see a close-up of the grooved throat of the beast—beached and lifeless, its throat hangs in inert sags. Crew members work to butcher the animal, and we see how they use their sharpened instruments to flay its skin and then deftly separate blubber from meat. The credit sequence concludes with two panning shots that survey the aftermath of the slaughter.

In one, the camera slowly sweeps across the skinned, deblubbered carcass, the whalers' swift work having transformed the living creature into a massive slab of exposed muscle. The final image is a long shot overlooking a handful of men engaged in their individual tasks, while we see a pile of discarded skin, fat, and entrails, with the docks drenched in blood. The shots appear to be colorized and are accompanied by mournful string music, two choices that aesthetically frame the archival footage as an elegiac look at Iceland's industrial past. Seeing a whale hunt through this nostalgic filter, the viewer understands whale hunting to be part of a bygone era, and the shots therefore depict a kind of labor that has virtually died out in modern Iceland. The grainy, desaturated archival images also serve to provide a historical backdrop of environmental violence and trauma that will haunt the present. The over-the-top homicidal brutality that will play out aboard the decommissioned whaling ship through the course of the film is, the opening sequence suggests, part of a historical continuum deeply rooted in Icelandic cultural history that first manifests itself as an ecocidal and unsustainable taste for whale meat.

Depicting a beginning-to-end visual narrative of a single whale hunt, the credit sequence is also an effective piece of processual filmmaking, to borrow the terms of Salomé Aguilera Skvirsky's recent book *The Process Genre: Cinema and the Aesthetics of Labor*. In Skvirsky's account, the "process genre" is a "sequentially ordered representation of someone making or doing something."[7] The capaciousness of this definition allows the genre to encompass many types of media, including instruction manuals, the chronophotographic motion studies by the likes of Marey and Muybridge, a number of subgenres of reality television, and a whole slew of documentary and fiction films that are fixated on the sequential completion of a task. More relevant processual intertexts may be found in George Franju's documentary short about a French slaughterhouse, *Le sang des bêtes* (*The Blood of the Beasts*, 1949)—a film that scholars have connected to the visceral impulses of modern horror films[8]—or, in a Nordic film context, the opening sequence of Aki Kaurismäki's *Rikos ja rangaistus* (*Crime and Punishment*, 1983), which focuses on the process of butchering meat. Skvirsky notes that our current media landscape is "awash with examples of the process genre"—a ubiquity that signals a widespread interest in the changing forms of labor in the twenty-first century: "These are all attempts to grapple with a new reality of work as the status and meaning of labor in the twenty-first century and across the globe is changing. The new landscape is defined by technological developments, advancing automation, and the dramatic growth of the immaterial labor sector."[9] The growing cultural currency of labor-oriented processual media, then, is at least partly motivated by a widespread desire to rematerialize work and labor in a digital and increasingly immaterial labor economy in the developed world.

In terms of process, the opening sequence of *Reykjavik* presents whale hunting as a predictable sequence of labor that is characterized by several distinct phases. First, there is the journey out to sea. Leaving the security of land, the whale hunters place themselves out in the feeding grounds of the massive marine mammals. However, by floating above them, surveilling their movements, and aiming their weapons at the creatures, they are clearly taking an anthropocentric and environmentally apathetic view that has become increasingly problematic in contemporary society. Upon arriving at the feeding grounds, the whale hunt begins the second phase of the process: pursuit. In this phase, the whale hunters use optical instruments to spot the whales and isolate them for an attack, while other crew members maneuver the craft into the right position, and still others man the harpoon guns and launch the offensive in earnest. Once the beast has been harpooned, the third phase of the hunt begins, which involves tethering the carcass to the side of the boat and taking it back to land. Finally, the fourth phase begins: the most gruesome and gory part of the process, when the carcass is cut into, flayed, and butchered so that the beast can be divided up and its meat consumed by an eager and hungry public. If *Reykjavik* takes the form of one of the most flesh-obsessed and transgressive subgenres of horror—namely the slasher—the opening sequence of the film provocatively places this horrific kind of fictional human slaughter within a historical context of horrific marine mammal slaughter. Icelandic society, the sequence suggests, has long been engaged in the business of opening up the bodies of living organisms, disemboweling them, and putting this exposed flesh on display and up for sale. *Reykjavik* will recapitulate this sequence in its main narrative, showing how the murderous whalers have simply substituted human flesh for whale flesh in the modern world, undertaking a familiar sequence of pursuit, capture, and slaughter as they hunt their human victims and reduce their bodies to meat. Since *Reykjavik* is centered on the labor involved in resource management, food production, and meat processing—and the way these brutal processes have been hidden away as industrial labor has become increasingly automated, marginalized, and dematerialized in the public consciousness—beginning the film with an overtly processual sequence is a way of not only rematerializing human labor but also making visible the now hidden environmental violence that human industries engage in to provide food for the nation. What the processual filmmaking sequence that opens the film accomplishes, then, is to bring the long history of environmental violence in the Icelandic whaling industry to the surface.

Though whales have been hunted in the waters around Iceland since as early as the twelfth century, the history of modern ecocritical debates over whaling can be traced to the establishment of the International Whaling Commission (IWC) in 1949. The IWC is a multilateral organization that traces its roots to the postwar whale conservation movement in the United States, where the International Convention for the Regulation of Whaling was held in 1946. The founding articles of the convention give some sense of the impetus behind these efforts at international conservation, citing several motivations for the convention, including the "interest of nations of the world in safeguarding for future generations the great natural resources represented by the whale stocks"; the desire to prevent overfishing of any species in any area; the recognition that maintaining healthy levels of whale stocks is in "the common interest"; and the desire to "establish a system of international regulation" for the "proper conservation of whale stocks."[10] Though Iceland joined the IWC at its outset in 1949, decades of tension followed as the Icelandic whaling industry showed intransigence and inconsistency in adhering to IWC rules. In one emblematic dispute, Iceland simply refused to follow a rule adopted by the IWC in 1954 that banned all hunting of blue whales to allow the stock to rebound and repopulate the North Atlantic over the next several years. At the UN Conference on the Human Environment, held in Stockholm in 1972, a ten-year global moratorium on whaling was passed unanimously, though the measure failed to pass in the IWC, with the Nordic whaling nations of Iceland and Norway joining Japan, South Africa, and Panama in voting no. After the IWC was expanded to include more antiwhaling nations over the next decade, the commercial whaling moratorium was finally passed in 1982. Meanwhile, international opposition to the Icelandic whaling industry was increasing, with tensions boiling over in a dramatic incident in 1979, when commercial Icelandic whaling ships fired harpoons over protestors aboard the Greenpeace ship *Rainbow Warrior*, an act of aggression that was continued in the form of Icelandic naval ships monitoring and periodically seizing the *Rainbow*

*Warrior* at gunpoint. After the IWC refused to allow Iceland's request to hunt some 250 fin and minke whales in 1991, Iceland left the IWC, but found that in doing so, it could no longer export whale meat to IWC member countries. As a result, as well as a condition of rejoining the IWC, Iceland did not engage in research or commercial whaling for fourteen years, resuming research whaling in 2003 and commercial whaling in 2006. Since then, the United States and the UK have led diplomatic protests against the commercial whaling industry in Iceland, though within Iceland, the industry enjoys popular support.[11] As this brief history of modern whaling regulation in Iceland bears out, commercial whaling is a particularly acute site of transnational conflict and negotiation of the imagined boundaries of national sovereignty.

*Reykjavik* first hints at the persistence of reactionary pro-whaling factions early on in the film. Just after the doomed tourists board the whale watching boat to leave on their excursion, the film cuts to a decidedly less picturesque setting: a dingy, rat-infested kitchen and dining cabin aboard a boat. There we meet the disgruntled family of whalers, who will soon begin their attack on the unwitting tourists, as they cook and eat a greasy meal of boiled sausages. In the background, a news break plays on a radio, announcing the extension of the IWC ban on commercial whaling in Iceland. As she dishes out the sausage to her sons, the aged mother complains, "These American animal huggers have turned our government into a bunch of whale-loving sissies, leaving us with nothing but debts and a useless whale boat that's rotting away." She bemoans the depths of their economic humiliation, as they have been reduced to "making souvenirs for the tourist shops in Reykjavik." We see in subsequent scenes that these souvenirs are in fact carved wooden whale figurines that the brothers whittle from driftwood. Prevented from hunting and slaughtering whales by environmental regulation, they have taken to using their knives to carve kitschy keepsakes that commodify the gentle image of the whale for the growing ecotourism industry. Responding to the mother's complaint, one of the brothers moans that "once Icelanders were Vikings, brave hunters of these dirty stupid sea monsters. Now, we are nothing but crybabies." The other brother puts the argument in crasser terms: "You know what I call Greenpeace?" he asks rhetorically. "I call it green piss!"

More enterprising and economically flexible fishermen, we learn—such as Captain Pétur—have turned harpoons into plowshares by using their boats to take tourists out on whale watching excursions instead—a more environmentally friendly and sustainable alternative to whale hunting. From the abject decrepitude of the below-deck mess hall on the disgruntled whalers' boat, the film cuts to back to the whale watching tour, capturing the boat cutting majestically through a sun-drenched coastal seascape as Captain Pétur takes to the PA system to narrate the journey for his passengers: "Up until the whaling ban of the International Whaling Committee, Icelanders were among the three biggest whaling nations on earth, third behind Japan and Norway. Today things are very different. Today we are very proud to be number three on the list of the top ten whale *watching* countries in the world. And in fifty minutes, we will be in the feeding grounds of the lively and friendly minke whale." Captain Pétur's jovial commentary presents whale watching in an environmentally unproblematic light, breezily smoothing over the domestic debates and cultural resentments that have been stirred up by international intervention in Iceland's domestic affairs. The postwhaling industrial transition to whale watching, according to Pétur's tourist-friendly account, has been seamless—and has itself led to a new kind of international distinction for the island nation. This account is one of environmental absolution for a checkered past, as modern Iceland leaves behind its tradition of brutal extraction and slaughter of marine mammals. That this discursively decontextualized commentary ignores the actual conflicts and resentments bubbling to the surface in Iceland is hinted at by the subsequent shot, which cuts straight to the abject image of a seasick Japanese tourist vomiting overboard and on deck. Moreover, the rhetoric of nonviolence and environmental innocence is also belied by the subsequent scene of Björn's attempted rape of Annette. As he corners her and begins his sexual assault, Björn taunts her by speculating that Annette "likes it rough." Whale watching, then, is associated not only with an indirect kind of environmental violence—through the carbon emissions that are required for tourists to travel to Iceland and venture out into its waters on rusting old whaling boats—but also with a more directly predatory and sexualized kind of violence as well.

As an intervention into contemporary environmental discourse, then, *Reykjavik* provides a more complex and decidedly less savory counternarrative to Pétur's cheerful tour commentary. Whaling has not been fully superseded in Iceland, and the apparently benign image of tourists admiring the majesty of nature by watching whales in the waters off Iceland is not as innocent as it seems. These debates about whaling, the film hints, are central to understanding Icelandic identity and the uncertain place of Iceland in the twenty-first-century world—particularly because it was filmed in the midst of the spectacular collapse of the Icelandic economy in 2008. In her study of the cultural politics of whaling in Iceland, Anne Brydon argues that that pro- and antiwhaling debates in Iceland are suffused with a "reactive nationalist identification with a self-image of rationality."[12] Pro-whaling and antiwhaling factions both make the claim that their positions are backed up by value-free scientific data and research, while challenging the "disinterestedness of their opponents' science."[13] The self-image of rationality is particularly pronounced in the pro-whaling factions, however, who justify their own stance against the "alleged sentimentality and greed of international anti-whaling forces."[14] To use the terms set forth by Bruno Latour, pro-whaling discourse tends to ground itself in *matters of fact*—fixating on the rational basis for annual hunting quotas and viewing the whale in statistical rather than sentimental terms—while antiwhaling environmentalist discourse often appeals more overtly to *matters of concern* in its activist stance toward the whaling industry. According to Anne Brydon, the history of this debate since the 1970s has seen a gradual weakening of the "national solidarity behind the pro-whaling position in Iceland as whale-watching tourism proved successful," a shift that has "opened up the figure of the whale to multiple negotiations over its meaning."[15]

As a violent and bloody ecoslasher, *The Reykjavik Whale Watching Massacre* enters into this discursive fray and aims its satirical barbs at all the discursive positions in the debate: the internationalist environmentalists, with their naive sentimentality about the "gentle giants" of the sea, are lampooned along with the xenophobic, embittered, and sadistic pro-whaling fishermen in the film. The ecotourists who participate in the allegedly environmentally benign alternative industry of whale watching are similarly skewered—discursively and physically—as craven, selfish, and consumerist cultural outsiders who have come to Iceland not to commune with nature but instead to consume its natural resources and contribute to its natural degradation. Discursively, the film occupies a particularly pessimistic, even nihilistic position in the debate, framing all sides as equally driven by selfish, anthropocentric concerns, while not ostensibly advocating any position itself.

## THE NORDIC ECOSLASHER

In many ways, *Reykjavik* hews closely to the genre conventions of the slasher that were established in the 1970s and 80s by films like *The Texas Chainsaw Massacre, Halloween,* and *Friday the Thirteenth.* These conventions have been most memorably elucidated in Carol Clover's book *Men, Women, and Chain Saws,* where she isolates a number of key features of the post-*Psycho* (dir. Alfred Hitchcock, 1960) slasher film. The killer, writes Clover, is most often a man "propelled by psychosexual fury, more particularly a male in gender distress."[16] Though the killers "may be recognizably human," they are "only marginally so"—an inhumanity that is reinforced by the masks they usually wear, which hide both identity and expression, effectively figuring them as inhuman, monstrous foes. This monstrosity is reinforced by a quality of "virtual indestructability" as they survive self-defensive assaults from their victims that would neutralize a human foe. Clover also describes the setting of the slasher film, a paradigmatically "terrible place"—most often a confined space such as a house or tunnel—which is terrifying in its "Victorian decrepitude" and also because it is occupied by "terrible families—murderous, incestuous, cannabilistic."[17] The "terrible place" seems at first to be a safe haven, but "the walls that promise to keep the killer out quickly become, once the killer penetrates them, the walls that hold the victim in." This trap-like quality is reinforced by the conventional moment in slashers when the victim locks herself into a confined space such as a closet "and waits with pounding heart as the killer slashes, hacks, or drills his way in."[18] Since the "emotional terrain of the slasher film is pretechnological," writes Clover, the preferred weapons of the killer are penetrative instruments like knives, axes, ice picks, needles, and pitchforks—typically phallic weapons that will violate the flesh of victims in spectacular, bloody fashion. As the name *slasher* suggests, these are films that evince "a fascination with flesh or meat itself as that which is hidden from view." Clover describes this fixation on the spectacle of cutting into the human body not as a sadistic interest in exerting punishment, but rather as an epistemological fascination with bringing the invisible out into the open, as it is driven by the realization that "all that lies between the visible, knowable outside of the body and the secret insides is one thin membrane, protected only by a collective taboo against its violation."[19] As all of these elements suggest, one major distinction between the modern slasher film and historical antecedents such as *Psycho* is the direct, often over-the-top rendition of physical violence: "What can be done is done, and slashers at the bottom of the [horror] category, do it most and worst." Clover thus characterizes the new tone of slasher horror as one of shock—a sensation that emerges from the "rapid alternation between registers—between something like 'real' horror on one hand and a camp, self-parodying horror on the other." It is a subgenre that revels in "intentionally outrageous excess."[20]

*Reykjavik* adheres to virtually all of these conventions, confining its victims to a terrible place—a dilapidated whaling boat inhabited by a terrible, implicitly incestuous family—and dispatching them serially in grotesquely excessive ways. The ostentatious violence of these deaths is punctured by the campy, self-consciously tasteless one-liners that are typically uttered after the kill. To give one typical example, after Marie-Anne uses a flare gun to shoot a flaming projectile into Siggi's eye, the camera cuts to her in close-up delivery of her response: "I'd call *this* an emergency." The deaths themselves revel in bloody excess and almost always capture the postimpact gore in a lingering shot that forces the viewer to dwell for several moments on the shocking aftermath of the kill. One of the brothers, for instance, isn't just killed with a well-aimed bullet; he is subjected to a shotgun blast that pulverizes his head, leaving a gaping wound atop his shoulders that we see showering the deck with blood in a pulsing fountain of gore. Appropriately for the film's ecological framing, the least spectacular death in *Reykjavik* is the one that is carried out by the orca in one of the film's final scenes. After Marie-Anne aggressively aims a harpoon at the creature when it comes up to the surface—she is convinced that it is bent on killing her—she and the vessel get caught on the rope attached to harpoon, and the wounded beast pulls her underwater to her certain death. Rather than getting a shocking postfatality shot, we instead stay on the surface, the camera lingering on the traumatized Annette, who is bobbing on the surface of the water in her life preserver, now left alone to face the elements without Marie-Anne.

The most influential aspects of Clover's theorization of the slasher concern the victims and potential victims of the killer. The series of victims dispatched by the killer throughout the film tend to be teenage "sexual transgressors of both sexes," who are invariably "scheduled for early destruction."[21] The intimate connection between sexuality and victimhood is reinforced by the frequency of postcoital deaths in slasher films—a virtually ubiquitous trope that leads Clover to conclude that "killing those who seek or engage in unauthorized sex amounts to a generic imperative of the slasher film."[22] Even more crucial to the slasher film is the final girl, the lone figure who survives the killer's onslaught. Her longevity in the film means that she will witness the horrifying deaths of her friends and peers and will stave off the killer long enough to either be rescued or kill the attacker herself. Invariably female, the paradigmatic final girl nevertheless is boyish in her self-presentation, her name, and her energetic, active physicality: "Although she is always smaller and weaker than the killer, she grapples with him energetically and convincingly."[23] As the lone survivor of the killer's sensationally rendered serial murders, the ubiquity of the final girl figure also has the effect of tying the post-*Psycho* slasher film to a hero narrative.

In the last two decades, there have been a growing number of Nordic slasher films, most adhering quite closely to the slasher conventions Clover describes, with the notable exception of the puritanical sexual purity the films seem to advocate. As Gunnar Iversen writes, Norway has been a particularly prolific producer of slasher films, most of which take a decidedly un-Norwegian approach to the wilderness and rural landscapes. Films like *Villmark* (*Dark Woods*, dir. Pål Øie, 2003), *Fritt vilt* (*Cold Prey*, dir. Roar Uthaug, 2006), and *Død snø* (*Dead Snow*, dir. Tommy Wirkola, 2009) all feature groups of young city dwellers who go out into the wilderness to enjoy recreation in nature, only to be attacked and murdered one by one by sadistic backwoods killers. Instead of adopting the culturally orthodox view that wilderness settings and the Norwegian landscape are "uplifting, democratic, and open spaces," contemporary Norwegian horror presents an image of the national landscape as "threatening, violent, or negative." In Iversen's view, this menacing version of the Norwegian countryside in contemporary horror allows the genre to critique the "Norwegian conception of nature": "The new cycle of Norwegian horror films reinvents the Norwegian landscape, moving from pastoral to wilderness, and from sanctuary to a wild, uninhabitable space. Nature and landscape become a space without boundaries in which anything can happen—an amoral ground where danger, violence, and death loom large."[24] The notably un-Norwegian presentation of the natural environment Iversen describes here thus takes the form of a pessimistic and brutally de-idealized landscape. As Iversen writes, these films have largely stayed true to the conventions of the slasher that Clover identifies, though they have replaced the sexually virtuous final girl with a more mature and agential "final woman," who survives not "by becoming virtually masculine, or by being pure and virginal" but because of her "independence and sexual maturity."[25]

Pietari Kääpä has similarly described a backwoods fixation in contemporary Nordic horror, but he has adopted the term *ecoslasher* to describe a series of horror films that "evoke key themes in ecocriticism" and "give rise to reinterpreted versions of national narratives."[26] As Kääpä writes, one of the ways *Reykjavik* departs from the Norwegian wilderness slashers is that it is centered on the "context-specific ecopolitics" of twenty-first-century Iceland. Most notably, the film problematizes both the contested commercial whaling industry in Iceland—a traditional but highly controversial practice internationally—as well as the growing ecotourism industry, which includes whale watching along with other environmentally suspect excursions. Although it presents de-idealized and menacing natural land- and seascapes similar to those in Norwegian horror films, *Reykjavik* departs even farther from the final girl convention by ending with an image of profound isolation and vulnerability: "In contrast to the final girl triumphing over nature or descending into a state of animalism, she ends up floating on the ocean as potential game."[27]

In her chapter on rural horror, Clover develops one more concept worth mentioning here: the prevalence of what she terms *urbanoia* in such films. Urbanoia describes the way city dwellers in horror films approach the rural countryside and its inhabitants with a mixture of fear, aversion, and guilt. The prototypical country dweller of rural American horror is the sadistic hillbilly, a figure who "live[s] beyond the reaches of social law" and therefore ignores the "civilized rules" of personal grooming and treats the (sub)urban outsiders who encroach on his territory with a cruelty born of class resentment.[28] The confrontation between the urbanoiac city dweller and the terrifying, malign countryside through which he travels is represented as a class conflict between the bourgeois values and lifestyles of the (sub)urbanite and the lawlessness and abject cruelty of the hinterlands. Since the prosperity of the city has been gained at the expense of the shrinking wilderness and the disenfranchisement of the country folk, "the city approaches the country guilty in much the same way that the capitalist approaches the proletarian guilty (for plundering her labor) or the settler approaches the Indian guilty (for taking his land)."[29] In his ecocritical reading of the American rural horror films of the 1970s, Carter Soles is even more pointed in his description of the environmental guilt response that drives urbanoia. The brutality of these "urbanoia films," according to Soles, is really "a horrifying reflection of our own 'civilized' cultural anxieties about our own rape of the natural world."[30] While urbanoia is a useful concept for understanding the city/country divide in American rural horror—and *Reykjavik* has certainly translated the "sadistic hillbilly" figure into a specifically Icelandic iteration of the disenfranchised and now bloodthirsty former whaler—I would argue that the role of urbanoia is less pronounced in Nordic ecohorror for a number of reasons. The most important of these reasons is that one of the central pillars of Nordic identity is having easy access to the wilderness—via the tradition of Everyman's Rights—and therefore Nordic culture tends to approach the wilderness with exuberance and a longing for rejuvenation rather than guilt and fear. Rather than reading the xenophobia and sadism of the villains in *Reykjavik* through the lens of urbanoia, then, I would argue that the central confrontations in the film are not between the city and the countryside, but rather between the parochial attitudes of an isolated island nation and the transnational currents of global trade and culture that it is stubbornly resisting. As viewers, then, we are not meant to be preoccupied with guilt and fear of the countryside, but rather to be swayed by the film's parodic depiction of the hopeless nostalgia, environmental violence, and abject xenophobia that undergird the nationalist ideology of eco-isolationism.

## SCALING OUT: TRANSCORPOREALITY AND TRANSNATIONALISM

If discourses of environmental nationalism rely on an ecologically faulty illusion of national isolation—reinforced, in Iceland's case, by its status as a geographically remote island nation—the ecoslasher subgenre provides a particularly potent vehicle for spectacularly undoing that illusion. With its abject carnality and its fixation on corporeal violations, the slasher film reduces human bodies to writhing, bleeding masses of meat, their insides now indistinguishable from their outsides. This brutal ontological reduction of the human subject to its violated flesh, the ecoslasher posits, has the potential to be a kind of ecocritical corrective to the reactionary illusions of corporeal enclosure and isolation from environmental connection. One manifestation of cultural ecophobia is an anthropocentric yearning for corporeal enclosure. This stance of corporeal enclosure is one that Stacy Alaimo's notions of transcorporeality and insurgent exposure specifically seek to counteract.[31] As an ecoslasher, *Reykjavik* presents a particularly brutal version of transcorporeal interconnection—one in which society is bound together by shared practices of environmental violence. These violent forms of corporeal conflict are explicitly transcorporeal since they take the form of a transgressive and gory opening up of the human body to show how the flesh of living creatures is made to literally become one with its surroundings through acts of environmental violence.

With its nihilistic tendency to skewer all discursive positions and present all human actors as equally driven by greed and equally incapable of coopera-tion, *Reykjavik* implicates all of humankind in this collective violence. Just as Iceland's past has been characterized by a bloodthirsty, rapaciously extractive impulse to mine the seas for all the warm-blooded meat they can provide, Iceland's present is no less environmentally violent. Even disregarding the "terrible family," everyday Icelandic society is nourished by the financial influx provided by carbon-intensive ecotourism—a point the film makes in its final shots by showing Endo jetting back to Japan directly over the picturesque seascape where Annette is floating as a lonely island. Environmentalists, sim-ilarly, have blood on their hands: in one scene, while Annette's friend Hannah (Ragnhildur Steinunn Jónsdóttir) is having drinks with a group of concerned environmentalists who are bemoaning the ecological impacts of whale watch-ing tourism, she gets a call from a desperate Annette, who tells her all about the attacks and begs her to call the coast guard. Hannah assumes that Annette is high on drugs and hangs up on her, leaving her and the other victims to face their attackers alone.

One tangible way *Reykjavik* makes human bodies one with their surround-ings is by making the ontological reduction of humans to meat literal. This is a tried-and-true staple of the slasher film, of course, which has a long tradition of combining spectacular bodily violence with a sensational presentation of cannibalism. Cannibalism, *Reykjavik* posits, is a kind of logical extension of the whale-hungry traditional diet of Icelandic culture. There are hints early on that the killers are cannibals, as they eat sausages that are unsettlingly greasy and fleshy. The film reveals how those sausages are made as the film goes on, and it becomes clear that the killers have substituted human flesh for whale flesh in their diet, literally feasting on the carcasses of environmentalists when they are denied their whale meat.[32]

Just as the sadistic whalers are about to begin their pursuit of the stranded whale watching tourists, we see that their sublimated bloodlust—denied by the IWC's whaling ban—has been satiated by murdering and dismembering environmental activists. In one scene, one of the brothers retreats to a cabin aboard their whaler where a man is held captive, bound to a chair. As the brother comes into the room with his axe at the ready, the man screams, "No, you can't do this! No, please! I'm a friend of nature!" As the attacker brings his weapon back in preparation for the blow, he delivers his one-liner—"You can tell it to my axe!"—whereupon he plants the blade in the environmentalist's head. After we hear the telltale chop into flesh, we see *Guignolesque* splatters of blood spray across the attackers' clothes. Though we don't see the dismemberment, the film shows us the product of the slaughter in a subsequent scene. When the whalers have seized upon the stranded whale watching boat and picked up the unwitting passengers, claiming all the while that they are taking the traumatized tourists to safety, the camera pans into an interior cabin to reveal the severed head of the environmentalist packed on ice—on display like fresh fish at a seaside market. The shot is not only a revelation of the horrifyingly cannibalistic enterprise the whalers have turned to; it is also a further sign that *Reykjavik* is concerned with presenting horror through a processual focus on labor and productivity. In this case, *process* can be used as a verb as well—showing us how the slasher effectively *processes meat* to create a consumable product in the end, which can either be consumed by the laborer himself or commodified and sold at market.

This ontological reduction of human victims to consumable sea creatures is reinforced throughout the film as the members of the "terrible family" attack and toy with their victims. When the mother—credited only as Mamma (Guðrún Gísladóttir)—has pinned one of her victims on the floor of an underdeck corridor at the end of a harpoon, she holds the tip of the blade up to the woman's neck and repeatedly commands her to "sing! Sing like a whale!" When her son Tryggvi tells her to hurry up and finish the woman off, the mother replies that "an old woman is entitled to enjoy her catch." Later, when the perverse Siggi has captured Annette, he binds her by the wrists to the ceiling of a cabin, suspending her in the air like a side of meat waiting to be butchered. As he strips her topless and gleefully rubs blood onto her chest, he calls her a "strong fish" in a tone of admiration. The conflation of human and animal flesh, then, is figured by the film as a brutal kind of reductionism. Although *Reykjavik* does eventually pit man against beast in one fleeting appearance of an orca, the film is far from the kind of "creature feature"—like *Jaws* (dir. Steven Spielberg, 1975)—that shows nature taking revenge on human society. Instead, the film uses debates about animal rights as well as Icelandic dietary and industrial practices to show the ways in which human agents are implicated as bloodthirsty, animalistic organisms just like any others. Rather than ontologically elevating the animal—engaging in the kind of sentimental anthropomorphism and cultural admiration for particularly precarious animals such as various species of whale or the polar bear—*Reykjavik's* ecocritical maneuver is to reduce the human being to the status of a beast, effectively leveling the playing field between human and nature.

A more grotesque conflation of environmental politics and human slaughter occurs after the whale watching tourists are brought aboard the slaughter ship. After the crazed brother Siggi has impulsively planted his hammer in the head of a woman in front of all the onlookers—a murder that the film figures as a kind of premature ejaculation by the overexcited Siggi—one Japanese tourist grabs a life vest and jumps from the boat, attempting to swim to safety. As he struggles to get away from the horrific boat, another brother, Tryggvi (Helgi Björnsson), realizes he has the means to stop the man's escape: a harpoon gun. Tryggvi steadies his aim and pulls the trigger. The projectile is shown in a slow-motion tracking shot that follows its swirling trajectory toward the swimming tourist. The whaler's aim turns out to be devastatingly true, and the harpoon plunges right through the man's chest. The scene dwells on the ship's machinery, which slowly comes into motion after the harpoon reaches its target: the winch begins turning, the rope line is pulled taut, and the tourist's corpse is slowly hauled back to the ship. In a later shot, the film heightens its gory takedown of the sadistic whaling industry in a particularly dissonant landscape shot. In it, we see a calm sea in the foreground, which gives way to a dramatic backdrop of rocky volcanic mountains and the picturesque light of a setting sun. In its deep focus and panoramic view of the Icelandic coastal landscape, the image looks as if it could be taken from a postcard—except for the impaled body of the tourist that dangles from the deck of ship on the left side of the shot.

In one particularly gruesome scene, the mother impales a European and a Japanese woman on the same harpoon. As the dying women face each other, skewered on the same weapon, they are brought into fatal proximity—a figure of gory and painful intimacy as they cough blood onto each other's faces. The dying Japanese tourist, however, had strapped a makeshift explosive device to herself, which she ignites as the women are bound together at the end of the murderous mother's harpoon. As the device explodes, it engulfs all three women in a fireball, effectively reinforcing their corporeal intimacy in a violent death.

The impaled corpse of a Japanese ecotourist dangles at the end of a harpoon line from the ship in the foreground, while the camera captures a picturesque shot of the sun setting over the dramatic Icelandic coastline in the background. Frame grab from *Reykjavik Whale Watching Massacre* (dir. Júlíus Kemp, 2009).

*Reykjavik Whale Watching Massacre*'s apparent final girl, Annette, is left to float, isolated and adrift, at the end of the film, leaving the question of her eventual survival unresolved. Frame grab from *Reykjavik Whale Watching Massacre* (dir. Júlíus Kemp, 2009).

## CAMP, PLEASURE, AND THE ECOCRITICAL SLASHER

As Carol Clover has emphasized, the slasher revels in its status at the bottom of the horror barrel, freely combining grotesque and sensational violence with self-consciously tasteless and campy excess. Since it pits human against human in a bloody Darwinian struggle for survival against an implicitly inhuman—or marginally human—foe, the slasher tends to reinforce the dichotomy of human and nonhuman rather than challenging it. The advent of the ecoslasher in Nordic horror, as elaborated by Pietari Kääpä, seems to offer the possibility of a more environmentally aware and ecocritical variant of the slasher. And indeed, *Reykjavik* does bear out this assumption in certain ways, clearly situating its bloody narrative at the discursive and physical intersections between human and nonhuman. If we take Stephen A. Rust and Carter Soles's helpful definition of ecohorror, "Horrific texts and tropes are used to promote ecological awareness, represent ecological crises, or blur human/non-human distinctions more broadly," then *Reykjavik* more than qualifies for that label.[33] The film not only "blur[s] human/non-human distinctions" with gleeful abandon; it also situates horror within an ecopolitical discursive context, effectively raising environmental problems for debate in a horror analogue to the social realism of contemporary Nordic noir. As Kääpä emphasizes in his reading of *Reykjavik*, however, the ecocritical dimensions of the film are constrained by its reassertion of a certain anthropocentric logic and its fixation on telling a national narrative. To Kääpä's reservations I would add that the ecoslasher's fixation on the transcorporeal mingling of human bodies and environments depends on violently opening up and murdering the bodies, thus positing the interface between insides and outsides as an exceptional state only effected through homicidal acts of corporeal violation.

To be too precious about the ecocritical seriousness of an ecoslasher, however, would be to disregard the self-referential and campy tone these films cultivate—a tone the devoted audiences of such "low" genres take great pleasure in. In this sense, it may be more useful to approach the ecopolitics of such sensationalistic genre films through the lens of pleasure, as Bridgitte Barclay and Christy Tidwell have suggested in their ecocritical approach to "creature features." Citing Alaimo's plea for the importance of pleasure in a time of climate crisis—"If we cannot laugh, we will not desire the revolution"—and Donna J. Haraway's advocacy of "working and playing for a resurgent world,"

Barclay and Tidwell write that the hybrid and aesthetically "low" qualities of campy texts like creature features "offer an alternate route into" ecocritical issues.[34] As "bad environmentalism," in the terms of Nicole Seymour, messy and aesthetically unserious genres like the slasher "demonstrate that engagement with serious issues need not entail serious affect or sensibility."[35] Among other ways, Barclay and Tidwell suggest, the combination of nature and biological motifs with horror in such texts "acknowledges the seriousness of the underlying environmental issues they address and establishes community through intentional and unintentional camp," often with an aesthetic messiness that "offers a great deal of space for both pleasure and critical analysis."[36] Though its unseriousness means that we might need to approach *Reykjavik*'s ecopolitics with a grain of salt—as Kääpä writes—the discursive space for pleasure and critique that it allows means that *Reykjavik* and ecoslashers like it can perform important cultural work and reach audiences with horror that more heightened aesthetic ambitions might never reach. Those who do seek out a film like *Reykjavik* expecting to see a comfortingly silly, gleefully gory, and unpretentious genre exercise are also consuming—in a tonally broadened and heightened form—a set of culturally specific environmental issues that are in fact at the heart of contemporary ecopolitical conflicts. In a radically distilled form, the final shots of the film offer a memorable encapsulation of the film's ecocritical argument. Though the reactionary impulses of environmental nationalism posit the body politic and the national territory as an enclosed and insulated space, Annette's isolated, drifting body, struggling for survival in the midst of an inhospitable sea, is far from an island. As the jumbo jet flying above her floating form reminds us, she is intimately, transcorporeally connected with a global environmental commons.

# CHAPTER FOUR

# Migrant Labors

## Predatory Environmentalism and
## Eco-privilege in *Shelley*

Iranian-Danish director Ali Abbasi's debut feature *Shelley* (2016) is a film about the horrors of pregnancy and childbirth that sets a tone of malevolent, rural organicism from the very start. The film begins with a montage of landscape shots that ground the viewer firmly in an isolated, heavily forested Nordic countryside. We see the dappled light of a setting sun over a picturesque lake, filtering through the branches of a forest in the foreground. A zoom shot takes us in among the trunks of a dense grove of trees, gradually pulling us into the darkness of the woods. We get an elevated view of the forested islets that dot the surface of the lake. We see a shock of leafless branches reaching up toward the sky out of a grove of otherwise green and leafy trees, the canted roofline of a wooden homestead abutting the trees in the foreground. In case the menacing undertone of Abbasi's establishing landscape shots is not abundantly obvious, an eerie electronic drone, hissing with static, slowly crescendos underneath the shots as the sequence reaches its conclusion, whereupon the screen dissolves into a blood-red backdrop for the title card. As this unsettling precredit sequence makes plain, there is clearly some malign impulse at work in the bucolic woodlands of rural Scandinavia.[1]

As Abbasi explains in an interview, the source of horror in *Shelley* has everything to do with the internal tensions implicit in the Nordic approach to nature—tensions that are especially apparent to Abbasi as a cultural outsider working and living in Denmark: "[Something] that interests me about Scandinavia is that people live with advanced technology and in many areas are ahead of the curve socially and scientifically. But you all are also in close contact with nature. It is as if nature expands and becomes something almost religious for you all. And all horror films I have seen come out of religion."[2] Employing the Danish collective second-person pronouns *I* and *jer* (you all) to distance himself from Nordic environmental attitudes, Abbasi emphasizes the distinction between his own Iranian cultural frame of reference and Scandinavia's strange combination of material prosperity and privilege with a cultural preference for rustic living. What strikes him is the paradox of Scandinavians being so progressive and "ahead of the curve" technologically and socially yet being almost superstitious in their reverence for the natural environment. Nature is a kind of stand-in for God in famously secular Scandinavia, as recent scholarship has borne out, and for Abbasi, the intense, irrational feelings Nordic people attach to nature make it a useful jumping-off point for horror.[3] Social scientists Atle Midttun and Lennart Olsson have labeled these tensions between socioeconomic progress and reverence for the natural world in Nordic societies "eco-modernity."[4] Although the effort to reconcile socioeconomic progress with environmental sustainability under the rubric of "sustainable development" has proved an elusive—if not paradoxical—goal, scholars such as Midttun and Olsson, along with establishment political leaders in the region, have continued to voice the optimistic proposition that eco-modernity is an achievable endeavor.[5] Abbasi's comments suggest that although Nordic societies seem to relate to nature through rationalist modes of discourse—aiming for "the sustainable management of the environment and development of natural resources," according to a recent branding document published by the Nordic Council of Ministers—their approach to nature is in fact haunted by the kinds of irrational impulses that can provide a jumping-off point for ecohorror.[6] And since it has become a social science truism that Nordic secularity has been key to the success of the region in terms of material prosperity, social equality, and happiness, Abbasi's film packs an even stronger punch.[7] These famously secular societies, the film suggests, aren't *really* secular; they have just "relocated" experiences of transcendence from the church to settings perceived as "pristine" and "natural." On top of that, Nordic environmental exceptionalism is actually manifested as a predatory regime of ecological privilege that comes at the expense of the socioeconomically vulnerable. So although *Shelley* draws a clear connection between horror and nature, the malevolence we sense lurking in the Scandinavian woodlands from the film's opening frames is decidedly anthropogenic.

To convey this outsider view of the persistence of the superstitious and the irrational in Scandinavian approaches to nature, *Shelley* focalizes on a young Romanian woman, Elena (Cosmina Stratan), a single mother who has moved to Scandinavia to earn money as a domestic worker and in-home nurse for the well-to-do couple Kasper (Peter Christoffersen) and Louise (Ellen Dorrit Petersen). Elena's hope is that the higher wages in Scandinavia will allow her to save money to buy an apartment in her native Bucharest for herself and her son, whom she has left behind in Romania in the care of her parents. Elena's main task is to care for the convalescing Louise, who has just undergone the psychological and physical trauma of a late-term miscarriage and emergency hysterectomy. Kasper welcomes Elena to their isolated lakeside villa by introducing her to their efforts to lead a pastoral, ecologically sustainable existence—they have eschewed the material comforts of electricity and running water, and they grow their own organic produce—and tells her unassumingly that he and Louise value the "peace and quiet" that their rustic lifestyle has afforded them. Although her new life unwittingly off the grid has cut Elena off from easy communication with her family in Romania as her cell phone battery slowly runs out, the rural isolation also draws Elena and Louise closer together, and they become fast friends in spite of their many cultural and socioeconomic differences. Elena learns how to light the gas lamps they use for illumination at night, how to keep dairy and other perishables fresh and bug-free in a mesh cage in the cellar, how to chop wood for the fire and gather eggs from the henhouse. As compensation for the hard work required to support their premodern, eco-friendly lifestyle, the couple and their new domestic worker are rewarded with uninterrupted quiet, panoramic views of the lake and forest, and all the *hygge* Nordic domestic life can afford—light-roast coffee, candles, wool blankets, and all.

The rustic idyll of Elena's new life in the Nordic countryside disintegrates after she enters into what seems like a mutually beneficial arrangement with Kasper and Louise. Having suffered from infertility for years before undergoing her recent miscarriage, Louise offers to purchase an apartment back in Bucharest for Elena if she agrees to serve as a surrogate mother for the couple, an offer Elena readily accepts. Almost immediately upon being implanted with the couple's fertilized embryo, however, the health and happiness Elena has started to achieve in her new life in the Nordic countryside give way to physical and psychological misery. As the pregnancy progresses, Elena is plagued by disturbingly gory dreams and aural hallucinations. She has unsettling new cravings that come upon her during her sleep, rendering her a ravenous sleep-walker estranged from her own body. She develops an alarming aversion to the sensation of water on her skin, breaks out in painful rashes, and starts to lose weight. She becomes convinced that the baby is trying to kill her and, in one frightening scene, starts pummeling her own abdomen until Louise manages to stop her. Although the doctors reassure Louise that the baby is a strong and healthy girl—"A real Viking," one of them remarks—Louise is frightened by Elena's hysterics and takes to keeping a close watch on what Elena eats and how she cares for herself. Elena decides she wants to return to her mother to wait out the rest of the pregnancy, but Kasper and Louise—afraid she will take in the baby as her own after delivery—tell her she needs to stay in their care until after the birth. The end comes sooner than anticipated, however, as an increasingly distraught Elena attempts to abort the baby herself with one of Louise's knitting needles. Elena is rushed to the hospital, where she dies from internal bleeding, though the baby, Shelley, is born unharmed. The film goes on to document the deterioration of Kasper and Louise's domestic happiness after Elena's death and the arrival of their baby, proceeding inexorably toward a gruesome denouement that showcases the brutal desperation of Louise's desire to be a mother.

At first glance, *Shelley* registers as a film about the physical and psychological horrors of pregnancy and childbirth, drawing on the "occult film" subgenre theorized by Carol J. Clover—a tradition in which a girl or young woman becomes a portal to the supernatural as her body is possessed by an evil spirit (as in *The Exorcist*, dir. William Friedkin, 1973), becomes impregnated with the spawn of Satan (as in *Rosemary's Baby*, dir. Roman Polanski, 1968), or becomes a conduit for psychic or telepathic powers (as in *Carrie*, dir. Brian De Palma, 1976).[8] In its initial reception, however, a tendency in *Shelley* that escaped most reviewers was the film's fixation on the predatory motivations that lurk beneath the respectable, virtuous face of Nordic environmentalism. Reading *Shelley* through the lens of ecohorror, then, casts the film in a radically different light, deemphasizing questions of genre classification and instead bringing the cultural specificity of its environmental critique to the fore. The film frames its central conflict around the relationship between Nordic eco-sustainability and the immense privilege and power implicit in such a project. These environmental inequities are personified in the guise of Elena—a working-class single mother from Eastern Europe who aspires to a middle-class life through domestic labor and surrogacy—and her economically and socially privileged Scandinavian employers Kasper and Louise, a couple who possess the material resources required to live an ecologically sustainable, "back to the land" existence. As the film dramatizes through the physical and psychological torments Elena suffers during the pregnancy, Louise and Kasper's eco-friendly domestic life is only achieved through the suffering of the migrant laborer's body. Such a cultural confrontation centered on environmental privilege and migrant labor effectively frames discourses of Nordic environmentalism and sustainability as parasitic—a far cry from the reputation for environmental exceptionalism the region generally enjoys. Because of this, *Shelley* supports Anca Parvulescu's argument that the prosperity of modern Europe has been underwritten by the establishment of an exploitative market in reproductive labor that traffics in Eastern European women. The assimilation of Eastern European countries into a modern European collective is, then, predicated upon an inclusive kind of exclusion: Eastern women are invited in conditionally, as long as they perform the reproductive and traditionally feminine labor that women in more privileged and egalitarian societies have left behind. Such an inclusive exclusion of Eastern European women's bodies effectively highlights the inequalities in biopolitical value of Eastern and Western European bodies in a supposedly egalitarian Nordic social-democratic state. Like *Thelma*, the unsettlingly shifting and porous boundaries of the transcorporeal body become an index of social inequality; in the case of *Shelley*, however, the inequalities have to do with socioeconomic privilege and ethnic (and implicitly racial) identity rather than gender and sexuality, a difference that has everything to do with Abbasi's position as a cultural outsider working in the Scandinavian film industry. As the Scandinavians in Abbasi's film become greener in their lifestyle and achieve their material and familial desires, the migrant's body withers away and dies a violent death, tossed aside as unimportant as soon as it has brought a healthy Scandinavian baby into the world. In that sense, *Shelley* supports Anna Estera Mrozewicz's argument that "Russia and Eastern Europe serve as an important, though not always recognized, screen onto which the Nordic countries project themselves" in contemporary cinema and narrative media.[9] In *Shelley*, the juxtaposition of Western European privilege and the exploitation of bodies of Eastern European women calls into question the moral logic of Nordic environmental and biopolitical privilege.

In centering horror on the way such eco-sustainability is enabled by the physical labor and suffering of economically disadvantaged migrant workers, *Shelley* develops a socially critical form of ecohorror that reveals the brutal, predatory, and parasitic impulses implicit in Nordic approaches to nature. The malevolent forces at work in *Shelley* are all the more sinister because they appear in the guise of kindness, hospitality, and ecological responsibility. In this sense, the horror effects Abbasi achieves in the film are tied to an ecohorror aesthetic of overturned cultural tropes and an alienated picture of the Nordic wilderness. The figure of the benign Scandinavian environmentalist becomes the exploitative employer of migrant labor. The robust, vital physique of the Nordic body—idealized as the healthy Viking in the modern imagination—becomes the enfeebled, infertile body of Louise. The parasitic immigrant body imagined by right-wing populist discourse—including the nativist appeals of resurgent anti-immigration parties such as the Sverigedemokraterne (Sweden Democrats) and the Dansk Folkeparti (Danish People's Party)—becomes the fertile maternal body of Elena. The progressive and hospitable Scandinavian couple become a sinister pair who prey on a less fortunate migrant worker through an opportunistic surrogacy arrangement. The pastoral, forested countryside, fetishized in Nordic national Romanticism as one of the most symbolically important national landscapes of the region, becomes a malignant space seething with a native menace. That menace, it turns out, is not an inhuman foe lurking in the underbrush but rather the irrational, predatory, brutal, and exclusionary impulses that hide behind the respectable face of Nordic environmentalism.[10]

In order to understand Abbasi's critiques of Nordic approaches to the environment, this chapter examines the way bodies are depicted in *Shelley*. While earlier chapters in this book have focused on the ways Nordic ecohorror emphasizes the unsettling enmeshment of bodies and their environments as a critique of anthropocentric idealism and ecophobia (chapter 1) or the persistence of misogyny in contemporary Nordic societies (chapter 2), this chapter examines the ways discourses of nature, health, and vitality are tied to broader cultural strategies of racialization. In these discourses, (implicitly white) Nordic bodies are assumed to be healthier and more robust because of their proximity to supposedly "pristine" and "pure" natural environments, while those of Eastern European migrants (implicitly not white or European *enough*) are assumed to be weaker and less healthy because of their distance from and aversion to the supposedly salubrious natural environments of the

Nordic region. *Shelley* works to overturn these associations by showing how supposedly "healthy" and "natural" approaches to the environment are suffused with a predatory, self-reinforcing logic of Nordic privilege. This analysis underscores the appeal of Nordic environmentalism as a rich vein of ecohorror that has been mined by a spate of recent transnational horror narratives associating Scandinavian environmentalism with regimes of racial, ethnic, or biological purity and supremacy.[11]

## HEALTH, DISEASE, AND ECOFASCISM

To fully appreciate the critical gaze *Shelley* trains on Nordic culture, it is helpful to isolate a pair of basic assumptions about the natural environment in the contemporary Nordic cultural imagination. While these assumptions are not unique to the region, they represent attitudes and ideas that are foundational to Nordic nature mythologies and cultural identities. The first is that life in the rural countryside is healthier for the human body and soul than life in the city—a proposition that has its roots in nineteenth-century national Romantic movements, which were a response to the rapid industrialization of domestic economies and urbanization of the Scandinavian population. By highlighting the degree to which eco-sustainability can take the form of nostalgic yearning for a preindustrial way of life, *Shelley* examines an atavistic impulse in contemporary Nordic environmentalism. The second of these assumptions is that access to rural nature is a democratic right rather than a privilege. This "right to roam" has been codified in a robust legal tradition that has existed for centuries, a tradition that is the basis for the role of outdoor wilderness recreation in Nordic cultural identities. The prevailing belief—both inside and outside the region—in a kind of Nordic "environmental exceptionalism" bestows a sense of ecological virtue on the central role played by eco-sustainability in Nordic political discourse, public policy, and the habits of private citizens. Addressing each of these assumptions in turn, this chapter analyzes how *Shelley* uses ecohorror to complicate the discourses of rural living, ecological egalitarianism, and environmental virtue that prevail in contemporary Nordic cultures.

One way *Shelley* emphasizes the direct connection between Nordic environmentalism and privilege is by drawing on deeply held cultural assumptions about the health-promoting effects of rural nature in the region. These assumptions, as one scholar recently put it, are not only part of the Nordic region's self-conception but also central to how outsiders perceive the Nordic countries, with words like *clean*, *pure*, and *healthy* ranking high in terms of their association with the region.[12] But the organicist pastoral project undertaken by Louise and Kasper has deeper cultural roots than contemporary Nordic environmental exceptionalism. A crucial historical precedent can be found in the cultural manifestations of vitalism—a nature-based cult of physical health that led to the invention of modern exercise regimes, the rise of nudism, and a widespread cultural fascination with sunbathing and solar therapy that was especially influential in early twentieth-century Scandinavian cultures.[13] Drawing on life-affirming philosophical and scientific theories of vitalism from the likes of Friedrich Nietzsche, Henri Bergson, and Hans Driesch, vitalism was a wide-ranging cultural impulse that found expression in the natural sciences and the literary and visual arts. The basic assumption of this modern form of scientifically and philosophically oriented vitalism is that life is an independent substance or force immanent to the bodies of living beings, and this vital force or energy can be strengthened or depleted by a range of habits and ways of living. Central to vitalism's rhetorical appeal was that it was presented as a healthy alternative to fin-de-siècle decadence, promoting personal physical rejuvenation along with a broader cultural rebirth. Such a project of rejuvenation and rebirth, according to the rhetoric of vitalism, could only be achieved outside of the distracting, corrupting, enervating, and above all unhealthy domain of the modern city. As Danish art historian Gertrud Oelsner puts it, vitalism thus demanded a "return" to nature:

> "Nature" was the opposite, positive pole to the growing metropolises of the age, and therefore came to play a role at many different levels. Not only could man mirror himself in the great outdoors and thus claim a new artistic dignity; nature also became an important concept in the general idea that culture, after a period of decline, was to be saved by the cultivation of a life "close to nature" and of natural hygienic practices; while the landscape itself, with its cyclically unfolding seasons, could be understood as a framework for cultural rebirth.[14]

As scholars have pointed out, this ostensibly life-affirming discourse of personal and cultural rebirth—like the Romantic nationalist movements that preceded it—had an ethno-nationalist impulse at its core, expressing itself both in the relatively benign movements of nudism and *Lebensreform*—a social reform movement that extolled the virtues of vegetarianism, open-air recreation, and exercise—to more radically *völkisch* and protofascist programs of ethnic exclusion and racial hygiene.[15]

As many scholars have noted, nationalist ideologies are preoccupied with establishing and naturalizing an imagined connection between a particular nation-state's physical territory and a particular people, frequently figured as an ethnic or racial community. According to Ernest Gellner, nationalist ideology is a product of the urban industrial age.[16] Despite these modern origins, nationalist movements idealize the rural countryside rather than the modern city in their zeal to cultivate the image of a national landscape distinct from other territories.[17] Scholars have explained this rural turn in nationalism by noting that the urban middle class imagined "the countryside and the 'natural' life, as an antidote to the materialism and competitive individualism of city existence," and has therefore advocated "a return to rural folkways" as a crucial task in recapturing an "authentic" and "pure" national culture.[18] Nationalist nature imaginaries, then, rely on the construction of a fundamental urban-rural binary in which the modern city is thought of as unhealthy, inauthentic, and suspiciously cosmopolitan. The rural countryside, by contrast, is presumed to be health promoting, authentic, and a cradle of the nation's folk culture relatively unsullied by the influence of suspicious ethnic outsiders. This spatial move to the countryside is, of course, a temporal leap as well, from the "disenchanted modernity of the city to the nostalgic originality of the country, which comes to represent what has been lost and should be reclaimed through the nationalist project," in the words of Bernhard Forchtner and Christoffer Kølvraa.[19] Adopting this Romantic nationalist preference for life in the rural countryside, the Nordic vitalist tradition of the twentieth and twenty-first centuries has overtly connected the pastoral, organic, and folk-cultural aspects of rural life with the cultivation of physical health, strength, and vitality.

Louise and Kasper's choice to lead an eco-friendly, vegetarian, off-the-grid lifestyle can, then, be seen as a kind of neo-vitalist project aimed at achieving spiritual and physical well-being—one that is also suffused with the cultural impulses and nature mythologies of national Romanticism. Because of these associations between health and the countryside, Elena's journey out to the rural Nordic farmstead seems like it might well provide her with a therapeutic respite from the stress, pollution, and distractions of modern urban life. One ticking-clock indicator of Elena's retreat from modern life is the gradual depletion of her cell phone battery in the absence of electric current at the remote farmstead. As the battery slowly drains, Elena loses her umbilical connection to her life and family in Bucharest. The loss of access to modern communication media, however, also has the ostensibly healthy effect that she becomes more firmly present in her own embodied labor, anchored as she is in the demanding daily tasks of traditional rural life. Chopping wood, feeding chickens, and harvesting vegetables are part of daily life at the farm, activities that keep her body actively engaged all day. Although Louise has been weakened by her surgery and initially requires help from Elena to get dressed and get around her house, she is quickly back on her feet. The film frames Louise as a characteristically healthy and vigorous Nordic woman—just the kind of stereotypically robust "Viking" a nurse refers to later in the film in connection with the apparently strong and healthy baby growing in Elena's womb. Louise's rural Nordic vitality is implicitly contrasted with the unhealthy, enervated, distracted, city-dwelling body and mind of Elena.

In an early scene that shows Louise and Elena harvesting root vegetables together and discussing the couple's choice to lead a rural, electricity-free lifestyle, this contrast between Louise's traditional rural vigor and Elena's modern urban frailty is emphasized by their physical positions. Crouched over the earth and plunging in her gloved fingers to pull out the vegetables, Elena is positioned as small, enfeebled, and awkwardly unfamiliar with the physical gestures and work required to harvest one's own food. Her grimacing face also betrays her disgust at the grimy labor required to cultivate the vegetable patch, a sign that she is not a naturalized inhabitant of this particular territorial soil. The film's fixation on the connection between farming and ethnic belonging to the national territory recalls the troubling nature mythologies of the German *Völkisch* movement, which were later appropriated by Nazi ideologues in the invention of racial classifications that preached the transcendent superiority of the Nordic "race" and imaginatively connected that race to the act of tilling the soil in the *Blut und Boden* (Blood and Soil) cultural tradition. The camerawork doubles down on Elena's lowly physicality by framing her in high-angle shots where her hunched figure looks down at the earth she is tilling. Louise, by contrast, cuts an elegant, vertical figure as she stands on a rocky outcrop above Elena, surveying the work as she puts on her gloves in preparation for the toil she is about to join in. The contrast between the women extends beyond their differing physiques to their coloring and complexions: Louise has platinum-blond hair and eyebrows and pale blue eyes, while the blue-eyed Elena has dark hair and features. These contrasts imply an ethnic distinction between the two women to go along with the cultural, linguistic, and socioeconomic differences the film has already established. Seen through the Romantic nationalist lens of folk pastoralism, the difference between Elena's weakened, city-dwelling body and Louise's rustic vitality implicitly marks national or ethnic difference and references discarded racial categories that situate the Nordic race as biologically superior.

The implicit ideology of (white) Nordic supremacy in Louise's folksy, eco-friendly lifestyle is evident, then, in the contrast the film develops between the healthy rural body of the ethnic insider and the unhealthy urban body of the ethnic outsider. In Louise and Elena's ongoing dialogue as their friendship grows more intimate, Louise frames her choice to lead a radically rural life as motivated primarily by personal health and vitality. In one scene, Elena expresses her ongoing wonder at the couple's rustic lifestyle: "It must be hard work for you and Kasper to live like this. No power, no running water, no . . . everything takes a lot of time. No TV, no computer—isn't it boring?" Louise responds that she doesn't mind, adding emphatically, "I don't miss any of that." Louise also hints at an apparent biological sensitivity to electricity, explaining, "Electricity—I have to stay away from it." Louise's claim that she has to "stay away" from electricity is likely a reference to electromagnetic hypersensitivity (EHS), a contested condition in which sufferers attribute a variety of "non-specific symptoms to electromagnetic fields of anthropogenic origin."[20] Based as it is on a claim of biological aversion to the invisible electromagnetic fields that are the anthropogenic products of industrial urban modernity, EHS may be seen as a medicalized analogue to the Romantic nationalist turn toward rural folk life. Equating rural nature with health and urban modernity with disease, EHS draws on long-standing Romantic nationalist tropes, revealing a distinctly atavistic impulse within certain styles of Nordic eco-sustainability. The prominence of these antimodern and Romantic nationalist discourses in *Shelley* reinforces the ideology of ethno-racial supremacy that suffuses Louise's interactions with Elena. In that sense, Louise's rural flight can be viewed not so much as a manifestation of her love for the Nordic countryside as a kind of purity project, driven as it is by a desire to escape the supposedly corrupting effects of modern technology on the physical body.

In her search for physical vigor and rehabilitation, Louise not only adopts the rural folkways of farming and domestic work; she also seeks the help of New Age folk medicine in the guise of a spiritual healer named Leo (Björn Andrésen). The film emphasizes the distinction between Louise's belief in pseudoscientific healing practices and Elena's thoroughgoing skepticism, a distinction that figures the privileged Scandinavian woman as the more "superstitious" of the two. Indeed, the belief in such folk healing is depicted as an extravagance that the more economically constrained lack the resources to indulge in. As affluent Scandinavians, Louise and Kasper can afford to eschew the pollution and stress of city life, a choice they frame as environmentally virtuous and healthy. Constrained by single motherhood and fewer economic opportunities, Elena chooses to work as a domestic laborer in Scandinavia so she can afford to move out of her parents' home and buy an apartment where her son, Niko, can have his own room. Elena's response to the guidance and treatments Elena receives from Leo is predictably one of bemused skepticism. Constrained by her disadvantaged economic position, Elena cannot afford to luxury of cultivating New Age spirituality and leading an ecologically virtuous lifestyle. She can only look on in incredulity when she sees Leo laying his hands on various parts of Louise's body while repeating the mantra "in with the positive, out with the negative" and coaching Louise on the optimal type of breathing to balance out her spiritual energies. In a subsequent scene, Elena expresses her skepticism more directly. As Elena enjoys a colorfully organic dinner and a glass of wine along with her employers, Louise haltingly explains the rationale for her healing treatments: "You know, there's a difference between good and bad energies, and their balance has to do with, you know, the body's inner energies and all the energies that surround us." As Elena starts giggling at the pseudoscientific rationale behind these treatments, Louise smiles self-deprecatingly and insists that healing could help Elena too. Elena teasingly asks Louise if she "really really really" believes what she's saying, to which Louise shoots back that she "really, bloody" does. When challenged to state his own beliefs, Kasper offers, "Well, there's more to this world than what you see." Louise asks Elena why she is so skeptical, to which she replies that she's not skeptical, but she just doesn't believe in the type of spiritual healing Louise is receiving. Louise continues the good-natured teasing and suggests that Elena should just go ahead and "watch some TV and let your brain melt."

The trajectory of Elena's integration into Nordic society is derailed after she strikes the bargain with Louise to serve as surrogate mother for the couple. While Louise grows stronger as her rural convalescence progresses and she exorcises the negative energies of her body through spiritual healing, the pregnant Elena grows weaker and becomes increasingly estranged from her body and mind. Because of this structure, *Shelley* draws on a Scandinavian tradition of quasi-vampiric narratives centered on the parasitic antagonism between two intimately connected women, a tradition that encompasses August Strindberg's play *Den starkare* (*The Stronger*, 1889), Ingmar Bergman's *Persona* (1966), and Joachim Trier's *Thelma*, among other texts. The physical toll of the pregnancy begins for Elena as soon as one of Louise's fertilized eggs is implanted, a narrative turning point after which her body inexorably deteriorates until she reaches her bloody demise at the end of a knitting needle. In her first postimplantation medical exam, the only symptoms she reports to the doctor are fatigue and a metallic taste in her mouth. While Louise and Kasper celebrate the successful implantation the night after the exam by retreating to the marital bed to make love, Elena is tormented by increasingly disturbing dreams that fixate on themes of pregnancy and violent death. In the first of these, Elena walks out of the front door at night to toss out some used water from a wash basin. Standing on the steps outside the front door, she gazes out into the blackness of the forest around the home and hears the distant cries of a baby in the darkness. The cries of the wailing infant draw her out into the murkiness of the forest, with only a handheld lantern to light the way. As she goes farther, the cries get closer, and the croaking, droning undertone from the cellar scene returns. When the cries stop, Elena's gaze is drawn to the ground, where the light of her lantern illuminates a nude baby lying still, covered with leaves and dirt and crawling with worms and insects. We hear labored, infantile breathing as Elena reaches down and strokes the infant's ear, and the bugs continue to crawl across the inert surface of the exposed body. Elena wakes from the nightmare at this point, clutching at her abdomen in apparent pain. Combining as it does Elena's retreat into an estranged, hostile, infanticidal wilderness with the growing discomfort and weakness of her maternal body, the dream is one of many postpregnancy scenes that indicate the presence of a hidden malevolence lurking somewhere behind the benign face of Nordic rural life.

As the pregnancy progresses and the baby grows, whatever vitality Elena had is inexorably sapped from her body, a structure that figures the couple's request for surrogacy as a parasitic imposition on the young migrant. Elena's skin becomes dry and itchy, she is tormented by headaches, and the natural world seems to have fully turned against her. As she feeds the chickens in one scene, the creatures scurry, clucking furiously and pecking at her in apparent hostility toward her presence in the coop. Rather than the intimate relationship among outdoor recreation, rural living, and physical vitality posited by neo-Romantic nature discourses such as vitalism, *Shelley* shows how Elena's body is assailed and gradually deteriorates through its contact with the supposedly salubrious climes of the Nordic countryside.

Troubled by Elena's symptoms, Louise invites Leo to treat her, ostensibly to help with her headaches. Having already expressed skepticism about the efficacy of such pseudoscientific treatments, Elena nevertheless politely submits to the treatment. Leo begins, asking Elena to imagine that her head is a room and to tell him what she sees in it. Elena treats the dialogue as an opportunity to subtly poke fun at Louise's rustic lifestyle, saying she cannot see what is going on in her head because "it is too dark—there's no electricity." Unfazed by the gentle mockery, Leo continues, laying his hands on her head and telling Elena that there is an object in the room—a "dark thing, maybe an animal"—to which, Elena, now fully swept up into the suggestive influence of Leo's pronouncements, tells him, apparently sincerely, that the object is a dog. Leo places his quivering hands on either side of Elena's head and induces her to "take this object out of the room." Leo's hands demonstratively make a gesture of exorcism, sweeping forward repeatedly, as if to somatically will the object to be swept out of Elena's head. "I'm dragging the dog out of the room," he narrates in his ponderous voice. Elena, now fully immersed in the trancelike condition induced by the treatment, grimaces and shakes her head violently in all directions. The soundtrack comes to life with an unsettling, echoing drone and the wild barks and howls of a vicious beast. As Leo completes his treatment, Elena settles down and opens her eyes, and Leo asks her how she's feeling. She does not respond, leaving the question open for the time. In the next scene, she asks Louise what happened, to which Louise responds that "Leo was removing all the negative energies that manifested themselves in your body, and you had a strong reaction."

As Elena's physical and psychological distress mounts, however, it becomes clear that *Shelley* is not about the horrors of negative energies that happened to have "manifested themselves" in the body of an immigrant laborer. Instead, the film is about the ways Nordic societies invasively enter the immigrant body, imposing and implanting malign energies in that economically and socially precarious body, while the privileged Nordic body remains above the fray. The film, then, is driven by biopolitical concerns about the horrific relativity societies use when assessing the value of human life. While ethnic Scandinavians inhabit a biopolitically privileged position that leaves their bodies less exposed to the deleterious effects of modern life—and gives them the material security to enjoy the benefits of modern life, such as advanced fertility care and the ability to afford surrogacy—the immigrant body is fully exposed and ecologically precarious.[21]

As the pregnancy progresses and the physical changes of pregnancy become visible, the implicit cultural weakness of the city-dwelling Elena becomes more radically physical. Elena's rapid physical deterioration belies the cliché of the maternal glow that supposedly radiates from the benevolent, fertile body of the expectant mother. Elena's skin becomes dry and itchy, and Louise is troubled to see scratches all over Elena's back one day when she's helping her get dressed. In response to Elena's physical symptoms, Louise becomes more vigilant—probing her with repeated questions about whether she is still taking her iron supplements and monitoring her eating habits. Louise's surveillance of Elena's body can be read as either benign protectiveness or as probing, invasive vigilance that oversteps the boundaries of bodily autonomy. The possibility of such an ambivalent interpretation of Louise's motives as either kind or domineering shows what a fraught position Elena is in as an immigrant laborer and surrogate mother. Once she enters into the surrogacy arrangement, Elena's bodily autonomy erodes, and Louise takes a clear proprietary interest in Elena's body as a vessel that will temporarily host, give nourishment to, and then give birth to Louise and Kasper's biological child. Elena's loss of autonomy reduces her body to a kind of prosthetic womb for her Nordic employers, estranging her from her body and putting her even more securely under the thumb of Louise and Kasper. What is more, Elena's gradual physical deterioration can be seen as a manifestation of the slow violence perpetrated on the precarious body of the migrant laborer and surrogate. As the pregnancy progresses and Elena's body grows weaker, it becomes more obviously vulnerable and physically exposed to the environment. The abject transcorporeality and exposure of Elena's body is reminiscent of the unwilled bodily abjection of *Thelma*, except in this case it is an index of Nordic privilege and the parasitic traffic in Eastern European women's reproductive labor in contemporary Europe rather than the persistence of misogyny in Norwegian society. A major strain in recent Nordic ecohorror, then, is transcorporeal body horror in the service of a critique of Nordic societies.

The pain of Elena's new skin condition, though, is nothing compared to the nocturnal torments she faces. With Louise vigilantly overseeing Elena's food consumption and pushing back against her unhealthy cravings, Elena begins suffering from sleep disorders—unconsciously leaving her bed and ending up in the kitchen, where she gobbles up raw sugar by the handful. More terrifying than the sleep-eating episodes are the nightmares that continue to plague Elena, becoming ever more violent and disturbing as she gets farther into the pregnancy. In one of her nightmares, Elena walks into a room to find Louise gently cooing to an unseen baby she holds in her arms, then plaintively singing the traditional Norwegian lullaby "Den fyrste song," the melancholy lyrics of which draw a clear line from motherhood to death. In the first stanza of the lullaby, the speaker sings, "The first song I heard was mother's song at my cradle. / The tender words went to my heart, and they dried my tears." In the final stanza, though, the lullaby takes a turn from sentimental infancy to death and loss, as the speaker reveals that his mother is now deceased, though her death has not meant an end to her soothing melodies: "And as I doze . . . I hear the song drifting softly from Mother's grave." When she sees Louise leaning over and softly singing and cooing to an unseen something in her lap, Elena asks whom she's talking to. Louise responds, "Shelley. Isn't she amazing?" Elena sees the candlelit reflection of Louise grasping the baby's hand, an image that seems to be seen through a curtain. Then the camera unexpectedly racks focus to reveal that the curtains are actually streaks of blood dripping down the mirror, obscuring the beatified image of mother and child behind an oozing, crimson fluid. A cut reveals that Louise's blond hair is also covered with streaks of dripping blood.

When Elena wakes from the disturbing dream, she finds that her hands are dirty and the outside of her mouth seems to be caked with streaks and splatters of dried blood. The presence of the blood is not immediately accounted for, though there is a suggestion later in the film that Elena's nocturnal cravings have become more bloodthirsty. In this later scene, Louise awakens to the sound of a chicken clucking, which she follows down to the cellar. There she discovers a bloodied chicken trying to escape and Elena crouched in a dark corner with splatters of blood around her mouth, having evidently attempted to eat the bird alive. The mysterious bloodstains and scratches that have turned up on Elena's body during the pregnancy both seem to have found an explanation in this scene—a chain of causation that ultimately places the responsibility for Elena's nocturnal brutality and estrangement from her own body on Louise and her zealous oversight and repression of Elena's pregnancy cravings.

Elena becomes increasingly troubled by her strange symptoms as the baby grows and her own body grows weaker and more alien. She begins losing hair and weight and, in addition to the dry, scratched skin, develops a painful aversion to water. Elena is slowly reduced to a bedridden invalid with visibly hollow eyes and the desperate, incoherent gaze of somebody who has lost her mind. Elena becomes convinced that something is wrong and the baby wants to hurt her. In one scene, an obstetrician tries to reassure Elena and Louise, narrating the ultrasound images of the baby they are seeing in real time. She tells them that the baby "is doing just fine," that the "inner organs look just as they should—no irregularities whatsoever, absolutely nothing to worry about." When Elena protests that she "knows" and "feels" that something is wrong, the doctor dismisses her complaints and chalks everything up to a routine case of dry skin, chiding Elena for not moisturizing frequently enough. After revealing the sex of the baby girl, the doctor adds, "And a big one—strong and healthy, a real Viking." Despite this, the troubling symptoms she feels mean more to Elena that a doctor's reassurances.

The doctor's description of the unborn baby as a "real Viking" draws on the same ethno-nationalist tropes of the healthy Nordic race, connecting discourses of fetal vitality with the image of the robust Nordic racial type constructed by, among others, a state-sponsored racial biology research conducted in Uppsala in the early twentieth century.[22] The image the doctor uses also hints at the spirit of invasion and colonization that underwrites the entire surrogacy venture. If the baby is indeed a kind of Viking, it is one that has made its way to a foreign land—Elena's uterus—and staked an invasive territorial claim there. Kasper and Louise's invitation to Elena to serve as their surrogate thus takes on a completely different valence. What seemed merely an expedient bargain that both parties get equal benefit from—Elena earning a tidy sum to start a new life for herself and her son in Bucharest, and in return providing her time, body, and labor to bring the Scandinavian couple's child into the world—becomes a rapacious act of Nordic conquest. This shift in valence also hints at the economy of women's labor migration Elena is participating in, framing such a market as inherently predatory and even parasitic. It is fitting, then, that in her theorization of the "occult film"—in which a young woman becomes a portal to malevolent supernatural forces through possession or pregnancy—Clover notes that its fixation on the "processes of transmission" and its "fascination with contagion" mean that "these films have much more in common, and indeed overlap, with modern vampire, werewolf, and zombie films."[23] Though I began my analysis of Lars von Trier's experimental horror film *Epidemic* by drawing connections between outbreak horror and the trans-media narratives of Count Dracula's parasitic migration to London, *Shelley* takes us full circle in its critique of Nordic environmentalism. Rather than situating the parasite as the Eastern European migrant—with his sartorial, physical, and linguistic markers of cultural difference, as exemplified by Bela Lugosi's performance in *Dracula* (dir. Tod Browning, 1931) or Max Schreck's performance in *Nosferatu* (dir. F. W. Murnau, 1922)—*Shelley* situates white Northern Europeans as parasitically privileged, as manifested in their exploitation of Eastern European reproductive labor. Rather than being a portal to the supernatural, then, Elena's body is possessed not by the child of Satan but rather by the spawn of Nordic privilege. The malevolent presence infecting the Nordic landscape hinted at in the opening montage of *Shelley*, then, does not infect the land from the outside; it is a malignance that has been grown from within.

## ENVIRONMENTAL PRIVILEGE AND PERFORMATIVE EXPOSURE

One of the most deeply held beliefs about nature in the Nordic cultural imagination is that everyone should have equal access to it. Given the importance of this eco-egalitarian tradition to Nordic identity, it should be no surprise that in their efforts to integrate newly arrived immigrants, Nordic societies have turned to nature. If being a Nordic citizen means being close to nature—and possessing a set of attitudes, habits, and skills that facilitate that closeness—it makes intuitive sense that societies might turn to a kind of outdoor recreation training regime that would help migrants from far-flung locales adopt these same attributes. This need has been answered in the form of nature-based integration (NBI), a diverse set of initiatives that involve providing guided interactions with nature for immigrant groups as a formal part of social integration programs. According to Benedict Singleton, who has researched the increasingly prominent role NBI has played in Sweden, these practices are driven by two primary concerns: first, a worry "among certain social groups that citizens of 'modern' societies are increasingly cut off from nature"; and second, a conviction that "contemporary population movements between countries represent a 'problem' to be dealt with, representing 'crises' for welfare states and national identities."[24] Despite the possible pitfalls Singleton identifies—such as the potential for guided nature walks to reinforce cultural differences and spark cultural conflicts around diverse responses to the natural environment—it is clear that the growing role NBI plays in Nordic societies is bound up with the intimate connection between nature and cultural identity in the region. If new arrivals are to be cohesively integrated into Nordic societies, NBI implies, there is a pedagogical imperative to inculcate a set of characteristically Nordic environmental attitudes and disciplines that will allow these outsiders to "fit in" with the societies in which they seek a place. The integration of immigrants, then, has become an opportunity to reinforce and reify Nordic environmental exceptionalism, establishing outdoor recreation skills as a requirement for belonging in Nordic societies.[25]

Because *Shelley* is premised on the arrival of a cultural outsider to the rural Scandinavian countryside and her struggles to acclimate to her new life there, the film is structured around a sort of individualized, private nature-based integration program for Elena run by Louise and Kasper. Structured around this fish-out-of-water narrative premise, the film leads the viewer to identify with Elena, which makes it an especially useful lens for critically examining the role nature plays in Nordic cultures from an outsider perspective. Once we learn that Elena is new to Scandinavia, the combination of picturesque Nordic wilderness landscapes with an unsettling undertone of lurking evil and menace in the opening montage feels justified. The isolated, heavily forested countryside that beckons the outdoorsy Scandinavian as an inviting respite from the noise and stress of modern life strikes the new arrival as forbidding and alienating—an unwelcome retreat from the material security of the city. Elena brings with her a set of habits and attitudes that are characteristic of her life as a city-dwelling young Romanian woman. As we identify with Elena's outsider subject position, we commiserate with her over the strenuous farm labor she must perform to earn her keep. In one scene, Elena awkwardly wields a wood ax, revealing her unfamiliarity with the characteristically Nordic skill of chopping and stacking firewood.[26] As Elena becomes frustrated with the way Kasper and Louise's retreat to rustic living has deprived her of modern conveniences and lines of communication to her family back in Bucharest, we identify with her bouts of loneliness and alienation. In one scene, we see how Elena uses what little cell phone battery she has left to scroll through pictures of her son, Niko, and we sympathize with her growing sense of isolation and homesickness.

Elena's status as a cultural outsider also makes her an ideal vehicle for making the audience feel they are being inexorably drawn *into* an alienated, potentially malevolent Nordic wilderness. The isolation of that outsider subject position is key to making the horrific undertone of the Nordic wilderness palpable for the viewer. Such a position allows *Shelley* to overturn prevailing nature mythologies in Nordic culture, reversing the polarity from cozy (*hyggelig*) seclusion to uncanny (*uhyggelig*) isolation. The film does this by contrasting scenes in which Louise's material comfort in the secluded wilderness establishes a warm sense of *hygge* with scenes in which Elena is isolated from her Nordic hosts and subjected to the full, horrific brunt of an alien environment that seems out to get her.

In one characteristic scene, we see how Elena and Louise's differing cultural perspectives on the environment structure their own embodied interactions with their wilderness setting. After enjoying a candlelit dinner and a bottle of wine with Kasper, Louise and Elena head out for a swim in the lake together. With characteristically Nordic outdoorsy exuberance, Louise strips naked and heads straight into the water. She is bubbling over with the bodily pleasures offered by the nude plunge into the refreshing waters of the lake and encourages Elena to join her, telling her how fresh it feels. As she reluctantly accepts the invitation, Elena is more cautious in exposing her body to the lake, keeping her underclothes on and dog-paddling out to Louise with a pained grimace. As she swims out to Louise, Elena takes exception to her description of the lake as "fresh." She exclaims, "No—it's fresh in a not so nice way!" In this early scene, the women's different responses to the wilderness environment are a source of amusement and good-natured teasing, as Louise gently models for the young immigrant a properly Nordic, enthusiastic bodily interaction with nature. Nothing could be farther from the immersive sensory pleasure Louise gets from her plunge in the cold, dark waters of the lake than Elena's tentative, tortured reluctance to expose herself to full bodily contact with the water.

Stacy Alaimo has used the concept of *exposure* to analyze different styles of embodied interactions with nature, contrasting the enclosed, armored stance of "carbon-heavy masculinity" with the receptive stance of "insurgent vulner-ability" carried out—frequently in the nude—by environmental activists and artists.[27] While the discursive context of Elena and Louise's divergent bodily interactions with nature is quite distinct from the highly politicized, extractivist context Alaimo discusses, the notion of environmental exposure still provides a useful frame for understanding the scene. While Elena is hesitant to fully expose herself to the immersive, transcorporeal flows her nude body would be subjected to in the murky depths of lake, Louise cheerfully disrobes and plunges her fully exposed body into the water, citing the health-promot-ing effects and refreshing pleasure of her environmental immersion. Elena's physical discomfort in this scene, however, is tempered by the compensatory rewards of *hygge* and domestic comfort in the subsequent scene. After their chilly swim, Elena and Louise cozy up to a blazing fireplace in the next scene. They have dried off and wrapped themselves in wool blankets, and they sit together in intimate conversation, their faces aglow with the warm, crackling light of the fire. Basking in warmth, coziness, and the intimate togetherness of a new friendship is framed as the women's compensation for the mild physical discomforts incurred by interacting with the wilderness.

Many other early scenes, however, hint at a more sinister kind of terror that lurks in the shadows of the environment, ready to terrify Elena whenever she must navigate her uncomfortable new terrain without one of her hosts. In these scenes, Elena is tormented with material—as well as possibly metaphysical or supernatural—agents that unsettle and alienate the young woman, reinforcing her aversion to wilderness isolation. In one early scene, Elena climbs down to the cellar to return a jug of milk to the underground pantry. The rustic cellar is plunged in darkness, the only illumination provided by the gas lantern Elena carries with her as she makes her way down. When she opens a mesh cabinet where the dairy products are stored, she discovers disconcertingly that several beetles have found their way onto the cheese. She regards the insects with clear disgust and uses the side of a rolling pin to gently nudge them out of the cabinet. As she finishes this disquieting domestic task, her gaze is suddenly pulled into the darkness, where she thinks she hears a heavy object falling. As she uses her lantern to inspect her subterranean surroundings, Elena hears what sounds like the plaintive cries of a baby in the distance. As she anxiously stands there listening, a wet, wheezing undertone begins—a tone that is hard to identify but brings to mind audibly amphibian associations of toads croaking or the watery lungs of a pneumonia sufferer struggling to breathe. This first disconcerting suggestion of a spectral child haunting the isolated farmstead comes after the women have discussed Louise's recent miscarriage but before any suggestion that Elena might consider serving as a surrogate for the couple. By the time she makes that decision, then, Elena's solitary interactions with the remote setting have already been marked by discomfort, disgust, and a visceral sense of natural—and possibly supernatural—menace. Though such an isolated setting, the film suggests, may be welcoming, invigorating, and refreshing for a cultural insider, it appears to pose very palpably felt material and psychological threats to a cultural outsider. Though Nordic environmental attitudes have cultivated a deeply rooted cultural orthodoxy that wilderness is hospitable, therapeutic, and health promoting, *Shelley* poses the question, Hospitable *for whom?* Because of his Iranian upbringing and outsider cultural perspective, Abbasi is better situated than most filmmakers working in the region to see through the benign image projected by Nordic environmental attitudes. As we have seen, Abbasi himself remarks that *Shelley* grew out of his observation that Scandinavians cling to nature and rustic living the way other cultures cling to religion, and this quasi-religious reverence for the natural world—despite Nordic social and material progress—provides fertile soil for horror.

Contrary to Abbasi's bemusement at this paradoxical combination of rustic environmentalism and material prosperity, scholars and commentators have increasingly noted how lifestyles of environmental sustainability—as well as access to clean water, fresh food, and unpolluted air—are an effective index for racial and economic privilege. This idea has led scholars to argue that it is crucial to not only understand the concept of *environmental justice*—a goal many environmental and social progressives strive for—but also the complementary concept of *environmental privilege*. As one recent study defines the term, environmental privilege is "a form of privilege linked to other types of inequalities such as race and class that confers to certain populations *socially constructed advantages in relation to environmental access, management and control.*" Just like other forms of privilege, environmental privilege "is underpinned by particular mechanisms that naturalize this type of inequality."[28] According to the scholarly literature on environmental privilege, then, the confluence of environmentalism and privilege is no curious coincidence, as Abbasi's comments imply. Instead, access to the "peace and quiet" of the salubrious rural idyll prized by Scandinavians like Kasper and Louise is a luxury only accessible to those with immense reserves of economic and social privilege. As the values of such access to nature are passed on transgenerationally, along with material wealth, those inequalities become naturalized.

Contrary to Nordic eco-egalitarian ideals, the wilderness is not a space that is equally welcoming or accessible to all. We see this from the very beginning of *Shelley*, when Kasper drives Elena out to his and Louise's isolated home. Upon her arrival, Elena is greeted not with the sight of a humble cabin, but instead with a large wooden villa that perches domineeringly on a promontory overlooking a picturesque lake and the hilly woodlands beyond it. The home offers access to the lake via a private boat dock and shoreline. Though the rustic existence Kasper and Louise lead requires more manual labor than modern city life, it is a pastoralism that is underwritten by their personal wealth and material security. While the fact that a childless Nordic couple can afford a massive lakeside home is not surprising, the contrast between Louise and Kasper's material privilege and Elena's precarious existence as an Eastern European labor migrant provides an illuminating reminder of the global inequities that Nordic environmentalism can ignore or obscure.

This dichotomy between the economically precarious city dweller Elena and the elite, inaccessible rustic coziness of Louise's rural lifestyle is conveyed in subtle sartorial cues in many of the film's early scenes featuring the two women. Elena is most frequently depicted in a simple T-shirt and hoodie, sometimes with crushed velvet leggings and a cotton dress. Her clothing clearly reads as thin and inexpensive—the kind of fast fashion outfits that global supply chains and offshore factory production in the developing world have made affordable to the masses. Though Louise's clothing in many scenes is simple and practical—jeans and a work jacket while she harvests vegetables in the garden—her privilege is also evident in her clothing. As she convalesces from her recent surgery, Louise is frequently depicted with ornate wool blankets, embroidered shawls, handmade wool sweaters, and other garments that exude a sense of cozy luxury that is inaccessible to economically constrained migrant laborers. Many scenes, moreover, reinforce Elena's role as a domestic servant, showing that she is the one engaged in the work of clothing Louise in the cozy warmth of wool slippers, shawls, and blankets. Just as rustic environmentalism can be an accurate index for privilege—with those who participate in environmental organizations being wealthier and more likely to be white than the overall population—*Shelley* also shows that clothing, especially the degree to which it provides coziness and lasting warmth, sends clear signals about the unequal distribution of wealth and material security. So while we have already seen that Louise willingly exposes her body to nature through open-air nudity, her actual exposure to the real physical discomforts or threats of the environment is mitigated by her economic privilege, which provides the compensatory comforts of warmth, coziness, and protection from the elements in picturesquely pastoral domesticity.

In this sense, Louise's bodily exposure to the environment is a performative, short-term kind of exposure that poses no real threat to her person. Far from the "insurgent vulnerability" of eco-activists that Alaimo describes in her work on transcorporeal exposure, Louise's ecological exposure is closer to what Asbjørn Grønstad has described as "conditional vulnerability" in the films of Ruben Östlund—a kind vulnerability that "ensues from the erosion of advantages that may not have been entirely warranted in the first place." The kind of vulnerability Grønstad describes in Östlund's films—most of which focus on the humiliation and symbolic emasculation of privileged white Scandinavian men—may be regarded by some as "performed" and "inauthentic." Grønstad, however, writes that this kind of experience of lost status is "perceived and felt as a real thing," which means that it deserves to be taken seriously.[29] Unlike the men thrown into uncomfortable and potentially threatening situations in Östlund's films, however, Kasper and Louise's flight from the material comforts of modern society is not a perceived threat—on the contrary, it is a voluntary project of environmental exposure that is eased by the compensatory security of their own personal wealth and privileged social status. In that sense, it is a clearer example of the kind of performative vulnerability that Grønstad brings up—one that moreover goes hand-in-hand with the outdoorsy environmentalism that is a core element of contemporary Nordic cultural identity. The Nordic Council of Ministers hint at this intimate connection between the Nordic love of nature and material privilege in a recently published document, "Strategy for International Branding of the Nordic Region." According to the branding strategy, "the historically strong bond between the Nordic people and nature" is the result of the favorable labor conditions and material security guaranteed by the Nordic welfare state: "There is plenty of space in the Nordic region. There are vast plains, high mountains, dense forests, and large oceans, and people are free to spend a lot of their recreational time there, *because of a labor market model that allows time for both work and leisure.*"[30]

Louise strips off her clothing to take a swim and beckons the reluctant Elena into the water. Louise's exuberant, recreational exposure of her body to the temporary discomforts of the natural environment is underwritten by her own material prosperity and the compensatory coziness of her privileged and secure home life.
Frame grab from *Shelley* (dir. Ali Abbasi, 2018).

The material toll of surrogacy is clearly marked on the surface of Elena's increasingly enfeebled body, underscoring the way Eastern European women's reproductive labor has been one way Nordic countries have secured their own material privilege. Frame grab from *Shelley* (dir. Ali Abbasi, 2018).

## MIGRATION, PRECARITY, AND EXPOSURE

In the gradually deteriorating body of Elena, *Shelley* presents us with a more authentically "exposed" figure of socioeconomic and environmental vulnerability than those of her Scandinavian employers, who enjoy the peace and quiet of their rural home and willingly undertake domestic labor without the aid of electricity and modern appliances but submit to such temporary discomforts against the backdrop of material wealth and security. As a Romanian domestic worker who has been hired by a well-off Scandinavian couple to help with housework, Elena participates in a well-established economy of labor migration from Eastern to Western European countries that *Shelley* frames as predatory and parasitic. As Anca Parvulescu has convincingly demonstrated, the traffic of Eastern European women's reproductive labor has gone hand in hand with the growth of a postunification, post-Soviet Europe. These are Eastern European women who migrate—through voluntary legal and forced extralegal channels—in order to work as domestic servants, nannies, personal attendants, entertainers, sex workers, and surrogate mothers in Western European countries. As Parvulescu points out, they have largely filled labor roles traditionally performed by wives within the institution of marriage. The labor of these women is therefore, according to Parvulescu, nothing less than the labor of reproduction. By extension, it could be argued that the cost of the relatively high levels of gender equality in Western European countries is borne by the laboring bodies of the economically disadvantaged Eastern European women who come to work there.

When Elena enters into a surrogacy agreement with Kasper and Louise, then, the film frames the arrangement as the opportunistic and predatory exploitation of an economically disadvantaged migrant's body. Far from the mutually advantageous agreement Louise initially presents to Elena—where Elena can earn enough money to buy an apartment in Bucharest through serving as a surrogate—the film shows how the pregnancy precipitates Elena's physical deterioration. Not only does Elena experience the psychological discomfort of unsettling dreams and sleep disruptions in addition to the physical side effects that accompany any pregnancy; more radically, Elena's deterioration takes the form of the erosion of her own bodily separation from the environment, as her skin begins flaking off and she reacts violently to even the gentlest of physical stimuli, such as a warm bath. As the pregnancy progresses—and the doctors reassure Louise that despite Elena's complaints and discomfort, the baby is strong and healthy—it becomes clear that Elena is becoming ever more exposed and vulnerable. By the time Elena becomes convinced that the baby is trying to hurt her and attempts a self-induced abortion as an act of self-defense from the apparently parasitic fetus, it has become clear that the Nordic environmental privilege embodied by Kasper and Louise's sustainable lifestyle—their stated desire to enjoy the peace and quiet of a pretechnological lifestyle and the domestic fulfillment of biological children—is directly purchased with the physical deterioration of a migrant laborer's body. Indeed, as Louise seems to move breezily past Elena's violent death in her joy at being a mother to a healthy Scandinavian baby, the migrant body in a Scandinavian state is clearly figured as the kind of *homo sacer* Giorgio Agamben discusses in his influential political theory: the obscure, abject figures of Roman law whose lives were deemed to have so little value by the state that they could be killed with impunity.[31]

Far from the widespread cultural assumptions in the Nordic region that the rural countryside is a healthy alternative to modern life in the city and the eco-egalitarian notion that the natural environment should be equally accessible to all, *Shelley* paints a picture of Nordic environmentalism as potentially malignant and exploitative. If nature has indeed assumed the place of God in the modern Scandinavian imagination, as Ali Abbassi claims, the kind of reverence it inspires can assume the same kind of exclusionary fanaticism and ethno-racial violence that organized religions have sparked. For that reason, it may be productive to connect environmentally and socially critical horror narratives like *Shelley* not only with ecohorror but also with the resurgence of folk horror in recent years—a mode that, according to Adam Scovell's monograph on British folk horror, is defined by its use of an isolated landscape and its fixation on the "skewed belief systems and morality" that flourish in such spatial and social isolation.[32] As modern Scandinavians redirect their spiritual fervor from organized religion to cultural rituals of outdoor recreation and communion with nature, *Shelley* suggests that the predatory impulses and material privilege inherent in Nordic environmentalism may constitute the most skewed belief system of all.

CHAPTER FIVE

# Folk Horror
# and *Folkhemmet*

## White Supremacy and
## Belonging in *Midsommar*

Though it features numerous scenes with gore and graphic bodily violence, Ari Aster's Swedish folk horror film *Midsommar* (2019) ends with a smile. The enigmatic grin belongs to Dani (Florence Pugh), an American college student grieving the recent tragic loss of her entire family, as she watches a bright yellow wooden structure burn to the ground. The building is a folk temple dedicated to human sacrifice that contains her boyfriend, along with several other living and dead bodies, all of which will be immolated in a neo-pagan midsummer ritual. She has been a guest of a Swedish folk commune called Hårga for their days-long midsummer festival along with her boyfriend, Christian (Jack Reynor)—a graduate student in anthropology writing a thesis on folk ritual—and a small group of his friends from university, including Josh (William Jackson Harper) and Mark (Will Poulter). They were invited to the festivities by their Swedish friend Pelle (Vilhelm Blomgren), a member of the commune who has been studying abroad in America. Pelle frames the Hårga festival in reverential terms for his American friends, though he also warns them that they may find the folk rituals and costumes strange.

The film more than bears this out, showing the American visitors—and the viewers—that the close-knit folk commune is held together by the glue of human sacrifice and rigid, ethno-separatist isolationism. One by one, the outsiders are brutally sacrificed—after first witnessing the violent ritual suicides of aged commune members—and Dani and Christian are the last outsiders to survive in the final scene. After being crowned the commune's May Queen, Dani has been given the responsibility to condemn one of two people to be the final sacrifice of Hårga's bloody midsummer festival: she must choose between Christian and a randomly selected community member. Having been drawn into the perverse social collective of the commune in her grief, Dani chooses to sacrifice her boyfriend. After Christian's limp body—rendered docile by a paralyzing toxin—is clad in a sacrificial bearskin, then wheeled into the yellow wooden temple which has been built for the sacrificial fire, and is being consumed by the fire, the penultimate shot of the film, showing us a view of the burning temple, slowly dissolves to the final shot. In it we see Dani's smile, artfully framed in close-up by the ceremonial gown and crown of flowers in which she is clad as the Hårga May Queen. Echoing this final edit, the entire film may be seen as a slow dissolve of a different kind. As Dani works through the grief of losing her entire family in horrifying and tragic fashion—the victims of a double murder-suicide by her mentally ill sister—her own identity slowly dissolves into the seamless collective meld of the Hårga commune. No longer *merely* Dani the grieving American college student, she has not only been taken in by the Hårga *folk*—she has been *absorbed* by them.

The horror subgenre most frequently assigned to *Midsommar* is folk horror, a small but coherent tradition that has witnessed a resurgence in the last several years.[1] According to historians of the genre, folk horror originated with a trio of decades-old British horror films that have collectively come to be known as the "unholy trinity" of folk horror: *Witchfinder General* (dir. Michael Reeves, 1968), *The Blood on Satan's Claw* (dir. Piers Haggard, 1971), and *The Wicker Man* (dir. Robin Hardy, 1973). Though there is no widely accepted definition of the genre, Adam Scovell has tied it to the anxieties modern cultures retain about the threats posed by rural environments, writing that folk horror is about "the evil under the soil, the terror in the backwoods of a forgotten lane, and the ghosts that haunt stones and patches of dark, lonely water."[2] In his recent book on the subject, Scovell has pointed to several hallmarks of the genre, including the use of folklore (or folkloresque "fakelore") to imbue the work with "a sense of the arcane for eerie, uncanny, or horrific purposes"; staging "a clash between such arcania and its presence within close proximity to some form of modernity"; and creation of its "own folklore through various forms of popular conscious memory."[3] Robin Hardy's *Wicker Man*—by far the most popular of the three seminal films—has been particularly important in establishing the tropes of the conventional folk horror film, a template that *Midsommar* follows assiduously. In this template, an urban outsider is drawn to an ostensibly benign rural community where pre-Christian folk traditions, beliefs, and ritual are doggedly upheld in a folk community that sees itself as a bastion of tradition against the rising tide of cosmopolitan and urban modernity. By the end of the film, the apparently innocent traditions and rural isolation of the folk community have been revealed as a cover that hides more sinister and brutal folk practices, and the outsider is eventually sacrificed in a bloody or fiery ritual in devotion to the pagan gods of an agrarian cult. In generic terms, then, folk horror fits *Midsommar* as a description because it hews quite closely to the narrative expectations of the subgenre.

In another sense, however, *Midsommar* can be described as *folk* horror because it centers on the horrors of one *particular* imagined folk community, namely the Swedish concept of the *folkhem* (people's home), a metaphor of national belonging that has been central to Swedish identity and public policy over the last century. Though the concept of the *folkhem*—and the robust Swedish welfare state to which it gave rise in the postwar years—has traditionally been seen in a benevolent light as a social model that provides national cohesion and promotes material prosperity, its shortcomings have become a subject of cultural critique in recent decades, particularly because of the ways it excludes or fails marginalized groups such as minoritized racial communities, women, and children. *Midsommar* joins this chorus of voices criticizing the shortcomings of the Swedish *folkhem*, using a fictional folk commune as a vehicle for evoking the real-life phenomenon of resurgent right-wing populist (RRP) politics in Sweden in recent years. This Swedish variant of right-wing populism traffics in a form of national nostalgia that grasps for folk symbols and touts supposedly "authentic" and "traditional" values—many of which rest on white Nordic identity as an unstated foundation—in the name of reforming the Swedish *folkhem*. In the populist rhetoric of parties like the ascendent Sverigedemokraterne (Sweden Democrats, SD), a right-wing populist party that traces its roots to neo-Nazism in Sweden, a rigidly closed, ethnically homogenous, implicitly white vision of the Swedish *folkhem* is a central pillar, even if the overt white supremacy of this discourse has been softened by SD's efforts to achieve bourgeois respectability as it has gained more parliamentary power in recent years.

As with the provocative polemics forwarded by Nordic right-wing populism, folk horror stages cultural conflicts that play out along multiple fault lines. Besides the gender divide, there are clashes between tradition and modernity, rural and urban societies, pagan and Christian belief systems, Europeans and Americans, community members and outsiders, and white people and people of color. So while Aster has somewhat reductively described his film as a "Wizard of Oz for perverts" and a "breakup film" about the horrors of codependency within couples and families, the film's many lines of tense and agonistic togetherness mingle and intersect, tracing complex and tangled matrices.[4] In their eagerness to foment right-wing provocation, culturally conservative critics have seized on Dani's enigmatic smile at the end of the film as proof that *Midsommar* is in fact a moral indictment of the cultural emasculation of men in modern America. In *The American Conservative*, commentator Sohrab Ahmari writes that Dani's smile "burns with the contemporary American's subdued rage at weak, absent men and fathers."[5] To reduce the film to such a direct reading of Dani's smile and the apparent misandry of the pagan cult's sacrifices is not only to ignore Aster's obvious use of irony and cultural parody; it is also to turn a blind eye to the many other cultural divides in the film, which go far beyond a gendered, heteronormative conflict between women and men.[6]

This chapter focuses on the many lines of togetherness in *Midsommar*—not only lines that draw people together into social collectives that provide protection and a sense of belonging, but also the lines of tension and conflict that exist in any social collective. These lineated meshworks of coexistence and mutual dependence—as well as deadly conflict—are aptly expressed by the ecological materialism of British anthropologist Tim Ingold, who argues that the principle of human and ecological togetherness is the line, a model of interpersonal connection that joins organisms together in family unions and communities. Ingold's theory contrasts the social principle of the line with the traditional figuration of the living organism as a "blob," more or less distinguished from its surroundings and from other living "blobs" by its membrane-like surface. Ingold's theory of the ecological "mesh" resulting from the innumerable lines of correspondence and mutual dependence in the material world is a vision of symbiotic togetherness that allows for individual variation, individual will, and individual identity. Collectives that are figured as a mesh thrive because of their diversity, their complexity, and their internal tensions. This model of the social mesh contrasts with the classical sociological theory of Émile Durkheim, whose seminal methodological work rested on a notion of social organisms joined together into groups in which individual identities dissolve and the demands of "social facts" seamlessly join beings together into alloy-like social collectives that may be described as a "meld." The meld is indifferent to individual will and agency, since individuals can no longer be meaningfully parsed from one another within the homogenous social compounds described by Durkheim.

The two images of social cohesion described by Ingold and Durkheim—the mesh and the meld—provide a basis for my analysis of the depictions of horrifying togetherness in *Midsommar*. The horror of *Midsommar* centers on the ways social collectives that seem to be *meshed* together in symbiotic relationships of mutual dependence and generosity are suddenly revealed to be in fact sinister social *melds* bound together by an ethno-racial sense of shared identity. In the paradigmatic meld-like social collective of the film—the neo-pagan Hårga cult—individual identities, wills, and desires are subsumed into cultivating an ethnically homogenous collective folk identity. Moreover, the meld-like connection between folk identity and the rural landscape suggests that the film is preoccupied with what ecocritic Ursula Heise describes as a fetishistic "sense of place" in modern environmentalism. As the Hårga cult encourages ethno-racial identification with the soil of their territorial domain in a *Blut-und-Boden*-like model of belonging, the film fixates on the tight unity between ethno-nationalism and environmentalism in the Nordic cultures. Like *Reykjavik Whale Watching Massacre*, Aster's film fixates on the beguiling rhetoric of cultural isolationism in contemporary Nordic cultures. Even more importantly, *Midsommar* extends the Nordic environmental racism and privilege on display in *Shelley* to its logical conclusion. What makes *Midsommar* distinct from these comparison cases is the degree to which it couples the social critiques of Nordic ecohorror with a spectacle-driven and hypnotic iteration of modern folk horror. *Midsommar*, then, not only uses the tried-and-true plot devices of the folk horror subgenre but also focuses on the practices of exclusion and other forms of ethno-racial violence that have been perpetuated in the name of the Swedish *folkhem*. As this chapter argues, recent material-ecocritical theory on the mechanics and ethics of human sociality can provide more humane and ecologically sustainable alternative ontologies for human society.

## THE MELD AND THE MESH

The absorbing, violently attractive pull of the folk collective is on full display in a scene that sets up Dani's chilling and enigmatic smile at the end of *Midsommar* and her preceding decision to sacrifice Christian in a ritual blaze. In this scene, Dani emerges from her honorary carriage after the conclusion of the maypole dance and peers through the keyhole into a room where she catches sight of her boyfriend in flagrante delicto as he completes a mating ritual with a young woman of Hårga. Dani immediately collapses in anguish, overtaken by a primal and panic-tinged grief at Christian's betrayal. As she moans and screams in emotional agony, she is surrounded by a group of young Hårga women who usher her away from the scene. The women embrace her and begin to mimetically echo Dani's tormented screams and frantic breathing, ensconcing her in a circle of sympathetic grief until the worst of the panic subsides. Dani's private trauma becomes a shared affective experience. The boundaries between self and community blur as the circle encompasses Dani and they become a nearly indistinguishable cluster of women in anguish.

This scene of Dani's grief being absorbed into a communal expression of pain is important in a narrative sense because it sets the stage for her acceptance of her place in the new family-like collective of Hårga. More importantly for this chapter, however, the scene expresses a certain model of sociality and community that helps account for much of the horror of *Midsommar*. In this version of community, group identity is secured through the rejection and exclusion of difference, which results in individual agency and identity dissolving into communal experiences of emotion and ritual practices of social cohesion. In this model, individual experience is caught up in a seamless collective meld. Although this particular scene implies emotional support and acceptance, the rest of the film unveils the violent and exclusionary logic of this group identity, which derives from a cohesion based on racial and cultural homogeneity and is strikingly indifferent to the value of individual life within the all-encompassing collectivity of the community.

Similar notions of social cohesion are central to the classical sociological theory of Émile Durkheim, whose seminal methodological work helped lay a foundation for academic sociology. The actions and even feelings of any individual person, writes Durkheim, are constrained by duties, commitments, and beliefs that "existed before he did," an indication that they "exist outside him."

In this sense, "there are ways of acting, thinking and feeling which possess the remarkable property of existing outside the consciousness of the individual."[7] Because of their externality, social facts can be studied by empirical observation and subjected to rigorous analysis through the methods of scientific sociology established in Durkheim's *Rules of Sociological Method* (1895). Durkheim ends his first chapter with an unambiguous definition of sociology's object of study: "*A social fact is any way of acting, whether fixed or not, capable of exerting over the individual an external constraint . . . which is general over the whole of a given society whilst having an existence of its own, independent of individual manifestations.*"[8]

Durkheim's sociology fixates on the ways in which these "social facts," alien to the individual, nevertheless set the parameters for individual beliefs and practices. Because of this dynamic of an external entity structuring and even, in some sense, dictating or controlling individual choice, Durkheim repeatedly emphasizes that social facts are agents of coercion. As these external forces "are invested with a coercive power" and "exercise control" over the individual, their nature is to penetrate individuals' consciousness and intervene in their lives.[9] Durkheim writes that "it is indisputable today that most of our ideas and tendencies are not developed by ourselves, but come to us from the outside [and] penetrate us by imposing themselves upon us."[10] Here we see that an undercurrent of violence on the individual body underlies Durkheim's notion of the social fact. Social facts are an intrusive force that naturally arises in societies of all kinds, binding otherwise separate individuals to the social collective by means of penetrating the individual's mind and consciousness. Social cohesion, then, is figured as a penetrative force in Durkheim's *Rules*, an image that resonates with the penetrative bodily threats posed by various horror subgenres, most notably the slasher film. In *Midsommar*, we see this notion of the penetrating, binding pull of the "social fact" in the way Dani is drawn into the commune through a shared bodily performance of grief. As the women of Hårga encircle Dani and mimic her emotional outburst, her individual ownership of personal grief is ceded to the group, her own particular experience becoming indistinguishable from the collective performance of anguish.

Durkheim recognized that his notion of the social fact would meet resistance from liberal individualists and would be particularly hard to swallow for acolytes of Herbert Spencer, Durkheim's predecessor in sociological theory. From the perspective of the market-fixated liberal individualism of the industrial age (which Spencer argued for), the problem with Durkheim's *Rules* was that he failed to adequately retain some sense of an operative individual will, or even an individual consciousness as such. Violence lurks just beneath the surface of Durkheim's social collectives. Individual will and identity are obliterated as they are coerced into line with the collective consciousness. This illiberal tendency is apparent in Durkheim's chosen metaphors. He describes social coherence as a kind of melding in which individuals are melted down in their absorption into the alien entity of the society. "Whenever elements of any kind combine," wrote Durkheim in his preface to the second edition of the *Rules*, "by virtue of this combination they give rise to new phenomena." In their assumption into the collective of society, then, individuals no longer exist as individual agents; they are instead melded indistinguishably into the whole. As if to underscore society's indifference to the mere individual, Durkheim uses the metaphor of melting down separate metals and combining them to form an alloy: "The hardness of bronze lies neither in the copper, nor in the tin, nor in the lead which may have been used to form it, which are all soft or malleable bodies. The hardness arises from the mixing of them."[11] In societies, as in alloys, the qualities of individuals dissolve as component raw materials are blended together into a seamless whole that is greater than the sum of its component parts. As Durkheim says here, the hardness of the alloy far exceeds that of the individual metals brought together in the mixture. It is difficult to imagine an image more at odds with liberal individualism; classical liberals like John Locke and Herbert Spencer would be as horrified by this image of societal melding as latter-day neoliberals such as Margaret Thatcher and Alan Greenspan.

Cultural anthropologist Tim Ingold articulates an individualist rejection of the Durkheimian social collective in his theoretical work on social life. Ingold's critique is grounded not in the laissez-faire economics of neoliberal capitalism, however, but rather in an eco-materialist approach to art and creativity. Ingold points out that in classical liberalism, "individuals may transact with one another through external contact, as they do in the marketplace," whereas in Durkheim's model, society is "seamless."[12] Ingold rejects out of hand this idea that individual minds, identities, and wills are seamlessly fused in the society, as Durkheim's metallurgic metaphor would suggest. Ingold's own preferred images are instead the "blob" and the "line," a dualism upon which Ingold formulates his theory of social life.

Conventionally, writes Ingold, living things are thought of as blobs. Blobs have insides and outsides. They can clump together along their surfaces; they can "collide, aggregate, and meld." But for Ingold, this model of the blob is not sufficient to explain the vital interconnection of living organisms in the meshwork of organic life. What blobs cannot do, writes Ingold, is "hang on to one another, or interpenetrate": "For like drops of oil on the surface of water, whenever they meet they meld into a new blob in which their respective essences so run together that they are no longer distinguishable, while their surfaces dissolve in the formation of a new exterior. Or to put it in more general terms, blobs can have no direct access to one another's interiority save by their blending in the constitution of compounds in which any trace of joining immediately disappears."[13] Since social life, like biological life, depends on interconnections and the durable intermeshing of otherwise distinct beings, Ingold writes that we ought instead to think of the living organism as "a bundle of lines." These lines entwine with other lines "to form a boundless and ever-extending tangle" that Ingold terms *the meshwork*.[14] In Ingold's thinking, Durkheim's sociological method is too bounded and homogenously compounded. Durkheimian blob-like collectives fail to account for the mutual dependence of organisms in social and ecological meshworks.

Rather than the social fact, then, Ingold's principle of social cohesion is the knot. "In a world where things are continually coming into being through processes of growth and movement," writes Ingold, "knotting is the fundamental principle of coherence. It is the way in which contrary forces of tension and friction, as in pulling tight, are generative of forms."[15] Importantly, knots do not have insides and outsides, like blobs. Instead, they have *interstices*. The most important difference between Ingold's notion of the knot and Durkheim's melded collectives is that the knot allows for the persistence of individual identities even within enmeshed societies. Two strings that are joined together in a knot, after all, do not have their surfaces dissolved and their individual essences melted together in their joining. Rather, says Ingold, social coherence is defined by a principle of "interstitial differentiation," whereby "difference continually arises from within the midst of joining *with*, in the ongoing sympathy of going along together."[16] Ingold's collectives, then, are tangled meshes in which individual components express their individuality in response to ongoing social relationships with others. Social collectivity, then, does not dissolve individualism; it is a precondition for it.

But what of the images of social togetherness in *Midsommar*? How do Durkheim's blob-like, superorganic social collectives and Ingold's image of knotted lines that form more or less durable social entanglements help account for the horrors offered by the film? Looking more closely at how *Midsommar* frames different models of togetherness, it is clear that the film oscillates between these two models, turning vertiginously from the differentiated "mesh" of classically liberal communities to the seamless "meld" of holistic communalism in moments when Dani (and the viewer) are most unsettled. While Ingold's notion of living beings as bundles of lines that tangle with others in an ever-extending meshwork of vital interconnections might be unsettling to ideologies that posit the human individual as separate from and superior to nature, his theory still retains some sense of an individual identity even within a social and ecological web. Durkheim's model, by contrast, presents itself as more obviously challenging and often violent toward the individual, and in that sense has more potential as a source of horror. But *Midsommar* takes an eclectic approach to the problem of individuals and collectives, presenting multiple visions of what social cohesion can look like—be it within a couple, a family, a community, a nation, or an ecosystem. The horror of the film arises from the unexpected oscillation from one sense of cohesion to another, often from benign meshes to menacing and violent melds.

This type of oscillation can be seen in a sequence early in the film, just after Dani and the rest of the American travelers have arrived in the vicinity of Hårga. Almost immediately, they are offered psychedelic mushrooms by an apparently well-meaning host. Dani is reluctant to take any, urging the others to go ahead without her. But when Mark makes his annoyance clear and insists that everyone must start their trip at the same time, she quickly succumbs to the group pressure. In that sense, Mark serves as a stand-in for the "social fact" of Durkheim's social theory, bluntly expressing the expectations of uniform behavior within the social group.

What follows is the first of the film's multiple psychedelic sequences. It is also the subtlest and most aesthetically sparse of these hallucinatory scenes, yet also perhaps the most unsettling, since it serves as the first hint of the terrors that await Dani and the group during the midsummer festival. Dani's trip begins on a relatively calm foot. After the group simultaneously takes doses of the drug—an event ritually marked by calls of "cheers!" and "skål!" from the group—they all sit together listlessly on a grassy hillside next to a lone tree. Mark immediately becomes paranoid about the sun and blue sky at 9 p.m.—"That's not fine! Why is it like that? That feels wrong, I don't like that!"—but calms down when he lies down and basks in the late-evening sun. "Everybody else lie down," he insists to the group. "Guys, do it, it feels so nice!" Mark's behavior in this scene serves as a kind of insecure glue that holds the group together. As a villager walks by and jovially greets them—"Hej hej!"—Mark reacts with immediate suspicion and says, "I don't want new people right now!"

Despite this immediate sense of paranoia and anxiety, Dani's trip starts as a benign experience. The film's sound becomes amplified and echoed, emphasizing Dani's own exaggerated feeling of embodied immediacy on the drug. Her breathing becomes deep and slow, her body relaxes, and she closes her eyes, becoming lost in the sound of her own breathing and the gentle commentary of Pelle. "Can you feel that?" asks Pelle. "The energy coming up from the earth?" Dani looks down at her hand, which rests on the ground, and as the camera pans down to follow her gaze, we see that earth and flesh have become unexpectedly enmeshed: the grass appears to grow *through* her hand in the shot, an image that reads as a decidedly trippy vision of transcorporeality. This image of interconnection with the earth fits well with Ingold's model of the meshwork of social and ecological connection. The grass and Dani's hand do not become indistinguishably one in a Durkheimian experience of melding, as copper and tin are melded together to form bronze; instead, like Ingold's meshwork, the two organisms have become entangled in each other's mesh-like matrices. Even in the midst of their intimate enmeshment, Dani and the earth remain resolutely distinct entities.

Pelle's languid commentary continues, directing both Dani's and the viewer's gaze to a landscape suddenly enlivened with a vital pulsation. "Look! The trees too, they're breathing," he tells the group. Dani looks up at the tree next to her, which seems to be pulsing and fluid, its trunk and branches distorting into subtly surreal swirls, under which we hear Dani's slow and steady breath. "Nature just knows instinctually how to stay in harmony," Pelle continues. "Everything mechanically just doing its part." The camera cuts to a close-up of Dani's face, and we see that she is unself-consciously absorbed in gazing at the tree, while the grass in the background sways in the gentle breeze, continuing to swirl as the pulsing liveliness of the tree has now spread throughout the well-lit landscape.

At this point, however, the trip turns bad. Mark, who seems to have calmed down under the influence of Pelle's comforting narration, says from off-screen, "You guys are like my family. You're like my real, actual family." At the mention of family, Dani suddenly snaps back into hypervigilance—her eyes shoot open, and her breathing stops. Mark's comment precipitates an uncanny return of Dani's trauma after the horrific loss of her "real, actual" family the previous winter, and she is suddenly thrown into a drug-tinged panic attack. She jumps to her feet and looks over at Christian, whose face seems to have melted into a subtly distorted mask. Dani hurries away from the group and off through the fields, telling them she wants to go on a walk alone. Passing a nearby group of celebrants—presumably also under the influence of psychoactive substances as they sing along with accordion music—she berates herself under her breath in an attempt to calm herself down: "No, no, no, no, no. Don't think that! You're fine. It's almost your birthday. You're okay. You're fine . . . you're fine . . . you're fine. . . ." As she nears the group, they turn to Dani and seem to be laughing at her, so she turns away again, now even more panicky and paranoid. Ingmar, Pelle's brother, catches her attention and tries to comfort her, insisting that the group wasn't laughing at her. He then invites her to interact with yet another new group—"You wanna come meet my friends?"—and suddenly his face seems to have melted and stretched into a disconcertingly exaggerated smile.

Dani, now even more panicked, rushes away to a nearby outhouse. When she strikes a match and looks at herself in the mirror, she sees a fleeting, flickering image of her sister's corpse behind her in the mirror—the deadly tube filled with carbon monoxide still horrifically duct-taped to her face. Dani's face, like Christian's and Ingmar's, is now also unnervingly distorted in the mirror, her right eye having become enlarged and her face unrecognizably asymmetrical. The image reads like an allusion to Ingmar Bergman's famous composite image of Bibi Andersson's and Liv Ullmann's faces horrifically fused together in an asymmetrical mask from *Persona* (1966), a plausible connection given Ari Aster's well-documented admiration for Bergman.[17] Though *Persona* has no clear environmental or ecocritical message, the way it unsettles and mingles the identities of its two central characters as the women grow more and more intimately connected provides a potent template for psychological horror that environmentally conscious films like *Midsommar* and *Thelma* have drawn on both thematically and iconographically.

How can the horror of this scene be conceived in terms of Durkheim's and

Ingold's social theory? The sequence initially reads simply as a mushroom trip gone bad, which plunges Dani back into her traumatic experience of loss, opening up wounds that have hardly begun to heal. However, it is not merely loss and trauma that are threatening in this scene; it is also the pull of social connections that press in on the individual, threatening autonomy and bodily integrity. Horror thus arises from our own connections to other humans within couples, friend groups, communities, and families. Taking into account this emphasis on the social, it may be further observed that the sequence starts with a benign image of organisms becoming entangled in a mesh of sympathetic togetherness, much like Dani's vision of her hand permeated with living grass easily fits within Ingold's model of social cohesion, with its tangled lines and its maintenance of distinct individual identities. From there, the pleasantly mesh-like model of socio-ecological togetherness espoused by Ingold suddenly shifts to horrific images of social collectives as Durkheimian melds: individual bodies begin oozing into grotesque new forms that try to cling to Dani. Individual identities melt, and panic arises from Dani's inability to escape the social connections that press in all around her: the boyfriend who morphs into a stranger and calls out her name, the menacing joviality of the singers who seem to laugh at her as she passes, the acquaintance with a Cheshire cat smile who wants to introduce her to new friends, the uncanny return of her dead sister, and the sight of Dani's own unrecognizably distorted visage in the mirror. All of these forces of individual dissolution within the alloy-like bonds of social cohesion that relentlessly pursue Dani in her panic remind her of her own debilitating psychological and social dependencies on others. The terror of the scene for Dani is that it shows how social connections can go horribly wrong in experiences of self-estrangement and loss of identity.

## SECLUSION AND EXCLUSION

This early scene, in which Dani's drug-fueled panic attack reveals the social and ecological world around her as a melded collective entity, is just a hint of the more hostile and bloody horrors that await her and the other American tourists as they are invited into the Hårga commune's midsummer festival. Impelled by academic curiosity, since Josh and Christian are writing their anthropology theses on folk ritual, the American visitors continually ask Pelle questions about the spiritual beliefs and social practices of the community. For Josh and

Christian, the villagers are anthropological informants rather than existential threats. Among other things, they learn about the community's understanding of human life as cyclical and seasonal, with social policies that enforce a rigid sequence of the seasons of the human life span. From infanthood to age eighteen, Pelle tells them, members of the community are considered children in the springtime of their lives. From eighteen to thirty-six, they are sent on a pilgrimage in which they travel abroad and live in other communities. At that point, members of the community return to Hårga and enter their autumnal period from thirty-six to fifty-four, when they are considered productive, working members of the agrarian collective. Finally, from fifty-four to seventy-two, community members have entered winter and are considered mentors for the younger generations. When Dani asks the obvious question—"What happens at seventy-two?"—Pelle (in a joking tone) mimes the death of such aged-out members of the Hårga commune, slashing his hand across his throat and sticking his tongue out to mimic the face of a corpse.

Exactly what kind of death the elderly members of the community can anticipate is revealed to the horrified outsiders—and gorily captured for the viewers—in a scene at the film's midpoint, when the tourists are told they are to witness a ritual practice described simply as the *ättestupa*. Pressed on what this entails, Pelle only says, "It's too hard to explain. You'll get a better sense tomorrow." As non-Swedish speakers, all of the visitors are left in the dark about what this ritual involves—all except Josh, whose expansive reading on the beliefs of such communities has clued him in to what might be expected—until they are invited to witness the ritual in all its spectacular gruesomeness. The horrific spectacle is prefigured the night before, when Dani wakes up from a sleep made restless by the crepuscular semidarkness of summer nights in northern Sweden. Her eyes are drawn toward one of the many folk murals painted on the whitewashed wooden walls of the communal dormitory. The camera traces Dani's upward gaze in a vertical pan that shows us the painted scene: a pool of blood on the earth, which is revealed to be dripping from a sedate villager who has plunged a dagger into their own wrist while standing between two growing sunflowers. As the camera pans up, we see that the scene is watched over by a benevolently smiling sun, which radiates down on the agrarian community that fertilizes the earth—and marks its territory—with its own blood. The image resonates with the undercurrent of *Blut-und-Boden*-style ethno-communalism that solidifies the rigid and exclusionary group identity of the Hårga commune. Taking up the iconography of vitalistic nature worship discussed in connection with *Shelley* in chapter 4, *Midsommar* makes explicit the predatory and exclusionary implications of Nordic environmentalism, spectacularizing what remains a suggestive undercurrent of white supremacy in Abbasi's film.

The actual spectacle of the *ättestupa* is sprung upon the group the next day. After the first of a series of highly ritualized community meals—held outdoors at a rune-shaped arrangement of banquet tables—the two participants in the *ättestupa* enjoy a solemn toast and are carried off on honorary sedan chairs by robed men wearing flower-garlanded straw hats. The rest of the villagers and their visitors are led off to a chalky-white landscape, where they are pictured gazing up at a high cliff in front of them. As the American visitors look on from the rear along with their guide, Pelle, the film cuts to a shot of the crowd looking up at the cliff, and we see a young man who looks directly at the camera. Similar direct looks at the camera are repeated a number of times in the film, a metacinematic gesture that implicates the spectator in the brutality of the folk rituals we witness.

The participants in the *ättestupa* function as an ominous illustration of the brutal endgame to which members of the Hårga collective commit in staying with the community. The ritual is ostensibly a freely chosen sacrifice of individual life to the continued vitality of the community. Aster's focus—and the spectator's gaze—is thus directed at the grim aftermath: the compound fractures and smashed skulls that await commune members at the end of their life cycle. And because *Midsommar* is a horror film shot entirely in sunlight, the horrified spectators can see *everything*. Rather than relegating horror to the "blind space" afforded by darkness and strategically evasive cinematography, *Midsommar* creates a horror of hypervisibility.[18] In that sense, although the brutality and racism of the commune are never expressly stated aims, they are strikingly out in the open.

As Dani and the others watch Hårga's *ättestupa*, we see (from their perspective) the first of the two participants walk to the edge of the cliff. Dani's breathing becomes erratic and panicky as she looks up at the woman, who seems to lock eyes with Dani before plunging off the cliff and landing face-first on a large rock situated below. The British visitors, Connie and Simon, immediately start loudly objecting to the ritual—"Why are you standing there! What the fuck!"—and the camera cuts to a quick succession of slow-motion shots showing the gory impact and aftermath in transgressively gruesome detail. A similar spectacle is repeated for the second participant, who comes to the verge of the cliff a few seconds later and similarly plunges off the edge. His attempt is less successful, however—he only horrifically injures his leg in the fall, so a small group of villagers wielding a wooden mallet come to put him out of his misery with several blows to the head shown in graphic detail.

Beyond the spectacular body horror of the scene, the *ättestupa* is noteworthy for the way it indicates the style of togetherness that establishes the Hårga community. Drawn in as implicated spectators witnessing the bloody sacrifices crucial to the commune's sense of a coherent group identity, the visitors are compelled to make a choice either to continue to witness the rituals as disinterested observers (as the American visitors, driven by the academic ambitions of Josh and Christian, do) or to reject the community's values and attempt an escape (as the British visitors do). But this apparent choice is, of course, constrained by the genre conventions of folk horror, which dictate that outsiders—whether curious observers like the Americans of *Midsommar* or investigative antagonists like Sgt. Neil Howie in the genre-defining classic *The Wicker Man*—must be sacrificed by the rural folk commune in the end. As a genre, folk horror is structured according to the insider/outsider logic of closed communities. Although there is no wall overtly marking the territory of Hårga—only a sun-shaped wooden portal that visitors walk through as they enter—the village is located in a remote clearing apparently surrounded by woodlands, seemingly far removed from any other communities. There is no cellular service in the area—an important detail that most present-day horror films are now obligated to include—and the village is accessible only by hiking paths and one small dirt road. A sense of isolation is, of course, crucial to the terror experienced by outsiders drawn into rural communes in folk horror films; without this distance from civilization, terrorized visitors could easily escape, or even just scream to get the attention of the outside world. In folk horror, isolation situates outsiders in a location where no one except the commune members brutalizing them can hear them scream.[19]

There are numerous signs that this isolation from the outside world is not only an intentional choice of the community but one specifically rooted in the commune's xenophobic and racist ideologies. The signs of this racist undercurrent are at first only fleeting and marginal clues strewn throughout the early part of the film as "Easter eggs" for eagle-eyed viewers to catch.[20] In a scene before the Americans' departure for Sweden, for instance, a thick tome titled *The Secret Nazi Language of the Uthark* sits on the coffee table facing spine out. The book is captured in a wide-angle shot as part of an initially indistinguishable clutter of books on the coffee table in Josh and Christian's grad student apartment, only noticeable to most spectators upon a second or third viewing more attuned to marginal details than to the narrative center of the scene. The runic symbols that proliferate throughout the Hårga commune—as well as the twentieth-century ideas about the esoteric and mystical properties of such symbols captured in so-called Uthark theories—are thus early on connected with fascism and ethno-nationalism.

Another marginal clue about Hårga's xenophobia that appears before the group's arrival in the village is seen from the rental car that Pelle and his American visitors drive northward after landing in Sweden. In a remarkable aerial drone shot tracking the car as it drives into the region of Hälsingland, where Hårga is located, the camera sweeps over the car and rotates vertically to capture the car's path along the highway in a head-on, upside-down shot that lasts several seconds. After a cut to a reverse shot, the camera then sweeps vertiginously back into an upright position as the car passes under a banner that reads, "STOPPA MASSINVANDRINGEN TILL HÄLSINGLAND" (Stop mass immigration to Hälsingland) and urges passers-by to "RÖSTA PÅ FRITT NORR I HÖST!" (Vote for Free North this fall). This political banner promotes the fictional political party Fritt Norr (Free North), a name that possibly references the Fria Nationalister (Free Nationalists)—a network of aligned extreme right-wing political parties (including the party Nationell Norrland)—as well as the push for the political autonomy of Norrland that has gained steam in recent years, a movement driven by regional and cultural resentment toward the more populous and demographically diverse regions of central and southern Sweden. More broadly, the banner connects the type of nostalgic rural isolationism we see in Hårga to the rise of far-right anti-immigration parties in Swedish national politics in recent years.

This development is especially embodied by the unprecedented success of Sverigedemokraterna in the 2018 general election, in which SD secured sixty-two seats in the Swedish Riksdag. Like other radical right-wing populist parties that have gained a significant foothold in parliaments across Europe over the last several decades, the most salient feature of SD's political platform is a pronounced skepticism toward immigration and multiculturalism. According to the doctrine of ethno-pluralism that is one of the ideological cornerstones of RRP parties, the social cohesion and cultural identity of modern nation-states is under existential threat because of lax immigration policies and the opening up of international borders. According to the ethno-pluralist doctrine, this threat to national cultures can be alleviated only by drastically limiting immigration, particularly from non-Western cultures originating in largely Muslim countries of the Middle East and North Africa. According to this logic, ethnic groups should be contained in regionally bounded territories across the globe, and legal restrictions should be put in place to discourage mixture between these ethnic groups.[21] In the Swedish context, SD has exploited the metaphor of the *folkhemmet* (the people's home), an ideal of national solidarity and egalitarian social policy first articulated in the 1930s that has been a central pillar of Sweden's Social Democratic Party, the dominant political party for much of the twentieth century and the faction that did the most to build the modern Swedish welfare state. According to SD, the cohesion of "the people's home" in Sweden—and the generous safety net offered by the welfare state—has been undermined by a far too expansive view of who counts as people who belong in the national home. The unprecedented success in recent years of SD, a party with clear historical ties to neo-Nazism, is thus rooted in metaphors of nation connected to a national territory—with cultural blood being tied to a regional soil—whose boundaries must be rigorously policed, as well as notions of national identity with a clear distinction between insiders and outsiders. A central tenet of SD, then, is a radically restrictive sense of what it means to be a member of the collective body known as the Swedish *folk*. According to one recent study, this sense of belonging had much to do with cultural clichés of typical Swedishness such as the love of *fika* (coffee-based work breaks) and an adherence to the cultural notion of *lagom* (a sense of being content with "just enough") as well as more prescriptive metrics like speaking fluent Swedish.[22] Such a territorial and restrictive notion of belonging fits with Durkheim's model of collectivity, since ethno-pluralism creates ethnically homogenous collective blobs with clear territorial boundaries between them.

This highly circumscribed notion of social belonging is also a clear feature of folk horror. According to Adam Scovell's recent authoritative monograph on the subgenre, this sense of belonging is reinforced by the notable feeling of isolation that all folk horror films share. There is a sense in these films that characters have been "banished" to an isolated landscape that is figured as an "inhospitable place because it is in some way different from general society as a whole and not simply because of a harsher topography."[23] Though this isolation is most often reinforced by geographic distance—captured in the alternative name for the subgenre, "rural horror"[24]—folk horror films can also take place in urban environments. *Midsommar*, like most folk horror films, is situated in a geographically isolated, rural setting with an agrarian economy and a society that is based on a skewed system of morality.[25]

One of the innovations of *Midsommar* within the folk horror subgenre, however, is that it overtly highlights the racism and xenophobia that animates rural folk belonging in such isolated and skewed communities. Beyond the clear references to neo-Nazism and far-right, anti-immigration politics, *Midsommar* further unmasks the coded racism that lurks in the restrictive ethno-pluralism of RRP parties such as the Sweden Democrats in subtler and more indirect ways. The cloaked white supremacy of the Hårga commune is especially highlighted by the frequently blinding, bleached-out landscapes captured by cinematographer Pawel Pogorzelski. The summertime setting in northern Sweden justifies such a blindingly bright lighting scheme from a narrative perspective, but in the *ättestupa* scene, we see how other stylistic choices reinforce this sense of the oppressive, exclusionary whiteness of the folk commune.[26] Set among chalky cliffs and a sparsely vegetated setting, the *ättestupa* becomes a kind of crucible of white rural identity as the commune practices its sacred, brutal ritual and spills the blood of the old onto its territorial soil with the stated goal of guaranteeing the continued survival of the racially and culturally homogenous community. The implicit goals of the ritual are to reinforce a group identity founded on violence and racial purity, an ideology communicated by the chalky hills and the white clothing, which sets a baseline expectation of ultra-whiteness as a criterion for community inclusion.[27] Against this decolorized background, the highly melanated skin of Josh, as well as the British visitors Simon (Archie Madekwe) and Connie (Ellora Torchia), stands out as a damning marker of racial and cultural difference that the commune does not tolerate. These Black and Brown visitors are the only people of color to be found in Hårga during the midsummer festival, and they are significantly (and predictably) the first outsiders to be murdered.[28] Just as other ethno-nationalist movements in contemporary Scandinavia cultivate shared spaces that are implicitly white—that is, de facto spaces of exclusionary whiteness, rather than spaces that de jure exclude people of color—Hårga's brutal racism is expressed indirectly and implicitly.[29] Hårga is, in short, a community that hides its white supremacy behind the friendly face of folksy hospitality and ethnographic openness. *Midsommar*, then, centers its horrors on a kind of predatory hospitality strikingly similar to the parasitic environmentalism discussed in connection with *Shelley* in chapter 4. According to these two films directed by cultural outsiders to the region, when an outsider is welcomed into a Scandinavian society, such a welcome is highly conditional, predicated on an expectation that the outsider must either assimilate and be absorbed to the social collective or perform reproductive labor for the community before being killed (like Christian in *Midsommar*) or cast aside (like Elena in *Shelley*).

## CLOSED CIRCLES AND CLOSED COMMUNITIES

The midsummer festival at Hårga culminates in another ritual of rural white identity and communal cohesion: the exhausting spectacle of the endurance dance around the maypole, a contest in which the woman who is able to continue dancing the longest is crowned the commune's May Queen for the year. The ritual is deeply connected to the commune's mythology and sense of shared racial identity as upholders of a tradition of rural, agrarian paganism. One of the female elders inaugurates the dance by recounting a community folktale about how the "the Black One lured the youths of Hårga to the grass and seduced them into dance. And when they began, they could not stop, and they danced themselves to death."[30] The elder frames the current ritual in quasi-Nietzschean terms as an act of *livsbejakende* (life-affirming) defiance of Mörkret (the Black One, according to the subtitles, but which could also be translated as "darkness"), in which contestants literally dance until they drop.[31] Dani has been drafted into the ritual, despite her initial reluctance, and is given a shot of a drug-laced liquid described as "tea for the competition." The first view of the actual dance is an overhead shot showing the crown of the maypole pointing majestically up at the sky, while concentric circles of female dancers grasp hands down below and musicians off to the side are poised at their instruments. As the tea takes effect, Dani looks down at her feet, perhaps in an effort to steady herself before the dance begins. Instead she is met by the sight of her feet appearing to fuse with the grass. This second transcorporeal image of body fused with ground is no longer the benignly trippy image of her hand with single blades of grass poking out of it, but instead is a more troublingly seamless fusion in which the flesh of her legs seems to dissolve into grass. No longer a harmless image of environment entangling and knotting with the body in the mesh, Dani is confronted here with a hint of a Durkheimian meld threatening to absorb her. The sight also has more troubling existential implications for Dani now, as she has witnessed the horrific ritual suicide of community members whose lives and bodies are voluntarily and violently given to the earth and has also seen one after another of the outsiders go missing in recent days. At this point in the film, transcorporeal unions thus signal for Dani the possibly imminent threat of her own death and absorption into Hårga's richly fertilized soil. As Dani looks more closely to confirm her vision, she begins to hyperventilate.

Once the dancing begins, though, Dani is swept up in the movement and becomes happily distracted by the choreography she is forced to pick up on the fly. Aster and Pawel Pogorzelski capture the dancing in both overhead shots of the twirling circles of women and eye-level shots in which the camera spins around the pole along with the dancers. The overhead shots have a hypnotic quality as the concentric rings of women dance in alternating directions, an effect that both pushes viewers away and pulls them in. This push-and-pull quality—reminiscent of the dolly zoom technique made famous by Hitchcock and cameraman Irmin Roberts in Hitchcock's *Vertigo* (1958)—signals the ambivalent attraction and repulsion felt by the commune for the American outsiders and the dizzying effects of the hallucinogenic substances Dani and the other visitors are fed. We have also seen the visual motif of concentric circles in a tapestry the camera panned across earlier in the film depicting a young man caught in the thrall of a love potion administered by a young woman who has just reached sexual maturity. In the penultimate panel of the sequence showing the arc of the young man's wooing, we see the man's eyes filled with the swirling, concentric lines of a spiral. The swirling circle motif thus points to the treatment Christian is being subjected to during this same sequence, as he is pulled away to be propositioned by one of the female elders of the community, who tells him that he has been approved to mate with young Maja, who has taken a liking to him and already administered a dose of the potion to him—which includes her own pubic hair—baked into a pie.

As the sequence cross-cuts between the dance and Christian's interview with the female elder about the mating proposition, we see how the swirl of the women engaged in a dance also signifies the magical and coercive swoon that people are put under, and in that sense gestures toward the disarming of male agency in this ritual mating practice. Aster's claim that *Midsommar* is only a folk horror film from the perspective of the male visitors to the commune resonates here, underscoring the degree to which the subgenre is animated by a gynophobic terror of the coercive pull of female sexuality.[32] This is also evident in a well-known scene from *Wicker Man* where the prudish male detective is horrified by a female teacher who instructs a classroom full of girls about the phallic symbolism of the maypole, inculcating the children in their community's reverence for the reproductive role of the penis. From a male perspective, then, folk horror poses a threat because of the way it reduces men to their bodies, objectifying them in a way that runs counter to masculinist fantasies of transcending the body through intellectual mastery. In being drawn into the mating ritual, Christian is both getting the wish he expressed at the outset of the film—to find a woman who is more interested in sex than Dani is—and also being reduced to pure bodily functionality. He is useful to the community, then, only because he is capable of ejaculation. It is important to my reading of the film, however, to resist the pull of this folk horror interpretation; only by looking beyond the film as a genre exercise can we understand its richness and complexity as a film in which duplicity is baked in, according to the director. Any folk horror gynophobia must therefore be countered by Dani's fairy-tale-like retreat into a magical space where her pain and trauma are validated and sympathetically reflected in the matriarchal Hårga family she is subsumed into.

As the dancing continues and Dani increasingly becomes ecstatically swept up in the currents of the dance, we see that the synchronization of the dancers is secured by the dancers' hands, which grasp hold of their partners to keep the collective circles intact. The principle of togetherness exemplified in this scene can be analyzed in terms of Ingold's notion of the meshwork of social and ecological collectives, which are drawn together by the clinginess of the linear entanglements among living organisms. Citing the remarkably strong grasp of mammalian infants, who cling to their caretakers for affection and nourishment, Ingold argues in the opening paragraph of *The Life of Lines* that "in clinging—or, more prosaically, in holding on to one another—lies the very essence of sociality: a sociality, of course, that is in no wise limited to the human but extends across the entire panoply of clingers and those to whom, or that to which, they cling."[33] Given the importance of hands clinging and fingers "interdigitating" with one another to Ingold's description of the meshwork, it is no surprise that to illustrate his theory he relies on one of the most celebrated representations of dance in modern art: Henri Matisse's painting *Dance* (1909–10). Ingold writes, "Matisse had a very blob-like way of depicting the human form," describing the figures in the painting as "voluminous, rotund and heavily outlined." Despite these qualities, "the magic of the painting is that these anthropomorphic blobs pulse with vitality," an effect that is achieved "because the painting can also be read as an ensemble of lines drawn principally by the arms and legs."[34] Superficially, the dancers of *Midsommar* seem to resemble Matisse's anthropomorphic blobs, especially in the way they cling to each other in a swirling dance and in the way the cohesion and synchronization of their collective movements depend on the linear entwining of hands and fingers. We see how Dani relies on her tight grasp of her more experienced partners' hands to maintain the stop-and-start rhythm of a dance with which she is completely unfamiliar. Dani gets swept up into the circle, forgets the unsettling sight of her legs dissolving into grass, and becomes preoccupied by the perpetual swirl of the collective dance, just as Matisse's dancers do.

However, as Ingold observes, the pulsing, vital quality of Matisse's painting is achieved not only by virtue of the clingy linear entanglement of the figures through their hands and fingers, but because the circuit they dance in is not a closed circle—it is instead "perpetually on the point of closure—once the hands of the two figures in the foreground link up," yet this closure perpetually escapes Matisse's dancers.[35] Indeed, it could be argued that the dance itself is *motivated* by the lack of closure—the whirl keeps on going eternally because the dancers strive to achieve a closure that always escapes them, like a dog relentlessly chasing its own tail. The gap between the dancers' hands in the foreground, then, is the spark of life for the entire dance: life and movement are guaranteed by nonclosure. In contrast to Matisse's painting, the aim of the maypole dance in *Midsommar* is precisely to *maintain* the closure of the revolving concentric circuits of dancers. In the Hårga elder's introductory speech at the commencement of the ritual, the participants are told that in losing hold and falling down, they enact a symbolic death, the implication of which is that life and vitality depend on the collective closure of the circle through the clingy cohesion of the dance. It is the closure of the circle that helps Dani overcome her ignorance of the ritual to win the endurance contest. She can stay upright as long as she holds on, and as she maintains her firm grasp on her partners, she is swept along in their movements and learns the moves as she goes. As, one by one, those around her lose their grip and fall down, they metaphorically die and are expelled from the circle. At the end, by being the last dancer standing, Dani has survived all the others who have fallen along the way. The logic of vitality in the Hårga dance, then, is a reversal of Matisse's painting, which depicts the way longing and yearning can motivate collective action and movement.

If we read the dance according to the terms Ingold lays out, however, we see that this professed vitality achieved by closure is actually antithetical to health and vitality. The closure of the dance circle echoes the commune's rigorous policing of its own boundaries via the careful maintenance of a limited gene pool. Though a villager insists to one of the visitors early in the film that the commune respects the incest taboo, we later find out that the commune's oracle—a physically and cognitively disabled boy named Ruben—is in fact a deliberate product of incest. The given justification for this practice is that the oracle is supposed to have a mind "unclouded" by typical intellectual concerns, but the implicit reasoning seems to be that the holiest members of the community are those whose bloodlines are least corrupted by genetic material from outsiders. The maypole scene, then, signifies that despite the commune's superficial gestures of vitalist nature worship—with its emphasis on the life-giving benevolence of the sun and the earth and its fixation on fecundity and procreation—the closure of the community and the violent and exclusionary tactics used to maintain that closure show that its vitality is only skin deep, a veneer that hides a deep-seated impulse toward brutality, violence, and death. Founded on a mythology of life-affirming whiteness struggling against the forces of existential (and racial) darkness, Hårga is the type of closed community that represents an extreme version of the ideal of ethno-pluralist territorialism that would please the most ardent adherents of RRP politics. In all its brutality and violence, and its use of the benign rhetoric of cultural tradition as a fig leaf to obscure more troubling ideologies, Hårga is a horrific vision of the kinds of communities that the populist movements which have flourished in recent years seek to establish. The dance sequences in the final act of the film subtly reinforce this picture by framing the ritually important maypole dance competition around mythologies of racial superiority—as the dancers seek to affirm the vitality of their white bodies against the wiles of the "Black One" bent on their destruction—and the power of closed communities as they cling together in a collective fight against dark outsiders.

## ANTI-HOLISTIC COMMUNITY

The closure of the Hårga commune and its fixation on the good of the community at the expense of the lives and agency of individuals—a tendency most graphically on display in the *ättestupa* scene—may be seen more broadly as a model of collectivity that is actually quite prevalent today, well beyond far-right anti-immigration movements. This model can be summed up with the truism that the whole is always greater than the sum of its parts, which ecological philosopher Timothy Morton describes as "one of the most profound inhibitors of world sharing."[36] By way of explanation, Morton writes that versions of holism that operate according to this assumption prioritize wholes that often include humans and other beings as nothing more than replaceable component parts. In the case of certain holistic versions of community, for instance, when the whole is seen as greater than its parts, the human individuals who make it up only have importance insofar as they serve the imperatives of the community. Morton says that to counter this particular version of holism, we must not grasp for the "anti-holist reductionism that neoliberalism promotes: 'There is no such thing as society; there are only individuals.'"[37] This would include the versions of community espoused by Herbert Spencer—collectives that see society as a collection of "lots of little blobs," to use Ingold's terminology, which may fleetingly transact in the marketplace but never meaningfully interconnect with one another in any lasting sense.

Instead of this anti-holism, Morton writes that sustainable social collectives should function according to a new kind of "weak holism" that sees wholes as *physically* larger than their parts but *ontologically* smaller. Morton labels this version of holism "implosive holism," operating according to the principle of "subscendence." In *subscending* their parts, wholes do not magically exceed their parts (as in *transcendence*); instead, the whole is seen more loosely as a collective, rather than a strictly bounded and rigorously policed community with clear definitions of insiders and outsiders. The wholes that Morton describes here are "implosive" because they become ontologically smaller (their existential significance is always less) at their surfaces, with individual parts always having

During the maypole dance sequence from *Midsommar*, Dani's sense of belonging oscillates between benign images of enmeshment as she is pleasurably caught up in the community of the dance and more threatening images of being involuntarily melded to her surroundings. Screen grab from *Midsommar* (dir. Ari Aster, 2019).

During one of the pauses in the music during the maypole dance, Dani looks down at her feet to find they have become seemingly one with the earth. Her immediate response is to become visibly panicked at this unanticipated sense of being melded to her material environment. Frame grab from *Midsommar* (dir. Ari Aster, 2019).

more ontological value than simply their function within the whole. By way of illustration, Morton writes, "A street full of people is much more than just part of a greater whole called 'city.'"[38] Humankind, similarly, "is ontologically smaller than the humans who make it up." Writes Morton, "There is so much more that humans do other than be parts of humankind."[39] Implosive holism, then, is a vision of holism that is meant to draw our attention to parts and to discourage us from always seeking meaning in transcendent scales; rather, it invites us to instead think smaller, valuing individuals and collectives but not in a way that frames collectivity in strictly bounded terms.

The type of transcendent holism that Morton argues against here is crucially not only the provenance of regressive and xenophobic models of community like Hårga; it is also, according to Morton, a central premise of certain ecological philosophies, notably the Gaia hypothesis put forward by the British chemist James Lovelock. According to this theory, the biosphere is a collective and self-regulating system that may be likened to a vast living organism. This superindividual quasi-organism is seen as a transcendent whole in which human beings and other living creatures are mere component parts who must continue to serve their function within the whole if they are to remain valuable members of the biosphere. Morton writes that a conclusion such holists could conceivably reach—according to the logic of transcendent holism—is that viruses have just as much right to exist as do patients suffering from the diseases viruses spread. Such claims, writes Morton, have "nothing to do with actual ecological politics," but instead derive from a "concept of biosphere that is greater than the sum of its parts, in which every being is a replaceable component."[40] This indifference to the value of life at the level of the individual or even the species, according to Morton, is associated with "agricultural-age religion, the ideological support of the social, psychic and philosophical machination that eventually generated mass extinction."[41] The danger of transcendent holism, then, is that it is accompanied by a violent—even genocidal—impulse in which the exclusion or extermination of individuals or whole species deemed expendable within the holistic community is seen as an acceptable sacrifice for the greater good. If the community is an organism, then, a kind of surgical brutality is occasionally warranted to amputate infected extremities or remove malignant growths that threaten the closed, self-regulating system of the community.

The way in which ostensibly ecological practices can harbor the trademark brutality of transcendent holism is encapsulated in the final scene of *Midsommar*, when bearskin-clad Christian and the other human sacrifices (alive and dead) are being assembled within the temple to be burned in the cathartic ritual purge overseen by the surviving members of the community. Aside from the two living community members who have voluntarily placed themselves in the fire, every other sacrificial offering has been carefully decorated in notably transcorporeal fashion—their corpses having been hollowed out and stuffed with material bits of the Hårga landscape, including twigs, straw, and flowers. These transcorporeal assemblages are chilling illustrations of the type of brutal, pseudo-ecological collectivity espoused by the transcendent holism of the Hårga collective. No longer afforded the individual agency that accompanies the subscendent wholes advocated by Morton, or by the principle of "interstitial differentiation" theorized by Ingold within the meshwork of organic life, these human forms are hollowed-out husks only fit to be burned in service of the blob-like Durkheimian meld of the Hårga community. It is fitting, then, that the surviving members of the community observing the spectacle of the ritual immolation are not depicted as independent individual agents either, but instead are seen thrashing and screaming in a sympathetic echo of the screams of pain emitted from the temple as the living sacrifices are consumed by cleansing fire.

The final shot of the film, which features the close-up of Dani's enigmatic smile, punctures the folk horror ending of the burning temple with a note of genre dissonance. Since we have been following Dani closely throughout the film and have been led to sympathize far more with her than with the callous and emotionally disconnected male American visitors who accompany her, our horror at the brutal ritual is mitigated by a sense of relief that Dani is finally free of her romantic entanglement with Christian. In the burning of all her connections to her old life in America, there is also a suggestion of a cleansing purge of her trauma and grief, and a sense of being adopted into a matriarchal society that—while clearly harboring troublingly brutal and exclusionary elements—is at least free of certain remnants of toxic masculinity that had previously clung to Dani. But such a simple interpretation immediately breaks down when we reflect on the horrors of racist and xenophobic exclusion the community is founded on, suggesting that the gap between the fairy tale and the folk horror interpretations cannot be bridged. The nonresolution of the ending suggests, then, that we should not attempt to see *Midsommar* as a transcendent whole in which formal elements of the film are component parts serving a unified genre interpretation of the film. Instead, *Midsommar* is rather a ragged, subscendent whole made up of a remarkably diverse array of elements that are always ontologically more significant than the holistic package that contains them.

═══

# Nordic Ecohorror as
# Social Critique

Given the Nordic region's global reputation as a haven of social-democratic progressivism and as models of well-ordered societies, one of the more remarkable developments in global horror cinema in recent years has been the frequency with which it has turned to the Nordic countryside as a setting to terrify its viewers. In "Scandinavia's Horror Renaissance," folklorist Tommy Kuusela presents one explanation for the appeal of Nordic nature for horror films: "With its vast, remote landscapes seemingly devoid of human activity, Scandinavia certainly makes a terrific setting for a horror film. After all, what could be a more fitting hiding place for secretive cults and supernatural beings, for places and creatures untouched by industrialization and our modern society?"[1] In Kuusela's reading, isolation in the Scandinavian wilderness provides fertile ground for horror. Such rural horror situates its characters far from help, isolating them in a distant landscape where they are free to enjoy the peace and quiet of outdoor recreation, but also where they are profoundly vulnerable, since nobody can hear their screams. As a diagnosis for why isolation in the Swedish countryside in a film like *Midsommar* or the picturesque insularity of the Icelandic seascape in a film like *Reykjavik Whale Watching Massacre* might serve as an ideal setting for contemporary horror, Kuusela's argument makes a certain intuitive sense. This is why we feel terrified when Thelma is drugged and held captive in her rural childhood home by her abusive father in *Thelma*, when Elena is cut off from her family back in Bucharest by a slowly draining cell phone battery in *Shelley*, or when Dani and her American friends slowly realize that there is no way out of the rural agrarian commune in remote northern Sweden where they have become trapped in *Midsommar*.

In the contemporary popular imagination, however, it is much more common to associate the vast expanses of undeveloped wilderness in the region with the more wholesome and healthy pursuits involved in the vaunted Nordic love of nature. This point is borne out in the Nordic Council of Ministers' document on branding strategy for the region, which emphasizes the importance of the wilderness for the particularly Nordic approach to the environment: "There is plenty of space in the Nordic region. There are vast plains, high mountains, dense forests, and large oceans, and people are free to spend a lot of their recreational time there, because of a labor market model that allows time for both work and leisure."[2] With the cultural logic of *friluftsliv* (open-air life) in mind—a concept that associates life in the wilderness with personal freedom—it is striking that Nordic cultural discourses have largely integrated nature and the wilderness as sites of spiritual and physical rejuvenation. Indeed, so intimately have culture and nature been bound up in Norway, writes cultural historian Nina Witoszek, that "the sublimity of nature relieved Norwegians from having to apologise for their lack of cities, castles, ruins or libraries. The vast reserves of mountains, fjords and forest have functioned as the equivalents of castles and cathedrals, i.e., as national heritage."[3] Not only is the natural world generally regarded as nonthreatening in this Nordic tradition of ecohumanism; it is imagined as a crucial reserve to which the weary modern urbanite can habitually return to restore physical and mental well-being. This association of the wilderness with physical and spiritual rejuvenation—rather than a potentially threatening isolation—is part and parcel of what many consider to be a Nordic environmental exceptionalism. In the words of one Swedish interviewee quoted in a recent article on the "relocation of transcendence" to the outdoors in Nordic cultures, "My hypothesis has always been that we Swedes are different somehow. We find our refuge in nature. It absorbs us."[4]

This feeling of being absorbed in nature can, of course, be perceived in wildly divergent ways. One person's pleasurable immersion in the wilderness is another's worst nightmare—as in the scenes of *Midsommar* when Dani's body seems to unnervingly become one with the rural Swedish landscape under the influence of psychedelic drugs. As an explanation for why absorption in nature can be subject to cultural variation, a comparison between American and Nordic conceptions of the wilderness is instructive. Modern American horror has made use of what Carol J. Clover terms "urbanoia": (sub)urban people's overwhelming fear of the rural backwoods and those who live there. Clover suggests that the move from urban to rural settings in horror may well be a universal archetype evident in fairy tales like Little Red Riding Hood, which fixate on the journey of a vulnerable little girl through the "deep dark woods," during which she is captured and eaten—and in some versions of the tale, implicitly raped—by the big bad wolf, whom she is naive and foolish enough to trust.[5] In Clover's reading, "the point is that rural Connecticut (or wherever), like the deep forests of Central Europe, is a place where the rules of civilization do not obtain."[6] Clover's theorization of urbanoia is heavily conscious of the classism inherent in the urbanite's confrontation with the hinterlands—an approach in these films that usually figures the country dweller as a toothless, inbred hillbilly intent on terrorizing and sexually assaulting the urban intruder. In an ecocritical reading of the rural slasher film in American horror cinema, Carter Soles connects this trope of urbanoia to a "Puritan conception of wilderness" that is deeply embedded in American cultural history.[7] Citing Roderick Nash's influential study *Wilderness and the American Mind* (1967), Soles notes that the deep-seated American antipathy toward the wilderness sees the country as "spiritually and physically dangerous, 'a powerful symbol of [humanity's] dark and untamed heart.'"[8] The brutality of the low-budget "urbanoia films" of the 1970s, according to Soles, is really "a horrifying reflection of our own 'civilized' cultural anxieties about our own rape of the natural world."[9]

While the trope of urbanoia may be an illuminating concept for examining American backwoods horror, as both Clover and Soles do, the approach I take in this book is to read Nordic ecohorror through the lens of nature imaginaries and cultural-historical traditions that prevail in the Nordic region. I am less confident than Clover, for instance, that urbanoia is something like a universal archetype, or that horror can be assumed to make use of the rural backwoods of Connecticut in the same way it makes use of the forested hinterlands of the Nordic region. Nordic folktales have no Red Riding Hood, but they do have *Askeladden* (the Ash Lad), a small but resourceful young boy who goes out into the wilderness to outmaneuver and slay the dimwitted Norwegian troll. Nordic folklore, then, is suffused with a more optimistic approach to the wilderness—one that stipulates that while the monsters of nature might be fearsome, they can be defeated. Nor does Nordic literary or cinematic history present us with a figure of rural decadence and corruption akin to Marlon Brando's Colonel Walter Kurtz of *Apocalypse Now* (dir. Francis Ford Coppola, 1979), whose retreat to the lawless wilderness during the Vietnam War sees him descend into the Conradian heart of darkness. And while some recent

Nordic ecohorror has drawn our attention to civilization's "rape of the natural world"—particularly the supernatural Swedish eco-noir television series *Jordskott* (2015–17)—the persistent perception that the Nordic approach to nature is more sustainable and virtuous, and therefore less marked by guilt than other developed nations, means that the motif of urbanoia is much less pronounced in Nordic ecohorror than it is elsewhere.[10] This is not to say that Nordic societies have nothing to feel guilty about when it comes to the environment—the continued dependence on atomic energy in Finland and Norway's extraction of petroleum are two well-known sources of environmental guilt in the region—but a long tradition of environmental exceptionalism and ecohumanism has meant that approaching nature has traditionally been a less anxious prospect in Nordic cultures than it has been in American culture.[11] That is why a Swedish interviewee can openly opine that "we Swedes are different somehow" and speak of absorption in the natural landscape as a pleasurable rather than threatening experience.

This distinction between American urbanoia, rooted in the Puritanical fear of the wilderness, and the Nordic ecohumanist tradition, which sees nature as a site of rejuvenation for the modern city dweller, can be illustrated by comparing the role of the forest in two recent American and Nordic horror films. In his historical folk horror film *The Witch* (sometimes stylized as *The VVitch*, 2015), American filmmaker Robert Eggers takes us to colonial New England, where a family of English settlers has been banished to the wilderness following a religious disagreement in the Puritan colony in which they have settled. The family's banishment is the inciting incident that leads them to be terrorized by a coven of witches who kidnap, murder, and dismember their baby, setting off a cycle of paranoia and mutual distrust that eventually drives the oldest daughter to join the coven after killing her mother in self-defense. It is no exaggeration to say that the narrative premise of *The Witch* is that the family's puritanical fear of the wilderness is justified, and their retreat to the woods is figured as a horrific absorption into the moral corruption and physical menace of the American wilderness.

In contrast, in Ali Abbasi's *Gräns* (*Border*, 2018)—a follow-up to his debut film *Shelley*—we meet an unusual-looking woman named Tina (Eva Melander) who works as a border guard for the Swedish Customs Service and has a preternatural sense of smell, which she uses to sniff out guilt on those who attempt to smuggle contraband such as drugs, alcohol, or child pornography into the country. In the course of the film, Tina meets a man named Vore (Eero Milonoff), who seems to bear a family resemblance to her, and she soon learns that she (like Vore) is not a human but in fact a troll who has been taken in by a childless human couple and raised as their own. Though *Border* centers on some of the same issues *The Witch* does regarding the kidnapping and brutalization of babies and small children, the forest serves a completely different function in Abbasi's film. For Tina—whose status as a troll raised in human society has estranged her from both species and isolated her from potential friends and lovers—the forest is a site she returns to repeatedly throughout the film to commune with nature and bask naked in the woodland streams. It is the only site in the film where she can not only be her authentic herself but also feel an embodied connection to something larger than herself.¹² Although wilderness settings play an important role in *Border*, the film's horrors have nothing to do with an urbanoiac fear of the countryside. We must, then, approach international ecohorror without implying a false equivalency between Nordic and the American cultural contexts.

Against the backdrop of contemporary Nordic societies, what is so destabilizing about ecohorror is that it undermines the very notion of the autonomous individual—a figure that is the basis of social cohesion and stability in the Nordic region, according to Berggren and Trägårdh's theory of statist individualism. In film after film, individuals who suppose they can transcend nature—studiously avoiding the taint of physical contagion through techniques of physical enclosure and isolation from the physical world—emerge as unsettlingly precarious ecological subjects. Another way of phrasing this is that we see figures who, in their approach to the natural world, seem to occupy a space of environmental exceptionalism, seeing themselves as "different somehow," in the words of the Swedish interviewee.

We see this move from a stance of disembodied interiority and enclosure to one of embodied transcorporeality and environmental exposure in Lars von Trier's ground-breaking experimental metafilm *Epidemic*. As the idealistic young Doctor Mesmer leaves the protective walls of the city to enter the supposedly plague-infested landscape of the countryside—approaching the world through the Cartesian dualism of scientific epistemology—Mesmer discovers that he is the carrier of the virus and his leaky body has confounded all efforts at quarantine and containment, seeding the disease throughout the countryside. We also see this characteristic oscillation between anti-ecological

In Robert Eggers's American folk horror film *The Witch*, a Puritan family in seventeenth-century New England approaches their banishment to the wilderness with fear and trembling. Frame grab from *The Witch* (dir. Robert Eggers, 2015).

In contrast to the Puritanical fear of the wilderness evinced in *The Witch*, the protagonist of Ali Abasi's Swedish fantasy-horror film *Border* frequently retreats to the forest to find peace and physical and mental rejuvenation, and to commune with the gentle woodland creatures who inhabit the space. Frame grab from *Gräns* (*Border*, dir. Ali Abbasi, 2018).

enclosure and ecological exposure in Joachim Trier's telekinetic thriller *Thelma,* this time with a more pointed gender critique that is centered on the uncanny persistence of misogyny in contemporary Nordic societies. According to the logic of the film, Nordic social models and nature imaginaries are haunted by the specter of anthropocentrism and paternalism—ghosts that manifest themselves in a father's efforts to subdue his daughter's corporeality in the same way he has mastered the rural Norwegian countryside where he lives. In both of these films, horror is generated from images of smothering and suffocation—scenarios that bring to mind the unsettlingly closed-off body posited by the anthropocentric and ecophobic dualisms the films take to task. The emergence of a fully embodied, ecological subject in these films thus represents a recognition of the fundamentally vulnerable positions transcorporeal bodies occupy in the material world.

What is more, by critiquing the benign image of contemporary Nordic societies, ecohorror also unsettles the other pillar in Berggren and Trägårdh's social theory, namely that of the sovereign state authority and the entire ideology of Nordic environmental exceptionalism it espouses. Concepts such as sustainable development, which Nordic political leaders have deployed rhetorically in an effort to reconcile unfettered economic growth with environmental sustainability, are challenged by Nordic ecohorror's repeated insistence that the friendly face of environmentalism often serves as a cover for the hidden violence of eco-isolationism, predatory privilege, and ethno-nationalism. In the Icelandic ecoslasher *Reykjavik Whale Watching Massacre* the rural horror template of American "urbanoia" films of the 1970s is deployed in the service of a self-aware parody of Icelandic parochialism and environmental exceptionalism. By bringing the bodily violence of Icelandic whaling to the fore and equating it with a homicidal and cannibalistic impulse, the film resituates the hillbillies of American rural horror that Soles writes about to the maritime pursuits of Icelandic industry, lampooning the Icelandic traditions of self-reliance and isolationism as ecologically unsustainable in a modern, globalized world. Ali Abbasi's debut film *Shelley* takes a similarly transnational approach, centering a narrative about the horrors of pregnancy and surrogacy against the backdrop of the traffic in Eastern European women's reproductive labor in contemporary Western Europe. Against Elena's materially vulnerable position as an economically disadvantaged single mother, the performative vulnerability of her Nordic host family's retreat to rustic living is shown to be underwritten by immense reserves of material privilege. As Elena's body withers away—with the implanted Nordic baby growing in her womb figuring as a parasite—we come to see the horrific biopolitical inequalities manifested in the divergent health outcomes of Eastern and Northern European bodies. In American horror auteur Ari Aster's Swedish folk horror film *Midsommar*, the implicit eco-isolationism and ecofascism of *Reykjavik* and *Shelley* find expression in brutal spectacles of ritual violence rendered in unnervingly vibrant technicolor. Though the film initially frames its interest in Hårga as an academic fascination with the charmingly antiquarian folksiness of the initially innocent-seeming agrarian commune, the spectacular violence that unfolds during the midsummer festival reveals the ethno-separatist and white supremacist territorialism at its core. As these films suggest, it is not so much the Nordic *environment* that is scary, but rather the predatory privilege and brutal xenophobia that lurks beneath the innocent face of Nordic *environmental exceptionalism*.

Seen in this light, Nordic ecohorror is about not so much the feeling of being threatened by an alien environment, but rather the unsettling loss of protective boundaries that keep the self insulated from the world and the nation insulated from the globe. These boundaries, ecohorror suggests, were always illusory. The body has never been isolated from the physical world, just as culture could never fully transcend nature. Confronted with the ecological reality of transcorporeal enmeshment—at both an individual and collective level—the arbitrary borders drawn by anthropocentric humanism give way to an unsettling new reality in which humans can no longer stand separate from the physical worlds they inhabit in a position of transcendent privilege. Instead, they must emerge as fully precarious ecological subjects, capable of hurting the natural world and being hurt by the natural world in return.

# FILMOGRAPHY

*Antichrist.* Dir. Lars von Trier. Denmark, 2009.

*Antlers.* Dir. Scott Cooper. Mexico/United States, 2021.

*Apocalypse Now.* Dir. Francis Ford Coppola. United States, 1979.

*Blood of the Beasts (Le sang des bêtes).* Dir. Georges Franju. France, 1949.

*The Blood on Satan's Claw.* Dir. Piers Haggard. United Kingdom, 1971.

*Border (Gräns).* Dir. Ali Abbasi. Sweden, 2018.

*Carrie.* Dir. Brian De Palma. United States, 1976.

*Cold Prey (Fritt vilt).* Dir. Roar Uthaug. Norway, 2006.

*Cold Prey 2 (Fritt vilt II).* Dir. Mats Stenberg. Norway, 2008.

*Cold Prey 3 (Fritt vilt III).* Dir. Mikkel Brænne Sandemose. Norway, 2010.

*Crime and Punishment (Rikos ja rangaistus).* Dir. Aki Kaurismäki. Finland, 1983.

*Dead Snow (Død snø).* Dir. Tommy Wirkola. Norway, 2009.

*Dead Snow 2: Red vs. Dead (Død snø 2).* Dir. Tommy Wirkola. Norway/Iceland/United States/United Kingdom, 2014.

*Epidemic.* Dir. Lars von Trier. Denmark, 1987.

*The Fury.* Dir. Brian De Palma. United States, 1978.

*Halloween.* Dir. John Carpenter. United States, 1978.

*Häxan (Witchcraft through the Ages).* Dir. Benjamin Christensen. Sweden, 1922.

*Hour of the Wolf (Vargtimmen).* Dir. Ingmar Bergman. Sweden, 1968.

*Insomnia.* Dir. Erik Skjoldbjærg. Norway, 1998.

*The Kingdom (Riget).* Dir. Lars von Trier. Television series. Denmark, 1994, 1997, 2022.

*Lake Bodom (Bodom).* Dir. Taneli Mustonen. Finland, 2016.

*Lake of the Dead (De dødes tjern).* Dir. Kåre Bergstrøm. Norway, 1958.

*Lamb (Dýrið).* Dir. Valdimar Jóhansson. Iceland/Sweden/Poland, 2021.

*Let the Right One In (Låt den rätte komma in).* Dir. Tomas Alfredson. Sweden, 2008.

*Midsommar.* Dir. Ari Aster. United States/Sweden, 2019.

*Night of the Living Dead.* Dir. George A. Romero. United States, 1968.

*Persona.* Dir. Ingmar Bergman. Sweden, 1966.

*The Phantom Carriage (Körkarlen)*. Dir. Victor Sjöström. Sweden, 1921.

*Psycho*. Dir. Alfred Hitchcock. United States, 1960.

*Rare Exports*. Dir. Jalmari Helander. Finland, 2010.

*Reptilicus*. Dir. Poul Bang and Sidney W. Pink. Denmark/United States, 1961.

*Reykjavik Whale Watching Massacre (Harpoon)*. Dir. Júlíus Kemp. Iceland, 2009.

*Sauna*. Dir. Antti-Jussi Annila. Finland, 2008.

*Shelley*. Dir. Ali Abbasi. Denmark/Sweden, 2016.

*The Sinful Dwarf (Dværgen)*. Dir. Vidal Raski. Denmark, 1973.

*Terror in the Midnight Sun (Rymdinvasion i Lappland; Invasion of the Animal People)*. Dir. Virgil W. Vogel. United States/Sweden, 1959.

*The Texas Chainsaw Massacre*. Dir. Tobe Hooper. United States, 1974.

*Thelma*. Dir. Joachim Trier. Norway, 2017.

*Thriller: A Cruel Picture (Thriller: En grym film)*. Dir. Bo Arne Vibenius. Sweden, 1973.

*Trollhunter (Trolljegeren)*. Dir. André Øvredal. Norway, 2010.

*Twin Peaks*. Dir. Mark Frost and David Lynch. Television series. United States, 1990–91.

*Vampyr*. Dir. Carl Theodor Dreyer. Germany/France, 1932.

*Vertigo*. Dir. Alfred Hitchcock. United States, 1958.

*Virgin Spring (Jungfrukällan)*. Dir. Ingmar Bergman. Sweden, 1960.

*What We Become (Sorgenfri)*. Dir. Bo Mikkelsen. Denmark, 2015.

*When Animals Dream (Når dyrene drømmer)*. Dir. Jonas Alexander Arnby. Denmark, 2014.

*The White Reindeer (Valkoinen peura)*. Dir. Erik Blomberg. Finland, 1954.

*The Wicker Man*. Dir. Robin Hardy. United Kingdom, 1973.

*Wilderness (Villmark)*. Dir. Pål Øie. Norway, 2003.

*The Witch (The VVITCH: A New-England Folktale)*. Dir. Robert Eggers. United States, 2015.

*Witchfinder General*. Dir. Michael Reeves. United Kingdom, 1968.

*The Wizard of Oz*. Dir. Victor Fleming. United States, 1939.

# NOTES

═══

## INTRODUCTION

1. In his recent book on the influence of the Nordic model abroad, legal scholar Michael A. Livingston dedicates a whole chapter to the marketing strategies that have been used to "sell" a particular set of supposedly distinctively Nordic values to the outside world, including—drawing directly from a branding document released by the Nordic council—"trust in each other and also, because of proximity to power, trust in leaders in society"; "new ways of thinking, focusing on creativity and innovations"; "sustainable management of the environment and development of natural resources"; "compassion, tolerance, and conviction about the equal value of all people"; and "openness and a belief in everyone's right to express their opinions." Livingston, *Dreamworld or Dystopia?*, 25–26.

2. See the World Happiness Report (WHR) website for more details on the methodologies used and for an archive of reports from recent years. Although there is nuance to the findings of these reports, the most widely publicized annual marker of the WHR is its yearly Happiness Index rankings, which are most often topped by a Nordic country. On March 19, 2021, the WHR published a press release that highlighted this, titled "In a Lamentable Year, Finland Again Is the Happiest Country in the World." The rankings, then, serve as a kind of digest that simplifies the report for easy public consumption, a distillation that reinforces the utopian Nordic happiness narrative every spring when the WHR is released.

3. The height of the recent Nordic happiness bubble in the Anglo-American lifestyle publishing markets seems to have been between roughly 2016 and 2019. Representative titles of lifestyle books on the "secrets" of *hygge* include Wiking, *The Little Book of Hygge: Danish Secrets to Happy Living;* and Johansen, *How to Hygge: The Nordic Secrets to a Happy Life.* Books on *lagom* include Brantmark, *Lagom (Not Too Little, Not Too Much): The Swedish Art of Living a Balanced, Happy Life;* and Dunne, *Lagom: The Swedish Art of Balanced Living.* Books on *sisu* include Nylund, *Sisu: The Finnish Art of Courage;* and Pantzar, *The Finnish Way: Finding Courage, Wellness, and Happiness*

*through the Power of Sisu.* For a pan-Nordic approach to happiness, see Partanen, *The Nordic Theory of Everything: In Search of a Better Life.*

4. Quoted in Margolis, "Bernie Sanders Wants Us to Be More Equitable Like Sweden." See also Booth, "I Live in Denmark"; and Norberg, "Sweden's Lessons for America."

5. Brodén, *Folkhemmets skuggbilder,* 12.

6. Stougaard-Nielsen, *Scandinavian Crime Fiction,* 9.

7. The first two seasons of *The Kingdom* aired on the Danish public television service (DR) between 1994 and 1997. A planned third season was derailed due to the death of two of the lead actors of the series. More than twenty-five years after the series premiere, a third season, titled *The Kingdom: Exodus,* was announced by the production company Zentropa. The new season will again be directed by Lars von Trier and cowritten by von Trier and Niels Vørsel.

8. "Nordic ecohorror" is a term of convenience that I use to refer to media created by or dealing with the concerns of nonindigenous inhabitants of the Nordic region. Not only is horror a genre that is difficult to find examples of in Nordic indigenous cinema, but the nature mythologies and notions of individualism and community that prevail in the indigenous communities of the region are so distinct from those that prevail in nonindigenous communities—which bear the cultural imprint of modern Western anthropocentrism and humanism—that including indigenous media from the Nordic or circumpolar Arctic region would make it difficult to construct a coherent argument about the works discussed.

9. *Meshwork* is drawn from the eco-materialist theory of anthropologist Tim Ingold, who proposes the term as a descriptive designator for the complex web of ever-emergent, dynamic relationships of correspondence between living organisms, material environments, and tangible things. He proposes this term as a more vital and coresponsive image than the comparatively static imagery employed by the various "assemblage theories" adopted by eco-materialist theorists in the wake of Bruno Latour's actor-network theory (Ingold, "Toward an Ecology of Materials," 437). It also coincidentally resonates with the term *mesh,* which ecocritic Timothy Morton uses to describe the vast web of ecological interconnectedness that runs between things (Morton, *The Ecological Thought,* 15).

10. Alaimo, *Bodily Natures.*

11. The term *natureculture* was coined by Donna Haraway in *The Companion Species Manifesto* in 2003, in which Haraway shows how the joint lives of dogs and people effectively collapse the dichotomy between "nature" and "culture." As Latimer and Miele write ("Naturecultures?," 11), the term suggests "that nature and culture are not two different things, but a matrix of contrasts." Thus, an "individual human body is not the

product of the interaction of nature (body, biology, genes) and culture (nature, education, technology)," but is instead a site of "natureculture."

12. Alaimo, *Bodily Natures*, 2.

13. Morton, *Ecology without Nature*.

14. Tidwell and Soles, *Fear and Nature*, 5.

15. Hennig, Jonasson, and Degerman, *Nordic Narratives*, 5.

16. Sustainable development as a concept was popularized by the seminal 1987 UN environmental publication *Our Common Future*, a report on the environment headed by the former Norwegian prime minister Gro Harlem Brundtland that became a foundational text of modern multilateral environmental efforts. The report attempted to build on the emerging spirit of environmental diplomacy that was inaugurated with the United Nations Conference on the Human Environment, held in Stockholm in July 1972. The prominence of both the Stockholm Conference and the Brundtland Commission Report in the history of multilateral environmentalism has effectively reinforced the Nordic region's reputation for exceptional leadership in issues of the environment and sustainability.

17. Lindell and Karagozoglu, "Comparative Environmental Behaviour," 39.

18. Witozscek, *The Origins of the "Regime of Goodness,"* 53.

19. Witozscek *The Origins of the "Regime of Goodness,"* 53.

20. See Nordic Council, "Strategy for International Branding"; see also Heise, *Sense of Place and Sense of Planet*, 28–50.

21. See Visit Finland, "Everyman's Rights—The Right to Roam," https://www.visit finland.com/en/articles/finnish-everyman-rights-the-right-to-roam/; Visit Norway, "The Right to Roam: Joys and Responsibilities," https://www.visitnorway.com/plan -your-trip/travel-tips-a-z/right-of-access/; Visit Sweden, "Freedom to Roam," https:// visitsweden.com/what-to-do/nature-outdoors/nature/sustainable-and-rural-tourism /freedomtoroam/; and Visit Sweden, "About the Right to Access Swedish Nature," https://visitsweden.com/what-to-do/nature-outdoors/nature/sustainable-and-rural -tourism/about-the-right-of-public-access/.

22. This notion is borne out in a study of recent development patterns in Denmark, which that have chipped away at tracts of previously undeveloped land, leading Hojring to suggest that the vaunted tradition of Everyman's Rights has been significantly curtailed, a situation that poses real-life impediments to accessing nature and runs counter to the Nordic environmental ideal of "sustainable development."

23. Rust and Soles, "Ecohorror Special Cluster," 509–10, emphasis added.

24. Tidwell, "Ecohorror," 115.

25. Tidwell, "Ecohorror," 116.

26. Tidwell and Soles, *Fear and Nature*, 3; see also Williams, "Melodrama Revised."

27. Mossner, *Affective Ecologies*, 3.

28. Thunberg, "World Economic Forum 2019 Special Address," emphasis added. See also Tidwell and Soles's discussion of Thunberg's fear-based rhetoric in Tidwell and Soles, *Fear and Nature*, 5.

29. See the Klimabrølet website, https://klimabrolet.no/.

30. For the original manuscript version of the prose poem in the original Norwegian, see Munch, MM T 2367, https://www.emunch.no/HYBRIDNo-MM_T2367 .xhtml.

31. Other young Scandinavian climate activists have taken similar inspiration from Munch's expressions of angst and dread in confronting the image of a natural environment in pain. In response to the painting, the fifteen-year-old Norwegian climate activist Penelope Lea recently penned a text attributing her own concern for the environment to her first confrontation with the painting: "Now I stood with my eyes closed in front of *The Scream*. I opened them again. For a little while I felt like I was inside the painting. At the same beaches, tracks, stones, under the same pines, the sky. But now, everything I knew, everything I loved, screamed. It was at that exact time I first became a climateactivist [*sic*]." See Munchmuseet, "Environmentalist Penelope Lea Interprets *The Scream*," https://www.munchmuseet.no/en/The-Scream/environ mentalist-penelope-lea-interprets-the-scream/.

32. On the connections between Greta Thunberg's panic-based appeal and the concepts of eco-fear and ecophobia, see Tidwell and Soles, *Fear and Nature*, 5. See also Alex and Deborah, "Ecophobia," on the productive potential of eco-fear in indigenous worldviews.

33. Estok, "Painful Material Realities," 130, emphasis added.

34. Cohen, "Foreword," ix.

35. Tidwell and Soles, *Fear and Nature*, 5.

36. Berggren and Trägårdh, "Pippi Longstocking," 16. See also Berggren and Trägårdh's book-length articulation of the "statist individualism" argument in their provocatively titled study *Är svensken människa?* (Is the Swede Human?), translated into English as *The Swedish Theory of Love* (Seattle: University of Washington Press, 2022).

37. Berggren and Trägårdh, "Pippi Longstocking," 19.

38. See Haeckel, *Generelle Morphologie*.

39. Margulis, "Symbiogenesis and Symbioticism," 3.

40. Ingold, *Being Alive*, 29.

41. Clark, *Being There*, 53.

42. Clover, "Her Body, Himself," 189. See also Williams, "Film Bodies."

43. Clover, "Her Body, Himself," 189.

44. Ingold, "On Human Correspondence," 11.

45. Durkheim, *The Rules of Sociological Method*, 39.

46. Morton, *Humankind*, 101.

47. Heise, *Sense of Place and Sense of Planet*, 17–67.

48. Gustafsson and Kääpä, *Nordic Genre Film*, 9–10.

49. Nestingen, *Crime and Fantasy in Scandinavia*, 53.

50. Gustafsson and Kääpä, *Nordic Genre Film*, 4; Soila, "Introduction," 3; Iversen, "Between Art and Genre."

51. Gustafsson and Kääpä, *Nordic Genre Film*, 4.

52. One notable exception to this tendency is Alexis Luko's analysis of the acoustics of horror in *Persona* and *Hour of the Wolf.* Luko, "Listening to Ingmar Bergman's Monsters."

53. See Hakola, "Nordic Vampires"; Wright, "Vampire in the Stockholm Suburbs"; Karlsson, "The Vampire and the Anxieties of a Globalizing Swedish Welfare State."

54. Iversen, "Between Art and Genre," 336.

55. Kääpä, *Ecology and Contemporary Nordic Cinemas*, 67.

56. Joyce, "Re-enchanting the Nordic Everyday."

## *One* THE PLAGUE IS HERE

1. See Iversen, "Between Art and Genre"; Gustafsson and Kääpä, *Nordic Genre Film*, 1–4.

2. Alaimo, *Bodily Natures*, 2.

3. Alaimo, *Bodily Natures*, 146.

4. Ingold, *Being Alive*, 29.

5. Chen, *Animacies*, 2. Building on the notion of "animacy hierarchies" in the linguistic anthropology of Michael Silverstein, Chen has used the concept of animacy to "interrogate how the fragile division between animate and inanimate—that is, beyond human and animal—is relentlessly produced and policed and maps important political consequences of that distinction." Chen points out that categories such as race, gender, ethnicity, nationality, sexuality, disability status, and animality have been used in the service of an uneven distribution of biopolitical capital, forming a hierarchy that situates the healthy white male at the top as the most animate and "alive" form of life.

6. Stephen A. Rust and Carter Soles ("Ecohorror Special Cluster," 509) have argued against defining ecohorror narrowly as "those instances in texts when nature strikes back against humans as punishment for environmental disruption."

7. Estok, "Painful Material Realities," 131.

8. Estok, "Painful Material Realities," 131.

9. Estok, "Painful Material Realities," 134.

10. Wells, *The Horror Genre*, 114.

11. Reyes, *Body Gothic*, 52.

12. Tidwell, "Spiraling Inward and Outward," 42.

13. Wald, *Contagious*, 2.

14. Alaimo, *Exposed*, 94.

15. Ingold, "Toward an Ecology of Materials," 438.

16. Morton, *The Ecological Thought*, 28.

17. Morton, *The Ecological Thought*, 30.

18. Witozscek, *The Origins of the "Regime of Goodness,"* 53.

19. Witozscek, *The Origins of the "Regime of Goodness,"* 53.

20. As an aside, Claes seems to be anticipating the production reforms that would take shape in Denmark and the other Nordic countries with the introduction of the 50/50 production schemes and the restructuring of the national film institutes, changes that paved the way for a more genre-forward, commercially oriented—and often more gorily material—form of filmmaking in the region, as elaborated in Iversen, "Between Art and Genre"; and Gustafsson and Kääpä, *Nordic Genre Film*.

21. Moreover, the paracinematic discourse around *Epidemic* emphasizes the authenticity and documentary-like quality of *Epidemic,* as von Trier claims that the final shots depict an actor actually being hypnotized and becoming terrified for her life. See Bigelow, "Authorised Viewing."

## *Two* ABJECT ECOLOGIES

1. Beery, "Nordic in Nature," 95. See also Henderson and Vikander, *Nature First*.

2. Gelter, "Friluftsliv," 78.

3. Robinson, "Thelma's Director."

4. Carol J. Clover and Linda Williams have both described horror as a "body genre," since it appeals directly to the bodily responses of its viewers, which it often does by violating the integrity of bodies on screen and bringing bodily fluids—particularly blood—to the surface. See Clover, *Men, Women and Chain Saws;* and Williams, "Film Bodies."

5. Kristeva, *Powers of Horror*, 3.

6. Kristeva, *Powers of Horror*, 3.

7. Kristeva, *Powers of Horror*, 1.

8. Kristeva, *Powers of Horror*, 2.

9. Alaimo, *Bodily Natures*, 2.

10. Ingold, "Toward an Ecology of Materials," 437.

11. Ingold, "Toward an Ecology of Materials," 438.

12. Hennefeld and Sammond, *Abjection Incorporated*, 4.

13. Hennefeld and Sammond, *Abjection Incorporated*, 2.

14. Hennefeld and Sammond, *Abjection Incorporated*, 2.

15. Manne, *Down Girl*, xxi.

16. Manne, *Down Girl*, 18.

17. Manne, *Down Girl*, 3.

18. Alaimo, *Exposed*, 94.

19. Foucault, *Discipline and Punish*, 104.

20. Foucault, *Discipline and Punish*, 128.

21. Kristeva, *Powers of Horror*, 3.

## *Three* MEN, WOMEN, AND HARPOONS

1. Kääpä, *Ecology and Contemporary Nordic Cinema*, 72–76.

2. One recent indicator of the popular currency of the final girl trope was the publication of Grady Hendrix's *The Final Girl Support Group*, a New York Times best-selling horror novel that imagines the kinds of lingering psychological aftereffects final girls would suffer in their lives after escaping massacre.

3. Nordfjörd, *Dagur Kári's "Nói the Albino,"* 34.

4. Nordfjörd, *Dagur Kári's "Nói the Albino,"* 34.

5. Nordfjörd, *Dagur Kári's "Nói the Albino,"* 35–36.

6. As Pietari Kääpä notes in *Ecology and Contemporary Nordic Cinemas* (11), "The connection between nature and national identity is not a 'natural' one or in any sense economically or environmentally sustainable. By this I mean that national identity—especially when it comes to nature—is a constructed notion that depends on a range of factors to do with the global economy, geopolitics, transnational cultural flow and domestic consideration." In this sense, ecocritical approaches can play the crucial role of "denaturalizing" the connection between identity and landscape constructed by nationalist discourse.

7. Skvirsky, *The Process Genre*, 2.

8. See Mee, *The Pulse in Cinema*.

9. Skvirsky, *The Process Genre*, 4, 5.

10. For more background and for the founding documents of the ICRW, see International Whaling Commission, "History and Purpose," https://iwc.int/history-and-purpose.

11. "Iceland to Resume Whaling," CNN, August 16, 2003.

12. Brydon, "The Predicament of Nature," 226.

13. Brydon, "The Predicament of Nature," 229.

14. Brydon, "The Predicament of Nature," 226.
15. Brydon, "The Predicament of Nature," 227.
16. Clover, *Men, Women, and Chain Saws*, 27.
17. Clover, *Men, Women, and Chain Saws*, 30.
18. Clover, *Men, Women, and Chain Saws*, 31.
19. Clover, *Men, Women, and Chain Saws*, 32.
20. Clover, *Men, Women, and Chain Saws*, 41.
21. Clover, *Men, Women, and Chain Saws*, 33.
22. Clover, *Men, Women, and Chain Saws*, 34.
23. Clover, *Men, Women, and Chain Saws*, 40.
24. Iversen, "Between Art and Genre."
25. Iversen, "Between Art and Genre."
26. Kääpä, *Ecology and Contemporary Nordic Cinemas*, 67.
27. Kääpä, *Ecology and Contemporary Nordic Cinemas*, 74.
28. Clover, *Men, Women, and Chain Saws*, 134.
29. Clover, *Men, Women, and Chain Saws*, 134.
30. Soles, "Sympathy for the Devil," 248.
31. See Alaimo, *Exposed*, 94.
32. The film's fixation on meat production industries and the implication of cannibalism are just two of many references *Reykjavik* makes to *Texas Chainsaw Massacre* and other low-budget American rural slasher films of the 1970s. On the environmental politics of American rural slasher films, see Soles, "Sympathy for the Devil."
33. Rust and Soles, "Ecohorror Special Cluster," 509–10.
34. Alaimo, *Exposed*, 3; Haraway, *Staying with the Trouble*, 3; Barclay and Tidwell, "Introduction," 276.
35. Seymour, *Bad Environmentalism*, 232; Barclay and Tidwell, "Introduction," 276.
36. Barclay and Tidwell, "Introduction," 276.


*Four* MIGRANT LABORS

1. According to the film's credits, *Shelley* was shot on location in Copenhagen and Villands-Vånga, a rural municipality in southern Sweden. The film never identifies the fictional setting with place names, instead opting to establish a vaguely transnational Scandinavian setting, with local characters using English while speaking to Elena and a blend of Norwegian, Danish, and Swedish among themselves, a mixture that allows the film to take advantage of Nordic coproduction financing models. Though he was raised in Iran, Abassi has lived much of his adult life in Europe and is a graduate of the Danish Film School who speaks fluent Danish. In interviews about the film, he has spoken of having broadly Scandinavian cultural ideas in mind when making

*Shelley* and comparing his own Iranian frame of reference with his experiences as an outsider living in Scandinavia. See Hjort, "Debutanten."

2. Hjort, "Debutanten."

3. In a recent study, a group of social scientists studying recreation habits and spiritual beliefs in Denmark, Sweden, and Estonia argued that in these famously secular societies (supposedly among the least religious in the world), the experience of transcendence has not gone away but rather has been "relocated" from sites of organized worship to individual recreation in nature. The study also argues that these quasi-religious "experiences of transcendence" are no longer "confined to settings that we generally recognize as religious." Instead, settings that are generally regarded as secular, such as undeveloped "natural" spaces like the forest or the seaside, "are permeated by transcendence in a way that we and our interlocutors easily recognize as like religion." Thurfjell et al., "The Relocation of Transcendence," 191–92.

4. According to Midttun and Olsson ("Eco-Modernity Nordic Style," 205), when "realities are seen as not permitting pursuit of one without undermining the other," in contemporary Nordic societies, "short-term socio-economic, rather than long-term ecological, sustainability prevails." Though they acknowledge the difficult environmental realities that are obscured by the rhetoric of "sustainable development"—which has been central to Nordic environmentalism since the publication of the Brundtland report in 1987—Midttun and Olsson argue that "reconcil[ing] socio-economic and ecological sustainability in a pragmatic reorientation toward eco-modernity" may be aided by reorienting national climate efforts toward transnational Nordic environmental cooperation.

5. Just as environmental activists have critiqued the utopian rhetoric of eco-modernity and sustainable development as not being radical enough to meet the urgency of global climate change, ecohorror narratives such as *Shelley* have uncovered the hypocrisies of Nordic approaches to nature that are built on a paradoxical alignment of eco-sustainability and material privilege. One recent example of this critique of eco-modernity came after the UN Climate Conference (COP 26) in Glasgow, where newly elected Norwegian prime minister Jonas Gahr Støre argued that Norwegian natural gas reserves were not part of the problem but in fact could be part of the climate solution, especially when paired with the carbon-capture technologies now being developed. In response to Støre's speech before the assembly, in which he shared his business-friendly, sustainable development approach to climate change, the Climate Action Network named Norway "Fossil of the Day" for November 2, 2021, writing that "Norway likes to play the climate champion but behind closed doors, new prime minister Jonas Gahr Støre is gaining a reputation as a fossil fuel cheerleader." Climate Action Network, "Fossil of the Day 02 November 2021—Norway, Japan and Australia," https://climatenetwork.org/resource/fossil-of-the-day-02-november-2021/.

6. Nordic Council of Ministers, "Strategy for International Branding of the Nordic Region," 14.

7. Phil Zuckerman's book *Society without God* is one example of this line of reasoning.

8. See Clover, *Men, Women, and Chain Saws*, 65–113.

9. Mrozewicz, *Beyond Eastern Noir*, 2.

10. This culturally specific critique of Nordic privilege and its relationship to nature discourses in the region is what makes *Shelley* a more radically ecocritical film than Lars von Trier's infamous and influential *Antichrist* (2009)—a film that *Shelley* bears some superficial resemblance to, with its lingering shots of menacing-looking trees and its emphasis on the psychological horror of rural isolation. Like many of von Trier's films, the setting of *Antichrist* has an abstract, placeless quality. Though it was shot in southern Sweden, just like *Shelley*, its setting is meant to signify an ironically malevolent, cursed version of Eden. In *Antichrist*, it is precisely the emergence of "nature," whether in the form of a talking fox or a matrilineal female connection to witchcraft that poses the threat, whereas in *Shelley* the malign quality perceivable in nature ultimately has more to do with human attitudes toward the natural world.

11. To cite just a few recent examples: the Swedish supernatural crime-horror television series *Jordskott* (2015–17), the British-Norwegian folk horror film *Sacrifice* (2020), and American director Ari Aster's Swedish folk horror film *Midsommar*.

12. Livingston, *Dreamworld or Dystopia*, 93.

13. On the connections between vitalism and Scandinavian culture, see Bigelow, "The Voice of the Blood"; Hvidberg-Hansen and Oelsner, *The Spirit of Vitalism*; and Vassenden, *Norsk Vitalisme*.

14. Oelsner, "Healthy Nature," 159.

15. In vitalist body discourses, the robust, idealized Nordic body was defined with reference to the supposedly decadent or degenerate bodies of racialized others, including linguistic, religious, and cultural minorities with a long history in the region, such as Jews, the Sami, and the Finnish people. As a cult of health and physical/cultural rejuvenation, vitalism was informed by the moralizing, reactionary voices that sought to diagnose the cultural "sicknesses" of the decadent fin de siècle, including the Jewish-Hungarian physician and cultural critic Max Nordau, whose two-volume treatise *Entartung* (*Degeneration*, 1892–93) diagnosed a range of social and cultural ills of the age through moralizing case studies examining the "degenerate art" of figures like Friedrich Nietzsche, Oscar Wilde, and Henrik Ibsen.

16. Gellner, *Nations and Nationalism*, 190.

17. Forchtner and Kølvraa, "The Nature of Nationalism," 205.

18. Smith, *The Ethnic Origins of Nations*, 190.

19. Forchtner and Kølvraa, "The Nature of Nationalism," 205.

20. Dieudonné, "Electromagnetic Hypersensitivity."

21. Over the last two decades, the intersection of systemic environmental and racial inequality has been framed as "environmental racism" by scholars in many disciplines studying how pollution and industrial contamination affects communities of color, with most of the literature focusing on conditions in the United States. For representative examples see Waldron, *There's Something in the Water*; Zimring, *Clean and White*; and Checker, *Polluted Promises*. More recently, scholars have turned their attention to examples in other contexts, such as Eastern Europe. Dunajeva and Kostka, "Racialized Politics of Garbage."

22. See Kjellman, "A Whiter Shade of Pale."

23. Clover, *Men, Women, and Chain Saws*, 66.

24. Singleton, "Interpreting Taskscapes," 115.

25. This sense that environmentalism is equated with Nordic identity also manifests itself in public attitudes toward migrant (and perceived migrant) communities in the Nordic region, with polls showing that a majority assume migrant communities to be less environmentally conscious than ethnically Nordic communities.

26. The domestic and international success of Norwegian Lars Mytting's bestselling book *Hel ved* (translated into English as *Norwegian Wood: Chopping, Stacking, and Drying Wood the Scandinavian Way*) is one indicator of the association between Scandinavian identity and cultivation of outdoor skills like wood chopping and stacking. After the English translation received the British Book Industry Award for Non-Fiction Book of the Year, Mytting remarked that he was delighted and surprised at the success of the book outside Scandinavia: "In the beginning we said: 'Well, it's a book that could only have happened in Norway.' But now the interest is all over." Caroline Sanderson, "Mytting Emerges Chop of the Pile," The Bookseller, May 31, 2016, https://www.thebookseller.com/profile/mytting-emerges-chop-pile-330723.

27. Alaimo, *Exposed*, 94.

28. Argüelles, "Privileged Socionatures," 651, emphasis added.

29. Grønstad, "Conditional Vulnerability," 21.

30. Nordic Council of Ministers, "Strategy for International Branding of the Nordic Region," 19–21, emphasis added.

31. Agamben, *Homo Sacer*, 47–48.

32. Scovell, *Folk Horror*, 18.

## *Five* FOLK HORROR AND *FOLKHEMMET*

1. Discussing the recent popularity of folk and rural horror in such films as *Midsommar*, *The Witch* (dir. Robert Eggers, 2015), *Antlers* (dir. Scott Cooper, 2021), and the Icelandic production *Lamb* (dir. Valdimar Jóhansson, 2021), Erik Piepenburg writes that the genre has proven to be an enduring one: "As long as humans mess with Mother

Nature and keep regenerating old hatreds, horror will hold up its mirror." Piepenberg, "Modern Times Call for Folk Horror."

2. Adam Scovell, "Where to Begin with Folk Horror." British Film Institute, June 8, 2016, https://www.bfi.org.uk/features/where-begin-with-folk-horror.

3. Scovell, *Folk Horror*, 7.

4. See Aster and Eggers, "Deep Cuts"; Handler, "'*Midsommar* Will Be a *Wizard of Oz* for Perverts,'"; and Nicholson, "'Midsommar Is 'The Wizard of Oz' for Perverts.'"

5. Ahmari, "Ari Aster's Moral Horror." See also Ross Douthat's discussion of the film in *the National Review* for another example of the fascination with the film in the American conservative press. Douthat, "*Midsommar* Casts a Transfixing Scandinavian Spell."

6. Still, as Erik Piepenburg writes in "Modern Times Call for Folk Horror," there is a good reason why folk horror may lend itself more readily to being co-opted by conservative commentators: "Although there are rich folk horror cinema traditions around the globe, folk horror films have been mostly made by white men, often about white people's anxieties."

7. Durkheim, *The Rules of Sociological Method*, 51.

8. Durkheim, *The Rules of Sociological Method*, 59, emphasis in original.

9. Durkheim, *The Rules of Sociological Method*, 52.

10. Durkheim, *The Rules of Sociological Method*, 52.

11. Durkheim, *The Rules of Sociological Method*, 39.

12. Ingold, "On Human Correspondence," 11.

13. Ingold, "On Human Correspondence," 11.

14. Ingold, "On Human Correspondence," 10.

15. Ingold, "On Human Correspondence," 10.

16. Ingold, "On Human Correspondence," 13.

17. See Ehrlich, "Ari Aster"; Aster and Eggers, "Deep Cuts."

18. On the concept of blind space and how it has been utilized in cinematic horror—using Carl Th. Dreyer's seminal horror film *Vampyr* as an example—see Bigelow, "Lurking in the Blind Space"; and Peirse, "The Impossibility of Vision."

19. Scovell has described isolation as one of the key links in the "folk horror chain," writing that isolation is a necessary precursor to the "skewed belief systems" that folk horror is preoccupied with. Scovell, *Folk Horror*, 18.

20. For representative examples of internet sources that seek to educate viewers on how to spot these "Easter eggs" in *Midsommar*, see Cameron, "Midsommar"; Harkness, "Things You Only Notice the Second Time." The prevalence of such community-based decoding practices around *Midsommar* suggests that part of the spectatorial pleasure of watching the film is that its complexity could give rise to the type of interactive, internet-based fan discourse that Jason Mittell has called "forensic fandom" in connection with narrative complexity in contemporary American television. Mittell, *Complex TV*.

21. See Rydgren, "Radical Right-Wing Populism."

22. Tomson, "The Rise of Sweden Democrats."

23. Scovell, *Folk Horror*, 17.

24. Hutchings, "Ten Great British Rural Horror Films."

25. Scovell, *Folk Horror*, 18.

26. This is similar to the way the setting in northern Norway justifies the blinding white light of the neo-noir *Insomnia* (dir. Erik Skjoldbjærg, 1997), a surprising stylistic choice given the typical preference for low lighting and expressive shadows in film noir.

27. As Ulrika Kjellman has written in an article appropriately titled "A Whiter Shade of Pale," the Swedish State Institute for Race Biology (Statens Institut för Rasbiologi, SIRB) in Uppsala played a central role in visually constructing a white Nordic racial identity in the 1920s and 30s, an identity that was given scientific legitimacy by SIRB's photographic publications.

28. For a detailed discussion of blackness in horror films, see Coleman, *Horror Noire*.

29. On the concept of implicit whiteness and its place in ethno-separatist movements in contemporary Scandinavia, see Teitelbaum, "Implicitly White."

30. The English translations of the speech given here are taken from the subtitles included in the film. Much of the Swedish in other scenes is purposely untranslated, putting audience members who do not understand Swedish in the shoes of the American and British outsiders, who are frequently purposely excluded by the group members as they speak to each other in Swedish. That this speech—along with a few other ritual speech acts in the film—is translated indicates that all viewers are meant to learn some of the mythology of the commune, including this folk tale of the evil figure known as "the Black One." The dance is thus meant to signify a life-affirming rejection not only of a particular figure, but more broadly, of darkness itself. The slippage between darkness and Blackness evident in the English translation indicates that white supremacy and folk religion are seamlessly woven together in the commune's belief system.

31. As we have already seen in chapter 4, however, the life-affirming rhetoric of vitalism implicit in the elder's speech has cultural-historical connections to protofascist ideologies of racial biology.

32. This connection to a gynophobic/ecophobic approach to landscape in folk horror helps account for some of the praise of *Midsommar* in conservative political circles. The connection between gynophobia and ecophobia is particularly evident in Lars von Trier's *Antichrist*, which is something of an outlier in Nordic ecohorror in its depiction of the environment as truly malevolent. For an ecocritical reading of *Antichrist*, see Thomsen, "Foggy Signs."

33. Ingold, *The Life of Lines*, 3.

34. Ingold, *The Life of Lines*, 6.

35. Ingold, *The Life of Lines*, 6.

36. Morton, *Humankind*, 101.

37. Morton, *Humankind*, 103.

38. Morton, *Humankind*, 102.

39. Morton, *Humankind*, 103.

40. Morton, *Humankind*, 103.

41. Morton, *Humankind*, 103.

## CONCLUSION

1. Kuusela, "Scandinavia's Horror Renaissance."

2. Nordic Council of Ministers, "Strategy for International Branding of the Nordic Region," 21.

3. Witoszek, *The Origins of the "Regime of Goodness,"* 54–55.

4. Thurfjell et al., "The Relocation of Transcendence," 190.

5. Clover, *Men, Women, and Chain Saws*, 124. On the connection between Little Red Riding Hood and rape culture, see Marshall, *Graphic Girlhoods*, 49–61.

6. Clover, *Men, Women, and Chain Saws*, 124.

7. In *Landscapes of Fear*, cultural geographer Yi-Fu Tuan has described the woods as one of the archetypal "landscapes of fear." Fairy tales scholar Sara Maitland has drawn attention to the persistence of irrational fears of the forest into adulthood in *Gossip from the Forest*. And cultural historian Elizabeth Parker has approached the forest through the lens of the eco-gothic and dark ecology in *The Forest and the Ecogothic*.

8. Soles, "Sympathy for the Devil," 237.

9. Soles, "Sympathy for the Devil," 248.

10. For ecocritical readings of *Jordskott*, see Bruhn, "Ecology as Pre-Text?"; Souch, "Transformations of the Evil Forest."

11. There has indeed been a recent scholarly interest in the intersection of privilege and guilt in the Nordic cultures, the most notable expression of which is the interdisciplinary research project Scandinavian Narratives of Guilt and Privilege in an Age of Globalization, headed by Elisabeth Oxfeldt at the University of Oslo. For one outcome of that project that speaks specifically to Norwegian environmental guilt, see Rees, "Privilege, Innocence, and 'Petro-Guilt.'"

12. In her ecstatic communion with the woodlands, Tina's approach brings to mind a newly en vogue Nordic nature ritual known as a *skogsbad* (forest bath), a term that has recently made its way into the Swedish lexicon and has become part of the strategies of Nordic self-branding abroad. See Visit Sweden, "Immerse Yourself in the Swedish Forest," October 12, 2021, https://visitsweden.com/what-to-do/nature-outdoors/forest-bathing/.

# BIBLIOGRAPHY

Agamben, Giorgio. *Homo Sacer: Sovereign Power and Bare Life.* Translated by Daniel Heller-Roazen. Stanford, CA: Stanford University Press, 1998.

Ahmari, Sohrab. "Ari Aster's Moral Horror." *American Conservative.* September 25, 2020.

Alaimo, Stacy. *Bodily Natures: Science, Environment, and the Material Self.* Bloomington: Indiana University Press, 2010.

———. *Exposed: Environmental Politics and Pleasures in Posthuman Times.* Minneapolis: University of Minnesota Press, 2016.

Alex, Rayson K., and S. Susan Deborah. "Ecophobia, Reverential Eco-fear, and Indigenous Worldviews." *ISLE: Interdisciplinary Studies in Literature and Environment* 2, no. 2 (Spring 2019): 422–29.

Argüelles, Lucía. 2021. "Privileged Socionatures and Naturalization of Privilege: Untangling Environmental Privilege Dimensions." *Professional Geographer* 73, no. 4 (2021): 650–61.

Aster, Ari, and Robert Eggers. "Deep Cuts with Robert Eggers and Ari Aster," A24 Films, July 17, 2019, https://a24films.com/notes/2019/07/deep-cuts-with-robert-eggers-and-ari-aster.

Barclay, Bridgitte, and Christy Tidwell. "Introduction: Mutant Bears, Defrosted Parasites and Cellphone Swarms: Creature Features and the Environment." *Science Fiction Film and Television* 14, no. 3 (Autumn 2021): 269–77.

Barker, Andrew. "'Thelma': A Slow-Burning Nordic 'Carrie.'" Special Broadcasting Service, December 10, 2021, https://www.sbs.com.au/movies/article/2017/09/16/thelma-slow-burning-nordic-carrie.

Beery, Thomas H. "Nordic in Nature: Friluftsliv and Environmental Connectedness." *Environmental Education Research* 19, no. 1 (2013): 94–117.

Berggren, Henrik, and Lars Trägårdh. *Är svensken människa? Gemenskap och oberoende i det moderna Sverige.* Stockholm: Norstedts, 2015.

———. "Pippi Longstocking: The Autonomous Child and the Moral Logic of the Swedish Welfare State." In *Swedish Modernism: Architecture, Consumption, and the*

*Swedish Welfare State*, edited by Helena Mattsson and Sven-Olov Wallenstein, 10–23. London: Black Dog Publishing, 2010.

———. *The Swedish Theory of Love: Individualism and Social Trust in Modern Sweden.* Translated by Stephen Donovan. Seattle: University of Washington Press, 2022.

Berman, Patricia G. "*Mens sana in corpore sano*: Munchs vitale kropper." In *Livskraft: Vitalismen som kunstnerisk impuls*, 45–64. Oslo: Munch-Museet, 2006.

Bigelow, Benjamin. "Authorised Viewing: Lars von Trier's Models of Spectatorship." *Scandinavica* 61, no. 1 (2022): 19–37.

———. "Lurking in the Blind Space: *Vampyr* and the Multilinguals." *Journal of Scandinavian Cinema* 5, no. 3 (2015): 223–39.

———. "The Voice of the Blood: Vitalism and the Acoustic in Knut Hamsun's *Pan* (1894)." *Scandinavian Studies* 90, no. 4 (2018): 531–52.

Booth, Michael. "I Live in Denmark. Bernie Sanders's Nordic Dream Is Worth Fighting For, Even if He Loses." *Vox*, March 1, 2016.

Brantmark, Niki. *Lagom (Not Too Little, Not Too Much): The Swedish Art of Living a Balanced, Happy Life.* New York: Harper Collins, 2017.

Brodén, Daniel. *Folkhemmets skuggbilder: En kulturanalytisk genrestudie av svensk kriminalfiktion i film och tv.* Stockholm: Ekholm & Tegebjer, 2008.

Bruhn, Jørgen. "Ecology as Pre-Text? The Paradoxical Presence of Ecological Thematics in Contemporary Scandinavian Quality TV." *Journal of Aesthetics and Culture* 10, no. 2 (2018): 66–73.

Brydon, Anne. "The Predicament of Nature: Keiko the Whale and the Cultural Politics of Whaling in Iceland." *Anthropological Quarterly* 79, no. 2 (2006): 225–60.

Cameron, Jack. "*Midsommar*: Fifteen Hidden Details Everyone Completely Missed." Screenrant, March 4, 2020, https://screenrant.com/midsommar-hidden-details/.

Checker, Melissa. *Polluted Promises: Environmental Racism and the Search for Justice in a Southern Town.* New York: New York University Press, 2005.

Chen, Mel Y. *Animacies: Biopolitics, Racial Mattering, and Queer Affect.* Durham: Duke University Press, 2012.

Clark, Andy. *Being There: Putting Brain, Body, and World Together Again.* Cambridge, MA: MIT Press, 1997.

Clover, Carol J. "Her Body, Himself." *Representations* 20 (Autumn 1987): 187–228.

———. *Men, Women, and Chainsaws: Gender in Modern Horror Film.* Princeton, NJ: Princeton University Press, 1992.

Cohen, Jeffrey Jerome. "Foreword: Storied Matter." In *Material Ecocriticism*, edited by Serenella Iovino and Serpil Oppermann, ix–xiv. Bloomington: Indiana University Press, 2018.

Coleman, Robin R. Means. *Horror Noire: Blacks in American Horror Films from the 1890s to Present.* New York: Routledge, 2011.

Dawkins, Richard. *The Extended Phenotype: The Long Reach of the Gene.* Oxford: Oxford University Press, 1999.

Dieudonné, Maël. "Electromagnetic Hypersensitivity: A Critical Review of Explanatory Hypotheses." *Environmental Health* 19, no. 48 (2020).

Douthat, Ross. "*Midsommar* Casts a Transfixing Scandinavian Spell." *National Review.* July 25, 2019.

Dunajeva, Jekatyerina, and Joanna Kostka. "Racialized Politics of Garbage: Waste Management in Urban Roma Settlements in Eastern Europe." *Ethnic and Racial Studies* 45, no. 1 (2022): 90–112.

Dunne, Linnea. *Lagom: The Swedish Art of Balanced Living.* Philadelphia: Running Press, 2017.

Durkheim, Emile. *The Rules of Sociological Method.* Edited by Steven Lukes. Translated by W. D. Halls. New York: Free Press, 1982.

Ehrlich, David. "Ari Aster Breaks Down Nine Movies That Inspired 'Midsommar,' from 'The Red Shoes' to 'Climax.'" *IndieWire,* June 25, 2019.

Estok, Simon C. *The Ecophobia Hypothesis.* New York: Routledge, 2018.

———. "Painful Material Realities, Tragedy, Ecophobia." In *Material Ecocriticism,* edited by Serenella Iovino and Serpil Oppermann, 130–40. Bloomington: Indiana University Press, 2018.

Evangelista, Chris. "'Midsommar' is Not Like 'Hereditary,' But It Is 'The Wizard of Oz' for Perverts, According to Ari Aster." SlashFilm. March 24, 2019. Accessed August 31, 2022. https://www.slashfilm.com/midsommar-plot/.

Forchtner, Bernhard, and Christoffer Kølvraa. "The Nature of Nationalism: Populist Radical Right Parties on Countryside and Climate." *Nature and Culture* 10, no. 2 (2015): 199–224.

Foucault, Michel. *Discipline and Punish: The Birth of the Prison.* Translated by Alan Sheridan. New York: Vintage Books, 1979.

Gellner, Ernest. *Nations and Nationalism.* Malden, MA: Wiley-Blackwell, 1983.

Gelter, Hans. "Friluftsliv: The Scandinavian Philosophy of Outdoor Life." *Canadian Journal of Environmental Education* 5, no. 1 (Summer 2000): 77–92.

Grønstad, Asbjørn. "Conditional Vulnerability in the Films of Ruben Östlund." In *Vulnerability in Scandinavian Art and Culture,* edited by Adriana Margareta Dancus, Mats Hyvönen, and Maria Karlsson, 19–31. Cham: Palgrave Macmillan, 2020.

Gustafsson, Tommy. "Slasher in the Snow: The Rise of the Low-Budget Nordic Horror Film." In *Nordic Genre Film: Small Nation Film Cultures in the Global Marketplace,* edited by Tommy Gustafsson and Pietari Kääpä, 189–202. Edinburgh: Edinburgh University Press, 2015.

Gustafsson, Tommy, and Pietari Kääpä, eds. *Nordic Genre Film: Small Nation Film Cultures in the Global Marketplace.* Edinburgh: Edinburgh University Press, 2015.

Haeckel, Ernst. *Generelle Morphologie der Organismen: Allgemeine Grundzüge der Organischen Formen; Wissenschaft, Mechanisch Begründet durch die von Charles Darwin Reformierte Deszendenz-Theorie.* Berlin: G. Reimer, 1866.

Hakola, Outi. "Nordic Vampires: Stories of Social Exclusion in Nordic Welfare States." In *Nordic Genre Film: Small Nation Film Cultures in the Global Marketplace,* edited by Tommy Gustafsson and Pietari Kääpä, 203–16. Edinburgh: Edinburgh University Press, 2015.

Handler, Rachel. "'*Midsommar* Will Be a *Wizard of Oz* for Perverts,' Says Director Ari Aster." Vulture, March 22, 2019, https://www.vulture.com/2019/03/ari-aster-new-a24 -movie-midsommar.html.

Haraway, Donna J. *The Companion Species Manifesto: Dogs, People, and Significant Otherness.* Chicago: Prickly Paradigm Press, 2003.

———. *Staying with the Trouble: Making Kin in the Cthulucene.* Durham: Duke University Press, 2016.

Harkness, Jane. "Things You Only Notice the Second Time You Watch *Midsommar.*" Looper, April 12, 2021, https://www.looper.com/246758/things-you-only-notice-the -second-time-you-watch-midsommar/.

Heise, Ursula. *Sense of Place and Sense of Planet: The Environmental Imagination of the Global.* Oxford: Oxford University Press, 2008.

Henderson, Bob, and Nils Vikander. *Nature First: Outdoor Life the Friluftsliv Way.* Toronto: Natural Heritage Books, 2007.

Hendrix, Grady. *The Final Girl Support Group.* New York: Berkley, 2021.

Hennefeld, Maggie, and Nicholas Sammond, eds. *Abjection Incorporated: Mediating the Politics of Pleasure and Violence.* Durham: Duke University Press, 2020.

Hennig, Reinhard, Anna-Karin Jonasson, and Peter Degerman, eds. *Nordic Narratives of Nature and the Environment: Ecocritical Approaches to Northern European Literatures and Cultures.* Lanham, MD: Lexington Books, 2018.

Hjort, Anders. "Debutanten bag den danske gyser 'Shelley': 'Usympatiske kvinder er enormt spændende.'" Soundvenue, October 28, 2016, https://soundvenue.com/ film/2016/10/debutanten-bag-den-danske-gyser-shelley-usympatiske-kvinder-er -enormt-spaendende-226424.

Hojring, Katrine. "The Right to Roam the Countryside—Law and Reality Concerning Public Access to the Landscape in Denmark." *Landscape and Urban Planning* 59, no. 1 (2002): 29–41.

Hutchings, Peter. "Ten Great British Rural Horror Films." British Film Institute, August 21, 2015, https://www2.bfi.org.uk/news/10-great-british-rural-horror-films.

Hvidberg-Hansen, Gertrud. "Hellas under Northern Skies." In *The Spirit of Vitalism: Health, Beauty and Strength in Danish Art, 1890–1940,* edited by Gertrud Hvidberg-Hansen and Gertrud Oelsner, 59–87. Copenhagen: Museum Tusculanum, 2011.

Hvidberg-Hansen, Gertrud, and Gertrud Oelsner, eds. *The Spirit of Vitalism: Health, Beauty and Strength in Danish Art, 1890–1940*. Copenhagen: Museum Tusculanum, 2011.

Ingold, Tim. *Being Alive: Essays on Movement, Knowledge, and Description*. London: Routledge, 2011.

———. *The Life of Lines*. London: Routledge, 2015.

———. "On Human Correspondence." *Journal of the Royal Anthropological Institute* 23 (2016): 9–27.

———. "Toward an Ecology of Materials." *Annual Review of Anthropology* 41, no. 1 (2012): 427–42.

Iversen, Gunnar. "Between Art and Genre: New Nordic Horror Cinema." In *A Companion to Nordic Cinema*, edited by Mette Hjort and Ursula Lindqvist, 332–50. Malden, MA: John Wiley, 2016.

Jakobsen, Samina. "Biografanmeldelse: Thelma." *Ekko*, November 29, 2017, https://www.ekkofilm.dk/anmeldelser/thelma/.

Johansen, Signe. *How to Hygge: The Nordic Secrets to a Happy Life*. New York: St. Martin's Griffin, 2017.

Joyce, Stephen. "Re-Enchanting the Nordic Everyday in *Beforeigners*." *Kosmorama*, February 21, 2021.

Kääpä, Pietari. *Ecology and Contemporary Nordic Cinemas: From Nation-Building to Ecocosmopolitanism*. London: Bloomsbury Academic, 2014.

Karlsson, Helena. "The Vampire and the Anxieties of a Globalizing Swedish Welfare State: *Låt Den Rätte Komma in* (*Let the Right One In*) (2008)." *European Journal of Scandinavian Studies* 43, no. 2 (2013): 184–99.

Kjellman, Ulrika. "A Whiter Shade of Pale: Visuality and Race in the Work of the Swedish State Institute for Race Biology." *Scandinavian Journal of History* 38, no. 2 (2013): 180–201.

Kristeva, Julia. *Powers of Horror: An Essay on Abjection*. New York: Columbia University Press, 1982.

Kuusela, Tommy. "Scandinavia's Horror Renaissance and the Global Appeal of 'Fakelore.'" *Foreign Policy*, October 28, 2021.

Latimer, Joanna, and Mara Miele. "Naturecultures? Science, Affect and the Non-human." *Theory, Culture and Society* 30, nos. 7–8 (2013): 5–31.

Lindell, Martin, and Necmi Karagozoglu. "Corporate Environmental Behaviour: A Comparison between Nordic and US Firms." *Business Strategy and the Environment* 10, no. 1 (2001) 38–52.

Lismoen, Kjetil. "Thelma veksler sømløst mellom uskyld og mørke drifter på mesterlig vis." *Aftenposten*, August 20, 2017.

Livingston, Michael A. *Dreamworld or Dystopia? The Nordic Model and Its Influence in the Twenty-First Century*. Cambridge: Cambridge University Press, 2022.

Luko, Alexis. "Listening to Ingmar Bergman's Monsters: Horror Music, Mutes, and Acoustical Beings in Persona and Hour of the Wolf." *Journal of Film Music* 6, no. 1 (2013): 5–30.

Maitland, Sara. *Gossip from the Forest: The Tangled Roots of Our Forests and Fairy Tales.* London: Granta Books, 2012.

Manne, Kate. *Down Girl: The Logic of Misogyny.* New York: Oxford University Press, 2018.

Margolis, Jason. "Bernie Sanders Wants Us to Be More Equitable Like Sweden. Could It Work?," Public Radio International, February 9, 2016.

Margulis, Lynn. "Symbiogenesis and Symbioticism." In *Symbiosis as a Source of Evolutionary Innovation,* edited by Lynn Margulis and René Fester, 1–14. Cambridge, MA: MIT Press, 1991.

Marshall, Elizabeth. *Graphic Girlhoods: Visualizing Education and Violence.* New York: Routledge, 2018.

Mauss, Marcel. *The Gift: The Form and Reason for Exchange in Archaic Societies.* Translated by W. D. Halls. London: Routledge, 2002.

Mee, Shannon Jane. *The Pulse in Cinema: The Aesthetics of Horror.* Edinburgh: Edinburgh University Press, 2020.

Midttun, Atle, and Lennart Olsson. "Eco-Modernity Nordic Style." In *Sustainable Modernity,* edited by Nina Witoszek and Atle Midttun, 204–28. London: Routledge, 2018.

Mittell, Jason. *Complex TV: The Poetics of Contemporary Television Storytelling.* New York: New York University Press, 2015.

Morton, Timothy. *The Ecological Thought.* Cambridge, MA: Harvard University Press, 2010.

———. *Ecology without Nature: Rethinking Environmental Aesthetics.* Cambridge, MA: Harvard University Press, 2007.

———. *Humankind: Solidarity with Nonhuman People.* London: Verso, 2017.

Mossner, Alexa Weik von. *Affective Ecologies: Empathy, Emotion, and Environmental Narrative.* Columbus: Ohio State University Press, 2017.

Mrozewicz, Anna Estera. *Beyond Eastern Noir: Reimagining Russia and Eastern Europe in Nordic Cinemas.* Edinburgh: Edinburgh University Press, 2018.

Mytting, Lars. *Hel Ved.* Oslo: Kagge, 2011. Translated by Robert Ferguson as *Norwegian Wood: Chopping, Stacking, and Drying Wood the Scandinavian Way.* New York: Abrams Image, 2015.

Nash, Roderick. *Wilderness and the American Mind.* New Haven, CT: Yale University Press, 1967.

Nestingen, Andrew K. *Crime and Fantasy in Scandinavia: Fiction, Film, and Social Change.* Seattle: University of Washington Press, 2008.

Nicholson, Tom. "'Midsommar' Is 'The Wizard of Oz' for Perverts, Says Ari Aster." *Esquire*, February 8, 2019.

Norberg, Johan. "Sweden's Lessons for America." *Cato Institute Policy Report*, January–February 2020.

Nordau, Max. *Entartung*. Berlin: Carl Dunder, 1893. Translated as *Degeneration* (London: William Heinemann, 1895).

Nordfjörd, Björn. *Dagur Kári's "Nói the Albino."* Seattle: University of Washington Press, 2010.

Nordic Council of Ministers. "Strategy for International Branding of the Nordic Region, 2019–2021." Copenhagen: Nordic Council of Ministers, 2019.

Nylund, Joanna. *Sisu: The Finnish Art of Courage*. London: Gaia, 2018.

Oelsner, Gertrud. "Healthy Nature." In *The Spirit of Vitalism: Health, Beauty and Strength in Danish Art, 1890–1940*, edited by Gertrud Hvidberg-Hansen and Gertrud Oelsner, 158–97. Copenhagen: Museum Tusculanum, 2011.

Oxfeldt, Elisabeth, ed. *Skandinaviske fortellinger om skyld og privilegier i en globaliseringstid*. Oslo: Universitetsforlaget, 2016.

Pantzar, Katja. *The Finnish Way: Finding Courage, Wellness, and Happiness through the Power of Sisu*. New York: Tarcher Perigree, 2018.

Parker, Elizabeth. *The Forest and the Ecogothic: The Deep Dark Woods in the Popular Imagination*. Cham, Switzerland: Palgrave Macmillan, 2020.

Partanen, Anu. *The Nordic Theory of Everything: In Search of a Better Life*. New York: Harper, 2016.

Peirse, Alison. "The Impossibility of Vision: Vampirism, Formlessness and Horror in *Vampyr*." *Studies in European Cinema* 5, no. 3 (2009): 161–70.

Piepenburg, Erik. "Modern Times Call for Folk Horror." *New York Times*, October 30, 2021.

Pitkänen, Kati, Joose Oratuomi, Daniela Hellgren, Eeva Furman, Sandra Gentin, Eva Sandberg, Hogne Øian, and Olve Krange. *Nature-Based Integration: Nordic Experiences and Examples*. Copenhagen: Nordic Council of Ministers, 2017.

Rees, Ellen. "Privilege, Innocence, and 'Petro-Guilt' in Maria Sødahl's Limbo." *Scandinavian Studies* 88, no. 1 (2016): 42–59.

Reyes, Xavier Aldana. *Body Gothic: Corporeal Transgression in Contemporary Literature and Horror Film*. Cardiff: University of Wales Press, 2014.

Robinson, Tasha. "Thelma's Director Explains Why He Made a Dreamy Gay Coming-of-Age Superhero Story." *The Verge*, November 10, 2017.

Rugg, Linda Haverty. "A Tradition of Torturing Women." In *A Companion to Nordic Cinema*, edited by Mette Hjort and Ursula Lindqvist. Malden, MA: Wiley/Blackwell, 2016.

Rust, Stephen A., and Carter Soles. "Ecohorror Special Cluster: 'Living in Fear, Living in Dread, Pretty Soon We'll All Be Dead.'" *Interdisciplinary Studies in Literature and Environment* 21, no. 3 (Summer 2014): 509–12.

Rydgren, Jens. "Radical Right-Wing Populism in Denmark and Sweden: Explaining Party System Change and Stability." *SAIS Review of International Affairs* 30, no. 1 (2010): 57–71.

Scovell, Adam. *Folk Horror: Hours Dreadful and Things Strange*. Leighton Buzzard, UK: Auteur Press, 2017.

Seymour, Nicole. *Bad Environmentalism: Irony and Irreverence in the Ecological Age*. Minneapolis: University of Minnesota Press, 2018.

Singleton, Benedict E. "Interpreting Taskscapes: The Rituals of Guided Nature-Based (Dis)Integration in Sweden." *Innovation: The European Journal of Social Science Research* 34, no. 1 (2021): 111–31.

Skvirsky, Salomé Aguilera. *The Process Genre: Cinema and the Aesthetic of Labor*. Durham: Duke University Press, 2020.

Slotek, Jim. "Thelma a More Sexualized Carrie, with Scandinavian Melancholy." Last modified November 15, 2017, https://www.original-cin.ca/posts/2017/11/8/thelma-is -carrie-with-scandinavian-melancholy-and-metaphor.

Smith, Anthony. *The Ethnic Origins of Nations*. Malden, MA: Wiley-Blackwell. 1983.

Soila, Tytti. "Introduction." In *The Cinema of Scandinavia*, edited by Tytti Soila. London: Wallflower Press, 2005.

Soles, Carter. "Sympathy for the Devil: The Cannibalistic Hillbilly in 1970s Rural Slasher Films." In *Ecocinema Theory and Practice*, edited by Stephen Rust, Salma Monani, and Sean Cubitt, 233–50. New York: Routledge, 2012.

Souch, Irina. "Transformations of the Evil Forest in the Swedish Television Series *Jordskott*: An Ecocritical Reading." *Nordicom Review* 41, no. 1 (2020): 107–22.

Stougaard-Nielsen, Jakob. *Scandinavian Crime Fiction*. London: Bloomsbury Academic, 2017.

Teitelbaum, Benjamin R. "Implicitly White: Right-Wing Nihilism and the Politicizing of Ethnocentrism in Multiracial Sweden." *Scandinavian Studies* 89, no. 2 (2017): 159–78.

Thomsen, Torsten Bøgh. "Foggy Signs: Dark Ecological Queerings in Lars Von Trier's *Antichrist*." *Journal of Scandinavian Cinema* 8, no. 2 (2018): 123–34.

Thunberg, Greta. "Greta Thunberg's World Economic Forum 2019 Special Address." Filmed January 24, 2019, at the World Economic Forum, New York, NY. Accessed August 31, 2022. http://opentranscripts.org/transcript/greta-thunberg-world -economic-forum-2019/.

Thurfjell, David, Cecilie Rubow, Atko Remmel, and Henrik Ohlsson. "The Relocation of Transcendence." *Nature and Culture* 14, no. 2 (2019): 190–214.

Tidwell, Christy. "Ecohorror." In *Posthuman Glossary*, edited by Rosi Braidotti and Maria Hlavajova, 115–17. London: Bloomsbury Academic, 2018.

———. "Spiraling Inward and Outward: Junji Ito's *Uzumaki* and the Scope of Ecohorror." In *Fear and Nature: Ecohorror Studies in the Anthropocene*, edited by Christy Tidwell and Carter Soles, 42–67. University Park: Pennsylvania State University Press, 2021.

Tidwell, Christy, and Carter Soles, eds. *Fear and Nature: Ecohorror Studies in the Anthropocene*. University Park: Pennsylvania State University Press, 2021.

Tomson, Danielle Lee. "The Rise of Sweden Democrats: Islam, Populism and the End of Swedish Exceptionalism." Brookings Institution, March 25, 2020, https://www .brookings.edu/research/the-rise-of-sweden-democrats-and-the-end-of-swedish -exceptionalism/.

Tuan, Yi-Fu. *Landscapes of Fear*. Oxford: Basil Blackwell, 1979.

Vassenden, Eirik. *Norsk Vitalisme: Litteratur, Ideologi og Livsdyrking 1890–1940*. Oslo: SAP, 2012.

Wald, Priscilla. *Contagious: Cultures, Carriers, and the Outbreak Narrative*. Durham: Duke University Press, 2008.

Waldron, Ingrid. *There's Something in the Water: Environmental Racism in Indigenous and Black Communities*. Winnipeg: Fernwood Publishing, 2018.

Wells, Paul. *The Horror Genre: From Beelzebub to Blair Witch*. London: Wallflower Press, 2000.

Wiking, Meik. *The Little Book of Hygge: Danish Secrets to Happy Living*. New York: Harper Collins, 2017.

Williams, Linda. "Film Bodies: Gender, Genre, and Excess." *Film Quarterly* 44, no. 4 (Summer 1991): 2–13.

———. "Melodrama Revised." In *Refiguring American Film Genres*, edited by Nick Browne, 42–88. Berkeley: University of California Press, 1998.

Witoszek, Nina. *The Origins of the "Regime of Goodness": Remapping the Cultural History of Norway*. Oslo: Universitetsforlaget, 2011.

World Commission on Environment Development. *Our Common Future*. Oxford: Oxford University Press, 1987.

Wright, Rochelle. "Vampire in the Stockholm Suburbs: *Let the Right One In* and Genre Hybridity." *Journal of Scandinavian Cinema* 1, no. 1 (2010): 55–70.

Zimring, Carl A. *Clean and White: A History of Environmental Racism in the United States*. New York: New York University Press, 2015.

Zuckerman, Phil. *Society without God: What the Least Religious Nations Can Tell Us about Contentment*. Cambridge: Cambridge University Press, 2022.

# INDEX

—

# NEW DIRECTIONS IN SCANDINAVIAN STUDIES

This series offers interdisciplinary approaches to the study of the Nordic region of Scandinavia and the Baltic States and their cultural connections in North America. By redefining the boundaries of Scandinavian studies to include the Baltic States and Scandinavian America, the series presents books that focus on the study of the culture, history, literature, and politics of the North.